On Garbage

On Garbage

John Scanlan

To Rebekah Sterling
May your 'missing stuff' never become garbage.

Published by Reaktion Books Ltd
79 Farringdon Road, London EC1M 3JU, UK

www.reaktionbooks.co.uk

First published 2005, reprinted 2005

Printed and bound in Great Britain by CPI Bath Press, Bath

British Library Cataloguing in Publication Data
     Scanlan, John
     1. Civilization, Western 2. Knowledge, Sociology of
     3. Philosophical anthropology. 4. Refuse and refuse disposal
     I. Title
     909'.09821

     ISBN 1 86189 222 5

Contents

Garbage can overflowing with 'filth' (discarded pornographic literature), Las Vegas Strip, 2000.

Preface

'Why garbage?' is a question that is frequently asked when I mention this project to friends or colleagues. Just as common as this reaction is the assumption that I must be studying 'the garbage problem', perhaps as part of some greater ecological or environmental concern. Although the book presents a perspective on garbage that will be of interest to those concerned with environmental (and other) wastes, the origin of my interest in this area, and the subsequent development of the project, has a more unusual history. In 1999 I had been doing a lot of thinking about chance, and specifically about the experience of chance within the context of Reason or, even, what is taken to be *reasonable*. What I had come to realize was that reason (our intellectual means of organizing the world we experience) actually produced chance as the residue or 'uncombinable' aspect of its ceaseless drive to colonize the unknown and confusing.

I was at this time working on my doctoral thesis at the University of Glasgow, and had recently written a large piece on chance and disorder that attempted to pursue this theme in two quite separate areas: in the representation of gambling in literature and culture and in the modernism of Marcel Duchamp and Zürich Dada. Somewhere in these early attempts to understand chance I had used the expression 'chance is merely the rubbish of reason'. However, there was no indication yet that I was going to develop the interest in chance and disorder into a focus on rubbish, or as it would become, garbage. But that changed. One day I had a meeting with my academic supervisors, Harvie Ferguson and Gerda Reith, to explore how I might take my project further. It was felt that my work on chance and disorder up to this point had looked at ideal and aesthetic aspects of the theme of disorder, and that it should attempt to move into a new area that was still connected to the central focus of disorder but could direct the work towards materiality. It was shortly after this that Harvie Ferguson became quite animated and began throwing out these words 'scum', 'filth', 'flotsam', 'the stuff that floats on the top', 'garbage'. Gerda and I sat around and stared blankly for a minute or so, not knowing how to react to this. Almost as an aside to fill the void of silence she said 'there is a group called Garbage . . . ' – and then something clicked. 'Trash', I said. 'Have you heard it? The song by the New York Dolls?' I had been listening to the appropriately trashy New York rock'n'rollers, and found myself unable to get the chorus of this song out of my head. Rather more unusually it became clear that this was because it also brought to mind the philosopher Immanuel Kant. The lyric of the song seemed to sum up my understanding of how Kant's notion of a universal and bounded Reason works, in that what Reason values rests squarely on the *disposal* of doubt, error, uselessness, and so on:

Trash, don't pick it up
Don't throw your life away

Or, at least this is what I thought the words were. The singer of the song, David Johansen, spewed out the word 'trash' in a gloriously un-restrained way. It actually sounded more like *traaaeeeuuyuusshhhh-hh*, followed quickly by the rest of the line. But I had misheard it. So beguiled was I by his magnificent rendering of 'trash' that I never got the fact that it was followed by the words 'won't pick it up, don't try to throw my life away'. Was the song *urging* that we should all become trashier? Devote our lives to decadence – or perhaps that we might retreat from trash? This is something I still find perplexing today, but in the end it matters little. Perhaps, after all, it did not echo Kant in suggesting that it was from a kind of disposal that meaning, or value, emerged as that which is retained.

An idea was born, nevertheless (encouraged, no doubt, by some-thing else Harvie Ferguson had reminded me on another occasion – 'Weird is good; as long as it's good weird and not bad weird'). In this book I take this idea of the fundamental importance of disposal and suggest that if we look for connections amongst the variety of hidden, forgotten, thrown away, and residual phenomena that attend life at all times (as the background against which we *make* the world) we might see this habit of separating the valuable from the worthless within a whole tradition of Western ways of thinking about the world, and that rather than providing simply the evidence for some kind of contem-porary environmental problem, 'garbage' (in the metaphorical sense of the detached remainder of the things we value) is everywhere.

Indeed, our separation from it is the very thing that makes something like a culture possible.

It will also be seen that the creation of garbage results from a more or less imperceptible contest between life and death – because death constitutes the human return to matter, and is in a sense, the 'garbaging' of the body. Which is to say death is *that which has to be avoided to maintain life*. From this avoidance of death arise a number of paradoxes. Thus, we see on closer examination that when Western societies attempt to use the accumulated knowledge of the workings of nature to combat death and disease, and to improve health, the very thing that creates the spur to action (death) ends up a century or so later being seen as almost an affront to life, instead of the necessity that no one avoids. Likewise the 'great cleanup' of the nineteenth century, which eventually forced food retailers to save food from contaminants and premature wasting by utilizing newly developed packaging and means of storage, paradoxically creates more material garbage, which in turn constitutes part of the greater problem of environmental degradation that we are told threatens life on a far larger scale. What this book does, therefore, is ask us to consider the possibility that the surprising core of all we value results from (and creates ever more) garbage (both the material and the metaphorical). This book, then, might be read as a shadow history of Western culture as a history of disposal, of garbaging.

In chapter One an attempt is made to map the metaphorical terrain of garbage. The reader is warned that the chapter begins with a series of descriptive snapshots. At this stage we still do not see very clearly what garbage is; these snapshots could also be taken as examples of the ways in which we may unwittingly glimpse garbage, but without fully realizing its implications. The point is to show that garbage is everywhere but, curiously, is mostly overlooked in what we take to be valuable from our lived experiences, and crucially, in the ways we (or Reason, this dispersed will to order) organize the world. We then proceed by looking at garbage through a set of notions that symbolize the cut-off and detached remainders of living. It may be objected at times that the language of garbage (which includes commonly associated terms like 'waste', 'rubbish', 'trash', and so on) is sprinkled indiscriminately here and there without proper regard for historical context (or, indeed, for disciplinary subtleties). First of all this would be a false impression, as examples are always related to their context. What we are dealing here is the referential power – and limitations – of language, of words. The language of garbage – the various terms that point to residues, remainders, and so on – is difficult to pin down. This is for the very good reason that its utterances refer to the excrement of meaning itself. For example, it is when something means nothing *to you* that it becomes 'filth', 'shit', 'rubbish', 'garbage', and so on. In any case, the most rudimentary philosophy would advise us that particular words refer to more general concepts, and this becomes clear when we see that whilst the uses of the word garbage have changed over time, all its instances nonetheless retain a general conceptual unity in referring to things, people, or activities that are separated, removed and devalued. The point is that the chiefly metaphorical use of garbage that is employed here is the only way to reveal the power of this word for organizing the other, shadowy, part of life we normally overlook. It is entirely unproductive to say that because 'garbage' means something quite different now from what it did in the fifteenth century (when it was imported into English) that to then speak of garbage in a general sense degrades its original meaning. Such an approach would surely entail that we have no legitimate right to depart from its Old French origins because, perhaps, its fifteenth-century English usage degrades *that*. Clearly, the reason why words change across contexts and move between languages is because of their connection to a more conceptual notion that supports the functioning of the word within many and varied contexts. Can one imagine any communication at all where language does not operate in such a fluid and metaphorical manner?

In what follows I attempt to track garbage along a number of thematic lines. Chapter Two, 'Garbage and Knowledge', looks at the work of knowledge in cleaning up the conceptual landscape, and here we see that Western metaphysics (which, broadly speaking, effects the separation of the human from the natural), is the great garbager that roots both the experience of the self with reality, and the development of the technological appropriation of nature. Chapter Three, 'The Aesthetics of Garbage', considers the variety of residues, rubbish and apparently senseless acts and meaningless language that informed the work of a number of twentieth-century artists. In chapter Four, 'Garbage Matters' (as the title implies) we encounter the actual material of physical garbage, and discover the reasons for some of the unusual uses it can be put to. The final chapter – 'Garbage and the Uncanny' – explores the experience of garbage in all its forms as illustrating the uncanny reality of an existence that, as history proceeds,

Pierre Daret, 'Man is Nothing But a Bit of Mud', engraving from Marin Le Roy de Gomberville, *La Doctrine des moeurs* (Paris, 1646).

seems to become further separated from its natural origin but that never really manages to fully detach itself, and as a consequence creates a present that is haunted by the spectre of garbage. As a result of such an understanding the environmental concerns that exercise the imagination of the present might be better understood within the context of this spectre of garbage when we can point to the fact that material garbage in contemporary society is the physical and objective counterpart of metaphorical garbage.

In other words, these spectres of garbage serve as a stark reminder of what we really are.

1 Garbage Metaphorics

Man that is born of woman hath but a short time to live,
and is full of misery. He cometh up, and is cut down, like a
flower; he fleeth as it were a shadow, and never continueth
in one stay.
The Book of Common Prayer, first anthem, 'Burial of the Dead'

WHOLES AND PARTS

'Garbage' is everywhere. It can be found in everything without exception, yet it is also largely invisible to most of us. Garbage enjoins some deep thinking about how we make the world we live in, and how this making curiously ends up so totally detached in one sense (but still nonetheless connected, even if this is an unwelcome hanging-on) from the things it creates. In an unproblematic sense garbage is leftover matter. It is what remains when the good, fruitful, valuable, nourishing and useful has been taken. Appropriation is the mother of garbage.

In another guise this is seen as a human propensity for differentiation (a complicated way of saying we choose or accept something whilst rejecting something else) that inaugurates a lifetime of cutting-off, disconnection and removal. Nevertheless, these activities become the principal means of marking off the valuable and worthy, and in this sense differentiation is what establishes culture. We only acquire or understand the valuable (or develop ideas of the relationship between the self and the object world) as the result of a galloping retreat from an *undifferentiated* mass of things (which may also be called 'nature') that could otherwise swamp us. This may be a trait belonging to modern society, yet born of the ancient world: the 'destining' of the West, as Heidegger said, and progenitor of the modern (if only in its role as a point of departure for conceptualizing our relation to the natural world). We arrive at this state of affairs – paradoxically, again – through

the connecting, but duplicitous, operations of a language and symbolism that, in a sense, steals the world for its own ends (and, to paraphrase
Schelling, such duplicity ultimately sees the world rise against us).[1]

Garbage is the formlessness from which form takes flight, the ghost
that haunts presence. Garbage is the entrails, the bits or scraps, the
mountain of indistinguishable stuff that is in its own way affirmed by a
resolute dismissal: it is *refuse-d* (not accepted, denied, banished).
Garbage is the tat, the lowly that has sunk to the depth of a value system
that is present (so far as we are aware) simply as a clean surface – mask-
like – much as the gleaming interiors of a thousand catalogue bath-
rooms; where 'white porcelain and bright polished metals [were] favored
because they reveal the presence of dirt: they were proof of their own
cleanliness'.[2] Yet such evident care does not hide the fact that garbage is
the mucky handprint of a being that carries on regardless, a dirty trace,
the wreck of beauty, and in the most recognizably banal sense, the excrement of a body. Garbage indicates the removal of qualities (characteristics, or distinguishing features) and signals the return of everything to
some universal condition, perhaps impersonal (and again, directly banal,
as in the case of pornography, which reduces the unique person to a
thing, a body with no interior life, no intellect, and thus a form devoid of
real beauty). This too marks the products of such a reduction as 'filth', a
distinction that spills over into related categories of sin, defilement and
abjection), and clearly – without complexity – a return to some material
condition (as when the representatives of God encapsulate the life cycle
as the same beginning and end – 'ashes to ashes, dust to dust'). At a
human level a violent stripping away of (positive) characteristics consigns
its victims to an indistinguishable mass, a state that ensures their treat-
ment as mere rubbish – social outcasts, foreigners, *others* – and like
representations of the damned in religious iconography simply *stuff* that
can be pushed around, co-mingled with its similarly valueless and
indistinguishable like, a pile of rubble to be moved from one place to
another (perhaps) as part of some eternal punishment; stacked up and
shovelled into a furnace, or in an example of the supreme efficiency of
instrumental evil, gassed through duplicitous instruments of hygiene.

If this outline of 'garbage' makes one thing clear it is that there is no
determinate and singularly applicable concept of 'garbage'. Indeed,
there is no 'social theory' or concept of garbage at all; nor is there a
readily accessible literature that lays bare the intellectual parameters for
a discussion of, or investigation into, the possibility that such a concept
might eventually be elaborated. In any case, the act of conceptualiz-

ing garbage actually transforms it into something else. Domesticates it. It is highly appropriate that we have to glean our material from the leftover or overlooked parts of a conventional academic discourse that is, I will argue here, itself fashioned from various bits or particulars into some whole. Nevertheless, the utility of this word 'garbage' in shifting our attention to the absent parts of our worldmaking is found in its comparatively limited original etymology (and which allows us to suggest that more common and related terms – such as 'rubbish', 'waste', 'trash' and so on – do not offer the same literary possibility because of their apparently greater precision). What, then, is 'garbage'? According to the *Oxford English Dictionary* (2nd edn, 1989), the word initially comes to English in the fifteenth century from Old French, and was first used to refer to food waste before it developed more general meanings:

> GARBAGE, *sb* 1. The offal of an animal used for food; esp. the entrails. Rarely, the entrails of a man. 2. Refuse in general; filth. 3. *fig* Chiefly in the sense of worthless or foul literary matter.

These three principal senses of garbage tell us one important thing and this is that the creation of garbage is the result of a separation – of the desirable from the unwanted; the valuable from the worthless, and indeed, the worthy or cultured from the cheap or meaningless. And it is because differentiation is a fundamental human activity that garbage is everywhere as the bits, scraps and leftovers of a variety of intact 'wholes'. (At this stage it is necessary to be abstract and general, but these 'wholes' will be elaborated throughout the text by use of examples.) But, more curiously, metaphorical garbage is also found in the most unlikely places as simply the formless, indeterminate, or protean – even where this is itself the token of some ultimate value, as is the case with gold or money. But why would money be a kind of garbage, you may ask. Because, as Christof Asendorf has noted, money only becomes freely mobile once it has been stripped of its actual character.[3] Money can become anything and this makes it nothing – the equivalent of waste matter ready to be re-fashioned into a new form. Or otherwise money, as Freud noted, is actually like shit (i.e., human garbage): not only because it is alienated from the person (like excrement is from the body), but also because the separation allows its further development into something that persists on its own – it gets everywhere because of the very absence of concrete properties. Money is like garbage in its formlessness, its existence outside of the parameters of *human time* (crucially, in so far as its value does not necessarily depend on immediate temporal constraints), and not least because it is in constant transformation.[4]

'Garbage' is also the retort of choice to yet another 'meaningless' artistic outrage, to the art that 'anybody' could make: like a creation by the British artist Damien Hirst, made from 'piles of ashtrays, empty beer bottles and newspapers strewn across the gallery', that was peremptorily unmade by a gallery worker who simply thought it was rubbish left over from a party:

> As soon as I clapped eyes on it I sighed because there was so much mess. I didn't think for a second that it was a work of art – it didn't look much like art to me. So I cleared it all into binbags and dumped it.[5]

There is no expectation within our general consciousness of the world, and outside of the suspension of these expectations when we willingly enter a gallery or a museum, that the gallery worker would be wrong. Rubbish is usually rubbish.

And yes, garbage is also the broken knowledge that lies in the wake of (and in the way of) progress, the bits that no longer fit or that get in the way of a truth that always lies just ahead (somewhere down the line in some undiscovered future). Garbage relates to the equivocal; it tells us neither one thing nor another, but merely effaces the status of our knowledge of the object world. Garbage is concerned with ends (and thus beginnings); it is where one thing becomes another, where the once known or admitted (objects of belief or faith, markers of certainty) unfold into a mess of incompatible parts. To repeat, garbage is neither one thing nor another, but instead is the remainder of such neatness, and this is one reason why it could be a dubious exercise to reconfigure it, to bring it back into our thinking – to make it something *to us*. The symbolic order is culturally (and historically) given and is understood principally to represent a system of signs and implied or overt meanings in which the sign itself stands for or represents some other object that has a place in a system of values. And because 'garbage' does not strictly refer to an *object,* but is a jumble of inexactness, a disordered condition (in the metaphorical sense), or degraded husk of some *former* object, it seems to lack conventional symbolic referents, and in a sense the stuff of garbage is the remainder of the symbolic order proper (which nonetheless is a condition of this symbolism functioning within a given culture or specific historical circumstance).[6] Garbage seems to reverse the real–symbolic dialogue because we can reveal more about it by seeing the way in which other things, judgements, and ways of living, symbolize *it*.

NOTHING

But, if even our commonly accepted tokens of value (such as money) can be considered, effectively, as garbage, it is nonetheless a temporary and contextual condition. By contrast, it is when those things of a more personal significance are rendered worthless that the reality of human moral and social degradation becomes apparent. In Ivan Klíma's *Love and Garbage*, the narrator (a writer moonlighting as a street-sweeper) is haunted by his knowledge of the fate of friends and family who perished in the war, reduced to the condition of worthless matter and other equally insignificant things. His personal

Buchenwald concentration camp at Weimar, Germany, April 1945.

descent into the world of garbage furnishes him with the awareness that the worst thing one person can do to another is to reduce them to the nothingness of garbage: 'When I learned after the war that all those I had been fond of, all those I had known, were dead, gassed like insects and incinerated like refuse, I was gripped by despair.'[7]

Yet equally we infer from the experience of the narrator that it is precisely because of the horrifying tendency of such events to intrude upon the orderly lives we strive to maintain that they should be banished from consciousness as if – like actually decaying matter – they appear contagious. The further he sinks into the life of a street-sweeper the more acute the metaphor of garbage becomes in describing everything that threatens our well-being. As a child, he recalls how he had 'lamented and mourned' the loss of a simple model aeroplane that had crashed to the ground in a 'heap of skewers, balsa wood and pieces of carefully stretched paper':

> it was then that Dad said to me: Remember that a man never cries! It was one of the few lessons I ever received from him. He laughed at the heap of rubbish as he picked it up, adding that that was the fate of things, and anyone worrying about it merely harmed himself.[8]

The 'fate of things' – their ultimate destination as part of some vast, all-consuming garbage pit – is to become nothing. This stands in marked contrast to a world revolutionized by advancing standards of hygiene and by the directing hand of public health agencies. The cleansed present and its uncanny other, garbage, seem also to reflect a duality that is strangely reminiscent of the Eden–Hell counterpoint that is found especially during the Middle Ages as part of the literature of Christianity. As Thomas H. Seiler has written, 'the Edenic, paradisiacal garden with its calm, its flowers, its light, its sweet smells is counterpoised by a chaotic and cacophonous place that is dark, dirty, and offensively smelly'.[9] In contemporary societies we strive for such a paradisiacal order not only through the agencies of public hygiene, but also through obsession with the health and maintenance of the individual body. Indeed, this obsession may be seen to go along with the abhorrence of dirt as a method of pushing back the time of the inevitable garbaging of this body. What does this tell us? Is it that if the body is not worshipped as a temple, then let it become a tomb? How far removed is this from those self-hating penitents of the Middle

Ages, who also – like our contemporary public health agencies – advocated respect for the body (but for the prolongation of 'life' in the next world), where great emphasis is placed on the unavoidably damnable aspects of everyday existence? To these Christians the human body was a living, moving, garbage receptacle, as we infer from the following passage quoted by Piero Camporesi:

> To be sure the body is very like a tomb and gives off noxious vapours in all directions. Hem! How vain is our toil! A tavern for worms, an inn for serpents, an hostelry for toads, a bilge full of dirt – thus it is to gleam, to be cosseted, to be proud? Is this wretched clod of earth, so dirty, so crumbly, thus to be clothed? Is such service to be paid the flesh, a mere servant, largely leaving aside the soul, bare and unclothed?[10]

In representations of hell, too, the body – the damned person – is just a kind of garbage. A contemporary visual illustration of this (which recalls numerous historical antecedents) can be seen in Jake and Dinos Chapman's *Hell,* where a pile of 'bodies' (actually action dolls) appear at first glance to be nothing other than a pile of rubbish, swept together before the furnace (see overleaf). In fact, as Madeline Pelner Cosman has written, the iconography of hell presents images that would have been familiar to the inhabitants of towns and cities during the Middle Ages precisely because of their familiarity with garbage. A description of the visible contents of the river Thames in London, for example – a disgusting, hellish, death-soup – could have stood just as well as a representation of a river in hell, containing as it did, 'sweepings from butcher's stalls, dung, guts, blood, drowned puppies, stinking sprats, all drenched in mud, dead cats, and turnip tops tumbling down the sluggish flood'.[11] Yet, if this recognizable garbage comes to signify the kingdom of hell, then how curious that contemporary writers see another kind of hell in the sanitized, anonymous spaces of modern society; the shopping malls, airports, and other places of transit, where the uniformity and lack of distinguishing characteristics mark these out as well as domains of *nothingness*, the waiting rooms of a hell of sensory blandness (rather than the Baroque hell of the five senses), as the architect Rem Koolhaas notes in the exposition of what he calls 'junkspace':

> Dedicated to instant gratification, Junkspace accommodates seeds of future perfection; a language of apology is woven

Jake and Dinos Chapman, *Hell* (installation detail).

through its texture of canned euphoria; 'pardon our appearance' signs or miniature yellow 'sorry' billboards mark ongoing patches of wetness, announce momentary discomfort in return for imminent shine, the allure of improvement.[12]

As in Dante's *Inferno,* where the sinners do penance or endure punishments on the mountain of purgatory prior to their ascent into paradise, so it is with the bland waiting rooms of the junkspace. As David Pascoe writes, purgatory can be projected into the depersonalization of the experience of the airport as a waiting room for a hopeful return to a real life beyond the junkspace: 'Charon, the functionary from Hell, is an animated version of those who stand at the numbered gate collecting identities before allowing passengers to board the aircraft.'[13] And 'airspace itself, rather than being a place of flow, is instead the site of psychological blockage, a zone where the individual is crystallized into blocks of time, losing sight of his personal and aesthetic identity'.[14] This kind of bland sameness, the reduction of qualities at the expense of homogeneity, corresponds to Marc Augé's conception of the 'non-places' of what he calls 'Supermodernity'; spaces that 'cannot be defined as relational, or historical, or concerned with identity'.[15] In these 'non-places', Augé suggests, we encounter an overlooked yet important part of modern experience that results in the establishment of 'solitary individuality [which submits to] the fleeting, the temporary and ephemeral':

A world where people are born in the clinic and die in hospital, where transit points and temporary abodes are proliferating inhuman conditions (hotel chains and squats, holiday clubs and refugee camps, shanty towns threatened with demolition or doomed to festering longevity); where a dense network of means of transport which are also inhabited spaces is developing; where the habitué of supermarkets, slot machines and credit cards communicates wordlessly, through gestures, with an abstract, unmediated commerce.[16]

And so on. Here, the temporary and ephemeral stand for the pervading sense of the disposability of it all; the admixture of discrete experiences describes a social reality that could just as easily be garbaged and reconstituted as something new. When we consider the metaphorical applicability of garbage to most aspects of contemporary experience, it is clear that without first settling on some principle of organization the material that could most clearly illustrate the centrality of garbage might be enough to overwhelm us. The domain of garbage seems so inexhaustible that in what follows I will attempt to outline a loose symbolism of garbage under several discrete, yet connected, headings. Given the nature of the subject it will be apparent

A detail from the Master of the Glorification of Mary, *In an Ideal Landscape, the Blessed are Taken into the Sky and the Condemned to Hell*, 1493, oil on canvas. Fondation Rau, Paris.

that this merely constitutes one way of approaching such a difficult enterprise, and that what is discussed under the respective categories could just as well appear (indeed, may reappear) under any of the others.

WASTE

The word 'waste' in Old and Middle English originally referred to a land or an environment that was unsuitable to sustain human habitation, but as the Middle English lexicon expanded to replace this older sense of the term with equivalents like 'wilderness' and 'desert', new uses of waste emerged that began to indicate moral censure.[17] But, if we are to generalize, we can say that in both its premodern and modern usages the notion of waste generally refers to an imbalance. In more specific terms we may locate this in our contemporary relationships to places, objects, as well as in behaviours and practices. For example, such an imbalance is reflected in a perceived excess of consumption – that is, where household rubbish, scrap heaps or other junk and clutter stabs through to consciousness the very profligacy of modern living. But whilst waste clearly stands for a remainder; a potential exhausted through use, 'to waste' is equally to squander in the distinct sense of not making the *best* use of something (time, resources, opportunities and so on) where the opportunity in question makes itself known but is ignored. Here, waste is a defect of effort in the face of the presence (or likely appearance) of something else that would bring one back into equilibrium with the world and so avoid a falling away into the pointless and futile. It would also constitute something like a notion of 'proper use' (of a thing, of time) as it applies, for example, to so-called wastelands.

Clearly, then, the meaning of 'waste' carries force because of the way in which it symbolizes an idea of improper use, and therefore operates within a more or less moral economy of the right, the good, the proper, their opposites and all values in between. In other words, all talk about waste – as we shall see – generally foregrounds a concern with ends, outcomes or consequences, and the recognition of waste indicates a need for attention to what usually remains unknown. However, the only way to try and work out the importance of waste within the metaphorical discourse of garbage (which is to say, of disconnections) is to look at how the idea of waste has been used to differentiate ideas about nature, about the proper use or harnessing of time, and in relation to material products.

There are two main aspects to any understanding of how meanings of waste operate, and have been related historically to an understanding of nature in general, and more narrowly to places and things. On the one hand notions of degradation point to the overuse of once valuable resources, where land, for instance, becomes barren or depleted through overuse, and where objects and places are exhausted of some capacity prior to being garbaged – that is, abandoned. On the other hand, there seems to be some idea of a kind of natural blankness – of nature having no existence beyond its human uses – and this has historically informed an understanding of the significance of wasteland, and to beliefs that certain parts of nature are inhospitable (meaning unfit for *human* habitation or sustenance) as in the *vast* of the oceans, the snow-covered lands and empty spaces. The impossibility of conceiving of waste outside of an economy of human values can be illustrated by considering the relationship between the self and natural space that emerged in the political philosophy of the seventeenth-century English philosopher, John Locke (and which later served to underpin the expansion of the American colonies). The first thing worth noting is that Locke's view of nature (and the human relationship to land) strongly reflected a Calvinist notion of stewardship that placed humanity at the service of the Almighty. For example, in his *Commentary on the Book of Genesis*, John Calvin perceived humanity to have been charged by God with the task of preserving nature and its bounty for future use: 'Let everyone regard himself as the steward of God in all things which he possesses. Then he will neither conduct himself dissolutely, not corrupt by abuse those things which God requires to be preserved.'[18]

Genesis 2:15, of which this is an interpretation, does not suggest that the earth, or indeed any natural resource, is anything other than the possession of God, but one can clearly read the obligation made explicit in Calvin's interpretation in the following passage: 'And the Lord God took the man, and put him into the garden of Eden to dress it and keep it.' Looked upon within a context of the history of ideas of nature, as Clarence Glacken has noted, such a view 'is closely linked with the responsibility that a temporary sojourner on earth has toward posterity', although in Locke's thinking the idea of *possessing* something – nature – and of this being an important aspect of self-hood, more emphatically moves the notions of natural space and its resources into the domain of individual freedom (with all the ramifications this has for the production of garbage, as we will see).[19] Locke's discussion of property in his *Second Treatise of Government* outlines the philosophical basis for claims to propriety over land (but also extends to a whole host of what we might call 'natural resources'). In Locke's terms, claims to property ownership rest on an idea of the proper use of land, which entails the appropriation (through the use of one's labour) of its previously unused potential. In an echo of John Calvin, Locke said that:

> God, when he gave the world in common to all mankind,
> commanded man also to labour, and the penury of his condition
> required it of him. God and his reason commanded him to subdue
> the earth, i.e. improve it for the benefit of life, and therein lay
> out something upon it that was his own, his labour.[20]

Implicit in this passage is the idea of a natural potential that would be squandered if human labour failed to make best use of it, something that Locke made clear in a later passage where he highlights the inherent wastefulness of a nature left untended: 'Land that is left wholly to nature, that hath no improvement of pasturage, tillage, or planting, is called, as indeed it is, *waste*; and we shall find the benefit of it amount to little more than nothing.'[21] Thus the idea of waste here corresponds to a particular economy of human values. In Locke's time – the seventeenth century – there appeared to be a general concern, especially within Christian thinking, that the fruits of nature are not simply given as a consequence of some existing state of abundance. In fact the belief is quite the contrary; that there is no such abundance – there is only waste – and without the vigilance of God expressed through his stewards on earth, 'the order of nature would be wiped out in a moment and would revert to the original chaos'.[22] But there is also a moral imperative at work in Locke's views of nature simply because it was taken to be the case that 'nothing was made by God for man to spoil or destroy'. So it is nature itself that is unruly or wasteful; but only insofar as its deterioration is permitted by what Calvin would have regarded as 'dissolute conduct'.[23] Thus, according to Locke, human endeavour (human labour, commonly taken as the opposite of moral dissolution in Locke's philosophy) is the quality that makes nature efficient, and that makes something out of a potentially vast natural uselessness.[24] The proper use of land is thus the fulfilment of God's will, and so Locke's understanding of spoilage and waste moves him beyond his political contemporaries, who also laid emphasis on the importance of the efficient use of nature for human ends, and 'into the uniquely Calvinist terrain of stewardship, just usage and divine calling'.[25]

Because Locke had made the moral case for the proper use of land, he was able to take his argument further, into a justification of the right to use untended nature, by employing the notion of waste in another sense that entailed both censure for the failure to put nature to use and the appropriation of land for those who would:

> If either the grass of his enclosure rotted on the ground, or the fruit of his planting perished without gathering, and laying up, this part of the earth, notwithstanding his enclosure, was still to be looked upon as waste, and might be the possession of any other.[26]

Following the will of God that (in the words of Calvin) 'nothing is more contrary to the order of nature, than to consume life in eating, drinking and sleeping, while in the meantime we propose nothing to ourselves to do', such an understanding links possession of land to 'proper use'. This connection between person and land, itself seemingly the source of accountability to God for one's efforts, allows us to highlight the theoretical unity of this idea of 'garbage' under the headings of this chapter – waste, imperfection, disorder and ruin – in that all are linked by what we find here in these ideas of waste – its *indeterminateness*, the references to places or things that belong to neither one person nor another, its being the original condition of nature's chaos. This is recognized in the tradition of gleaning, where the leftovers from harvesting were accepted as being the property of anyone that should come upon them. Sir William Blackstone's *Commentaries on the Laws of England* of 1768 tells us that 'The poor are allowed to enter and glean upon another's ground after the harvest, without being guilty of trespass.'[27]

Others have stressed that in fact there is no waste in nature, certainly not in the Calvinist sense employed by John Locke. To be sure, nature is subject to constant upheavals that are destructive, or that lay waste to natural features of the physical environment, but, as Glacken notes in his discussion of George Hakewill (a seventeenth-century natural historian and author of *An Apologie, or Declaration of the Power and Providence of God in the Government of the World*, first published in 1627), this is not the same as the 'waste' consequent upon failing to fulfil one's role as God's steward on earth. Hakewill was a notable, and according to Glacken, eloquent defender of the belief that the planet was not ageing (that is, not undergoing a process of deterioration), but undergoing changes that actually improved on its supposedly perfect original condition. This was because whilst 'the earth is the scene of great transports of soil from one place to another, in the wearing down of mountains, in the building up of deltaic plains . . . nothing is lost'.[28] Hakewill outlines the argument given by some of his predecessors who believed that nature was engaged in an irreversible decline as soon as Adam and Eve were cast out of Eden, and does this in an attempt to understand the corresponding view that nature, in a sense, rots away as it ages. This was a view of the perfection of nature that rested on the supposed superiority of originality as against maturation, suggesting a point had been passed after which the only inevitability remaining is natural degradation. Thus:

> the Creature the nearer it approaches the first mould, the more perfect it is, and according to the degrees of its removeall and distance from thence, it incurres the more imperfection and weaknesse, as streams of a fountain, the farther they run thorow uncleane passages, the more they contract corruption.[29]

Thus, while Locke's understanding of waste has come to be associated with a theory of property rights, it was nonetheless driven by the idea that any benefits that would result from such rights – including the bountiful goods of nature – were dependent on *duty* to a higher power. There is no indication that Locke shares the rather different view also found in the work of some seventeenth-century natural philosophers that the world had been in a long decline ever since its exit from the antediluvian paradise. One notable proponent of this view was Thomas Burnet, clergyman and author of *Sacred Theory of the Earth* (1753) who, according to Glacken, was:

> so obsessed with the idea that the earth is a pile of 'Ruines and Rubbish' whose mountains have not the 'least foot steps of Art or Counsel', a globe which is a 'rude *Lump*' a 'little dirty Planet', that he would grant it neither order nor beauty.[30]

Such concerns with the potential degradation of nature have continued into the present, again grounded in some idea of a lost or abandoned state of perfection, and can also be seen in the language and attitudes of preservationist movements. For example, leading figures in the development of the Council for the Protection of Rural England (CPRE) made the case for the stewardship of the English countryside by utilizing what David Matless has termed 'binary contrasts of good and evil, order and chaos, beauty and horror', which had the purpose of claiming a 'clear and absolute authority over landscape'.[31] Under the new conditions of the twentieth century, however, the idea of God as master of nature was replaced by an appeal for a new authority; namely central government. A leading figure in the CPRE, Clough Williams-Ellis, would claim that only an organization like the CPRE, backed by government legislation on the matter, could prevent disorder consuming the natural beauty of the countryside (which, of course, was not 'natural' at all, but the result of centuries of human 'interfering'):

> Discipline! How unwilling we English are to submit to even a little of it . . . But we do in the end submit; we did in the War and we should do so yet again in this matter of preserving England . . . In this matter, I say, we are petitioning to be governed; we ask for control, for discipline. We have tried freedom and, under present conditions, we see that it leads to waste, inefficiency and chaos.[32]

These preservationists were interested in *settling* the English countryside, and here this meant preventing it, on the one hand, from turning into a human building site, and on the other from lapsing uncontrollably into a destructive natural cycle, both of which threatened to permanently alter the face of the landscape. It was the threat of it all going to wrack and ruin through a neglect of duty that symbolized an unnecessary waste: the absence of an order that could be easily exercised over the unruly abundance of nature simply invited a natural 'will to disorder' to make itself apparent.

And within a broadly conceived understanding we see this neglect to apply also to the behaviour of the individual person. Thus, in history and literature, idleness (or doing nothing) creates its own garbage, and is often associated with generally unwanted, perhaps unseen, consequences. In Machiavelli's *The Prince,* for example, we read that the idleness of states that failed to arm and protect themselves adequately offered a corresponding opportunity to an ambitious and competing power to extend its domain.[33] This is a belief that was clearly understood during the Second World War. A good example of this is the series of posters, produced by the US War Production Board in the 1930s and '40s (see opposite), that echoes this Machiavellian warning by associating idleness not only with playing into the hands of the enemy, but also, by unwittingly inviting ruin through a failure to be aware of the consequences of laziness. Doing nothing is more generally the source of bad character (it has affinities with the *akrasia,* or weakness of will, found in Aristotle's *Ethics*) and can develop into a paradoxically active trait that erodes what is good and virtuous. At several places in Ivan Klíma's novel *Love and Garbage* – a novel that has the eventual decay of everything as its central metaphor – a parallel is drawn between neglect and garbage. Laziness here becomes characteristic of a void, or a pit into which one may sink, and where things (relationships, lives) also waste away or deteriorate. An example of this is the relationship between the narrator and his wife, which under a variety of external pressures (including the narrator's preoccupation with his inability to write) is falling to pieces. He is aware that his wife felt that their relationship had been consumed by apathy, in their taking each other for granted: 'she tried to convince me that what people, including we two, were lacking was ritual. For years we hadn't courted one another very much, and as a result, a mundane element had invaded our relationship.'[34]

So the absence of an intense or persevering will gives rise to a wasting. This theme emerges as well in another contemporary novel, Don DeLillo's *Underworld,* where garbage is a central metaphor, and in which we see adolescent Nick Shay (who as an adult becomes a waste consultant) in a scene with Father Paulus, a Jesuit priest responsible for his education:

> 'Have you come across the word velleity? A nice Thomistic ring to it. Volition at its lowest ebb. A small thing, a wish, a tendency. If you're low-willed, you see, you end up living in the shallowest turns and bends of your own preoccupations. Are we getting anywhere?'
>
> 'It's your confession, Father.'
>
> 'Aquinas said only intense actions will strengthen a habit. Not mere repetition. Intensity makes for moral accomplishment. An intense and persevering will. This is an element of seriousness.

Is This Your Machine? c. 1942–3, photomechanical print.

Constancy. This is an element. A sense of purpose. A self-chosen goal.'[35]

The need for an external and directing purpose also harks back to the reasons why many 'physico-theological' conceptions of nature were so prevalent in early modern society (not to mention the importance of the idea of wasteland in John Locke's theory of property), resting in large part on the idea that waste depends on an understanding that there has been a human failure; that waste results from a neglect of duty in failing to cultivate God's land.[36] But, as we have seen, that particular conception of waste operated within an economy of human values in which the consequences of doing nothing to prevent natural erosion was either known through experience, or for those who would hear them, from frequent reminders from the pulpit.[37] Something can only be wasted in this sense if it is already 'there' – present – to be worked upon and is ignored, neglected, or used improperly.

The particular sense of 'waste' that we derive from idleness does not avoid spilling over into the related notion of moral impropriety, in so far as the psychological equivalent of a physical failure to act to prevent nature's ruin – indifference to the needs of people around you – invites those things we usually value in relationships to come apart, as Klíma's narrator was aware: 'I returned to lies once more. There is nothing by which a person can justify a lie. It corrodes the soul just as much as indifference or hate.'[38] The metaphor of 'corrosion' forces us to see its opposite, solidity (or perhaps incorruptibility) as the equivalent of moral goodness and psychological health. 'To corrode' in its original meaning is, Klíma's narrator reflects, literally to 'gnaw away to pieces'.[39] And in terms of the relationship between Klíma's two central characters we see that it emanates from a debilitating human failure that can only be halted by a restatement of honesty and truth or, alternatively, the opposite courses of disengagement and abandonment.

The relaxation that permits the dropping of some moral standard (in resorting to lies, for example) cultivates an attitude of indolence. In this sense, to be guilty of laziness implies moral dissolution and the abandonment of virtue to nothingness. Intense work, or vigilance, must meet the lure of relaxation with fortitude if one is to avoid moral laxity, as the narrator of *Love and Garbage* notes:

I had never before been able to stay by the water for even a few hours, I was frightened by the void of laziness. I could not be totally lazy . . . I always had to escape the reach of the black pit which I invariably saw before me as soon as I was quietly relaxing anywhere.[40]

In John Keats's 'Ode on Indolence' the specific threat of the 'lazy' summer day is that it induces a numbness that leaves one unresponsive to all feeling and, like those who were perceived to have succumbed to the sin of sloth in the Middle Ages, potentially emptied of any goodness, and thus, we assume, at the mercy of anything that might fill up the void:

> My idle days? Ripe was the drowsy hour;
> The blissful cloud of summer indolence
> Benumb'd my eyes; my pulse grew less and less;
> Pain had no sting and pleasure's wreath no flower:
> O, why did ye not melt, and leave my sense
> Unhaunted quite of all but – nothingness?[41]

If this kind of numbness represents a state of being spiritually afloat between destinations, idleness is equally taken to be the result of being in too many 'places' in quick succession, or of thinking too randomly. Garbage, here, is once again symbolized by indeterminateness. What is common between these two apparent contradictory states – being disengaged and being over-engaged – is that they share in nothingness, in being – psychologically, or physically – without roots. As Montaigne suggested in his essay 'On Idleness': 'The mind that has no fixed aim loses itself, for, as they say, to be everywhere is to be nowhere.' In other words, leaving things alone – not *working* with a goal in mind – simply invites destructive tendencies to come to the fore. Montaigne compared *wasted land* with the idle mind, and noted how in nature 'ground that lies fallow, teeming, if rich and fertile, with countless kinds of wild and useless plants' requires the restraint and mastery of the human hand to keep wildness at bay. Thus, seeing the havoc that this can bring forth, the mind cannot be left to follow its own ruminations – as it is with nature, 'so it is with our minds. If we do not occupy them with some definite subject which curbs and restrains them, they rush wildly to and fro in the ill-defined field of the imagination'.[42]

Montaigne's essay anticipates Francisco de Goya's famous etching *The Sleep of Reason Produces Monsters* (c.1794–9) by a good two hundred years, but brings to life the ruinous consequences of the untended imagination in a vivid metaphor that displays how much we avoid the wasteful by ensuring the imagination is tethered for proper use. It is a lack of rational focus that allows the vacant mind to wander: 'like a runaway horse [the mind] is a hundred times more active on its own behalf than it ever was for others. It presents me with so many chimeras and imaginary monsters, one after another, without order or plan.'[43]

The physical state of being rootless, of being visibly outside community norms, is one thing that characterizes so-called 'wasters'. These people are usually itinerants of one sort or another who fail to conform to the social norms of stability and, as a consequence, are deemed to exist beyond the kind of controls and restraints that would make them reliable and trustworthy. So-called 'normal' society further excludes and distances itself from them. Such 'offenders against society' – everyone from vagabonds, wanderers, rogues, prostitutes, pimps, gamblers,[44] to people who refused to work for wages – were subject to a variety of vagrancy laws that attempted to solicit conformity. One such law defined vagabonds as:

> Idle and dissolute persons who went about and begged, runaways, pilferers, drunkards, night-walkers, lewd people, wanton and lascivious persons, railers and brawlers, persons without a calling or profession, visitors of tippling houses and houses of illfame, and wanderers.[45]

What we have lumped together here under a single catch-all category of 'vagrancy' is a whole host of potential offenders: those who want something for nothing; those who deny social conventions; rabblerousers and drunkards, and so on. A common element in perceptions of all such outsiders is that they do not take measures to sustain their lives against simply wasting away, without having achieved anything noteworthy or virtuous. And because of their inability to subject themselves to control, social morality (as well as the law) sees to it that the wasteful activities of such people are looked down upon disdainfully, and regarded as bad examples for the rest of society. If these examples are taken into consideration, then the symbols of waste all point to things that have eluded the guiding hand of human social organization, or indeed have simply got out of control, as is the case with the waste that is evident in the debris of unfettered consumption.

The idea of laziness also leads us to consider the importance of our civilized notion of linear time, and to the realization that it is principally time that structures the human orientation to waste; which is to say, as much as 'waste' requires some human (often moral or religious) standard to convey its power, its ability to communicate the gravity in a lapse actually rests on the fact that temporal experience has shown that all living matter (as well as natural and human made objects) deteriorates. Time is the proof that we do not escape these universal processes of generation and decay, and so laziness (by inviting time to corrode life) has to be resisted lest it reveal the futility of our attempts to master it. It is deterioration itself that has to be mastered. Shakespeare's 'Capricious Time' brilliantly captures this need for a vigilant attitude toward the future in guiding our conduct – as the only means, indeed, of postponing the eventual corrosive decline:

> Time hath, my Lord, a wallet at his back
> Wherein he puts alms for oblivion,
> A great-sized monster of ingratitudes:
> Those scraps are good deeds past, which are devoured
> As fast as they are made, forgot as soon
> As done. Perseverance, dear my Lord,
> Keeps honour bright: to have done, is to hang
> Quite of fashion, like a rusty nail.[46]

Thus, to avoid being consigned to the past – to avoided being disposed of, we might say, alongside those things and people that 'have done', to keep honour bright, to remain within the control of *present-ness* – is to keep up the good work; to keep working at it.

IMPERFECTION

Attempts to escape the destructive potential of time face a difficulty in the fact that the temporality of human existence ultimately runs on a different track to the abstract divisions of the clock and calendar that have, since the dawn of the industrial age, convinced us that there is a human time that may escape the eventual decay of everything 'natural'. Indeed, time is the primary agent of obsolescence where garbage correspondingly becomes (to the extent that it is visible, or an object of experience) the evidence of our failure to escape 'natural' time.

Deteriorating matter (whether in the form of faeces or discarded consumer goods) embodies a time that exists beyond our rational time: in this shadow world, time is always running matter down, breaking things into pieces, or removing the sheen of a glossy surface and, therefore, the principal methods of dealing with material waste throughout most of human history – dumping, burning, recycling, reducing the use of virgin materials – are simply ways of ensuring that this fact does not intrude too far into everyday experience.[47] In contemporary society the increase in the volume of consumer products may force a strict reorganization of time, in so far as the situation can be met by adherence to a regime that ensures the removal of these objects before they decay. We see an illustration of this in Don DeLillo's *Underworld,* where the central character Nick Shay and his wife have become obsessed with garbage: 'Marian and I saw products as garbage even when they sat gleaming on store shelves . . . we asked whether it is responsible to eat a certain item if the package it comes in will live a million years.'[48]

Such sentiments may be the mere recognition of the undeniable truth of the fact that contemporary society realizes an abundance of consumer products, which are all apparently differentiated by the surface branding that masks the very material consequences of such consumption. Aside from the packaging on food products, their other chief characteristic is that they exist in virtue of the ubiquitous sell-by date, meaning that product lives are fixed by a pre-assigned 'death'. Indeed, in terms of the introduction of new products and new lines, as Susan Strasser notes in *Waste and Want,* some manufacturers of consumer goods in the United States during the 1950s were already thinking in terms of 'product death-dates'.[49] Nowhere in advertising will this be made explicit (the characters of Nick and Marion in *Underworld* are, generally speaking, exceptional in their foresight), but in terms of the functional obsolescence of objects the development of new product lines is directed by the idea that new technology will improve our lives – or, indeed, that new fashions will make us feel better about ourselves. Curiously, then, fashion embodies one of the key ideas of modernity, in as much as the guiding idea is that the future (it is assumed) will be better than the past, and so in modern society the Christian notion of eternity has been secularized into one of irreversible time, a notion that holds out the promise that progress to the future entails the overcoming of error, defect and imperfection.[50]

A peculiar way of looking at modernity might see it as a kind of figment of the transcendental imagination; as Matei Calinescu says, a heaven that is not other-worldly, but located at some distant, unspecified, point in the future. Thus:

> Utopian imagination as it has developed since the eighteenth century is one more proof of the modern devaluation of the past and the growing importance of the future. Utopianism, however, would hardly be conceived outside the specific time consciousness of the West, as it was shaped by Christianity and subsequently by reason's appropriation of the concept of irreversible time.[51]

It is easy to see modernity then as the spectral double of its Christian predecessor, which by the advance of technology would overcome the decaying reality of temporal existence that Christianity offered only in the next world.[52] The salient point about such an entropic modernity is that under the conditions of experience it inaugurates, it becomes inconceivable that we could now occupy a world without obsolescence. With garbage banished to the past and imagination and desire set on the future, of course garbage is overlooked by history and in memory. How could it be otherwise? And if desire gets caught up in the pursuit of pleasure – of happiness – who can fail to recognize the irreducible truth, the aptness, of Nietzsche's observation regarding the close relationship between the necessity of disposing of what is past and successful self-affirmation.

> Anyone who cannot forget the past entirely and set himself down on the threshold of the moment, anyone who cannot stand, without dizziness or fear, on one single point like a victory goddess, will never know what happiness is . . . All action requires forgetting, just as the existence of all organic things requires not only light, but darkness as well.[53]

It seems, however, that in the twentieth century the emergence of psychoanalysis proved the failure of such attempts at total forgetting. Jean Baudrillard remarked upon this development as an aspect of our relationship to the abundance of a world that may appear to stand in opposition to the self:

Psychoanalysis itself is the first great theoritization of residues (lapses, dreams, etc.). It is no longer a political economy of production that directs us, but an economic politics of reproduction, of recycling – ecology and pollution – a political economy of the remainder. All normality sees itself today in the light of madness, which was nothing but its insignificant remainder.[54]

And so we may suggest that garbage provides a shadow history of modern life where the conditions for its production and the means by which it is rendered invisible cast it as an unwelcome double of the person; the uncanny and spectral presence that only in death recombines with the body to realize fully the modern hope of self-identity. An identity that fingers us as merely matter. Perhaps the most adequate theoretical conceptualization of garbage is to be found in the notion of the *uncanny*. If garbage is the unwelcome shadow that trails the present (its deformed or spectral double) then we may recognize it in Freud's understanding of the uncanny as the eerily familiar object, image or phantom that continually resists any of our attempts to disconnect from it – it is the remainder as unwelcome presence. 'In reality', Freud remarked, the uncanny is 'nothing new or alien, but something which is familiar and old – established in the mind and which has become alienated from it only through the process of repression.'[55] Uncanny garbage then becomes capable of inducing horror because of the presumed harmful effects it has on the bodies of personal and social order, indicating their fragile and transient nature.

If garbage in all its forms can be said to represent nature (including human existence) as an endless process of generation and decay, then this is only exaggerated by the fact that knowledge and reason involve a separation of the human from the natural. This is the result of our technological adaptability – where 'technology' is understood in its Aristotelian sense of *techne* – meaning both that which is distinct from the totality of nature (*phusis*), and nature made in the human image (as Heidegger wrote, technology is the *ordering of nature* for use).[56] This separation undergoes further refinement throughout the development of modernity, which from the medieval privy to the division of labour and the development of an economy of consumption illustrates a trend towards successive separations that lead to further differentiation at the individual level, which *at the same time* (and through the network of social associations that sustain life) results in an almost total abstraction from reality. As an aspect of the progress of

Western individualism, what begins with the rationalization and privatization of excremental waste ends in the ubiquity of fashion – both the water closet and the fashion boutique thrive on the power of disposal to abolish the past, and to cleanse, empty and adorn the present. Thus, where the modern household toilet expels the dead matter that exits from the body stripped of its positive, life-giving, properties, the machinery of fashion symbolically *flushes* the past. Like everything else in modern society fashion is established on the basis of a strict organization of time and the fashionable lives only by the sell-by date (which is to say, once again, its death is already anticipated).

The other side of obsolescence, of course, is found in desire, with the two combined in a dance of death. In the 'empire of fashion' – as Gilles Lipovetsky describes consumer society – products take on the force of magical charms, promising untold varieties of self-renewal:

> Along with the agitation that is characteristic of fashion there arises an order of 'autonomous' phenomena, responding only to the play of human desires, whims and wishes . . . Everything connected with appearance is by rights at the disposal of individuals who are henceforth free to modify the fleeting signs, to make them more sophisticated; the only limitations are contemporary standards of appropriation and taste.[57]

The genius of obsolescence is seen in the way it conceals garbage within this capacity of the individual to 'modify the fleeting signs', whilst at the same time promoting novelty in a way that obscures the horizon of finitude that situates all human experience. What is the result of all this? Clearly, the abolition of temporality under the conditions of a social organization of time in, for example, functional or planned obsolescence, feeds on and is sustained by fashion's endless procession. Yet in doing so, it produces ever more dead matter.

Again and again we return to the importance of time in all this. Time fundamentally conditions the creation of garbage in that it provides the framework within which things become corruptible and useless. The planned obsolescence of certain consumables will render them superfluous prior to any actual or obvious material degradation. When this occurs objects come to represent imperfection simply in virtue of the fact that by contrast with some new or improved version they fail to match up to the latest vision of perfection.[58] As design historians Ellen Lupton and J. A. Miller have noted, the early twentieth century saw the development of a new kind of consumer economy where 'waste became an essential component of the production cycle' because a market would otherwise fail when it reached saturation point, and thus 'industry . . . needed to shorten the natural "lifespan" of "durable" products, so that people would buy them not once but several times, thereby stabilizing the production cycle'.[59] Yet, aside from such planned failures (and forgetting for the moment our faith in perfectible technologies) do we have any right to expect that we can actually banish garbage? The truth is surely that the durability of any particular thing is contingent upon circumstances that cannot always be controlled. In other words, objects eventually exemplify imperfection because they break, develop defects or display other flaws.

We consume and discard more than consumer products, however. And we degrade more than spaces, places and things. The truth is that these behaviours and the processes they set in motion are also directed towards the incorporeal objects of knowledge. Thus corruptibility spills over from the material world of objects into the imperfection of useless knowledge and beliefs, where defective knowledge, at the extreme, may represent a threat to life.

We might easily overlook the fact that the wake of certainty – of reason – is error. In the history of knowledge what is often forgotten or passed over is the variety of defects that (despite their eventual uselessness) actually make a significant contribution to the progress of knowledge. Because language and knowledge are always engaged in a process of connecting to a world that is taken to be real (or, indeed, 'objectively' knowable), we can easily fail to remember the parts that are detached and consigned to the garbage pit of error and defect, rendered unimportant or insignificant. During the seventeenth century, for example, certain imperfections that could no longer slot into the more complete picture of the natural world that a new scientific understanding aimed for nevertheless drew the attention of the great minds of the time, the forerunners of our (far more specialized) contemporary scientists. Whilst useless knowledge exemplified an imperfect means of uncovering reality, it often, according to Rosalie L. Colie, stood as a validation of scientific experimentation simply by highlighting the tricks that natural phenomena could play on the imagination. Which is to say, these defective sources of knowledge – this garbage – revealed the inherent folly of not adopting scientific standards for the study the natural world. Examples included imitations of the marvellous effects of nature, which were presented in various 'houses' or 'chambers', such as those described in Francis Bacon's *New Atlantis* (1626). This work included the following revealing description of a 'Perspective-House', which represents the corruptibility of dubious 'facts'. It contained, Bacon wrote:

> All Delusions and Deceits of the Sight, in Figures, Magnitudes, Motions, Colours: All Demonstrations of Shadowes. Wee finde also diverse Means yet unknowne to you, of Producing of Light, originally, from diverse Bodies. We procure meanes of Seeing Objects a-farr off; As in the Heaven, and Remote Places; And represent things Neare as A-farr off, And things A-farr off as Neare; Making Faigned Distances.[60]

As Lorraine Daston and Katherine Park note, Bacon intended these imagined 'preparations and instruments to dampen rather than to feed the wonder he elsewhere called *broken knowledge*'.[61] The knowledge, in other words, that 'is nothing but contemplation broken off, or losing itself'.[62] Thus, chopped off from the main body of knowledge, these errors come to constitute the ruminations and dead ends of apparently pointless intellectual curiosity. And if, as the German philosopher Odo Marquard would say some two hundred years later, 'sense is just the nonsense we throw away', then such broken knowledge deserved to be seen as garbage.[63]

Whilst cabinets of curiosities and the like displayed the gullibility of a human mind that was unable to discriminate between, on the one hand, the fantastic wonders of nature (physical deformities, apparitions, and so on) and, on the other, an understanding of how nature might be classified for use, the division and ordering of knowledge had already been challenged by the invention of the printing press in the mid-fifteenth century. In his *Social History of Knowledge* Peter Burke notes that the consternation this technological innovation caused amongst scholars helped to develop the idea that knowledge would be totally useless without a great deal of tidying up, for the printing press was like an incontinent child discharging waste indiscriminately and without the ability to exercise any self-restraint. The 'disorder of books' that followed upon an unconstrained increase in printed matter demanded control.[64] The relationship between such a necessary clean up and the actual usefulness of the resulting knowledge is illustrated by the case of the encyclopaedia. Again Burke notes that the uncontrolled excess of the printing revolution had obviously made encyclopaedias more readily and more widely available [but also] made them even more necessary than they had been before the invention of the press. To be more precise, one of their functions became increasingly necessary, that of guiding readers through the ever-growing forest – not to say, jungle – of printed knowledge.[65]

What the encyclopaedia would offer stood in stark contrast to a simple and childlike fascination with the curious anomalies of nature – those bits of reality that by their abnormality or rarity no longer fitted: the encyclopaedia represented the possibility of a complete account of knowledge in all its totality and connectedness. The unexplainable curiosities were, by contrast, a kind of garbage: disconnected from their origin, they spoke of the unruliness of a nature that in its messiness belied the universality of the new science of causes championed by Bacon, which thus constituted a retreat into certainty.

In its positive elaboration, or in the reconstitution of some causal chain or network, knowledge produces its own picture. What Bacon's 'broken knowledge' tells us is that this is a picture that is always being remade, or retaken (in the sense that knowledge *takes* or withdraws itself from something greater; again, knowledge is the sense that is produced from nonsense). Among these endless acts of appropriation, the leftovers are the once constitutive but now expelled remainders; or, to use Nietzsche's analogy, the *costumes that we tried on* but found to be ill-fitting, not to our taste, and so on.[66] How then, do we understand this act of *taking,* yet still fail to see its remainders? Jean Baudrillard has remarked on this erroneous perception, common at the level of everyday thinking, which seems to conclude along the following lines: 'when everything is taken away, nothing is left'.[67] But the truth is, as we have seen, that there is always a leftover – because some*thing* (indeed, every *thing*), is distinguished from something else that stands apart from, or in opposition to, it.

The world we conceptualize, speak and philosophize about, like the physical world, consists of a vast storehouse of stuff, some of which (at any given time) will be known to us, some not so. As some of the philosophers of nature realized in centuries past, the world undergoes various traumas and upheavals – in the migration of earth and water, in the gigantic mountain ranges thrown up by tectonic unrest, and so on – but this is just matter moving around. In a sense, nothing disappears; nor does the planet import matter from elsewhere. Instead, matter is just reconstituted in new forms, perhaps in different places, and appears new to the human mind, which is taught the value of refashioning. From the inclusive point of view of an economy of human values, such remainders (material and conceptual) are, according to Baudrillard, a 'gigantic waste product'.[68] Thus, 'it is not that there is no remainder. But, this remainder never has an autonomous reality, nor its own place: it is what partition, circumspection, exclusion designate . . . It is through the subtraction of the remainder that reality is founded and gathers strength.'[69]

And so no thing that manages to constitute itself as a part of some totality of human understanding (or way of seeing the world) avoids the mark of impurity that makes it a living thing. All attempts to present a unity of knowledge, or an overcoming of error, results in the creation of garbage, in other words. Examples of this are found with political ideologies, in particular. One example of this, as Geoffrey Bennington has observed, can be seen if we consider the ideology of Marxism as a living, moving thing. As a 'body' of beliefs and values,

> [the] body of 'Marxism' . . . both secures and compromises its unity and integrity as a body by ingesting and expelling or excreting, leaving behind a trail of what it was in the form of the waste-product, the *déchet*, the dropping. The history of what Marxism itself expels, as its own 'deviations' (due to the absorption of foreign bodies) or its own 'vulgar' versions (generated by internal or intestinal malfunctions) could persuasively be read, in eminently materialist terms, as a history of digestion and eventually of shit.[70]

So it is that knowledge is more generally regimented for particular ends by the purging of the excess.

DISORDER AND CONTAMINATION

If we recall that garbage arrives at its fate because it either suffers or effects some disconnection – it is the separation of a part from some greater whole – we can see in the symbols of disorder the guiding power of garbage to, on the one hand, enforce the separation of part from whole, whilst at the same time rehearsing the steps that lead to the banishment of garbage. We might further understand garbage by exploring how it helps to organize the boundary between order and disorder across various aspects of experience.

A simple, but nonetheless illuminating example: how can we comprehend the written exhortation on the packing of a simple bar of soap, which claims to be capable of clearing a path to the fulfilment of any number of nameless desires? 'Break through all obstacles that present themselves,' declares the magical cleanser: 'no matter how difficult, and simultaneously cut all malign influences that may ensnare you.'[71] This soap is clearly powerful stuff, and its capacity for assisting the pursuit of personal freedom signals the importance of a notable *absence*, namely that which it claims to vanquish. In an example of good-humoured superstition that plays also to a common ambition to get on in the world, this soap merely declares slightly more forcefully what most of us are made aware of from early in childhood, and that is the disordering power of the unclean. Thus, the symbolic power of the message is delivered not only through the contrast between dirt and its opposite of cleanliness, but also through the awareness that soap *destroys* dirt. This also brings to mind something that the anthropologist Mary Douglas famously noted in her study of pollution taboos, namely that dirt *is* disorder: 'Where there is dirt there is system. Dirt is the by-product of a systematic ordering and classification of matter, in so far as ordering involves rejecting inappropriate elements.'[72]

It is easy to focus on dirt here and overlook the idea that it is more importantly an instance of disorder that provides the spur to order – or more precisely we need to be clear that order and disorder determine each other (because the order we settle on, for example, marks a point of exclusion). All social systems, Mary Douglas suggested, organized themselves around some basic acceptance of the pure and contaminating; although this need not be (as was the case with early developments in public health) because 'we are governed by anxiety to escape disease' but may rather be because 'we are positively re-ordering our environment, making it conform to an idea'.[73] Once again we are caught within a certain economy of values (meaning that the values within such a system are not rigid, but are subject to change and variation), and whilst dirt (or indeed, garbage) will have a variable status between cultures, it is nevertheless conditioned within cultural constraints by the creation of an order. We find much the same point made in a quite different analysis – Michael Thompson's less well-known book *Rubbish Theory* – in which the view is presented that 'the boundary between rubbish and non-rubbish moves in response to social pressures [but that nevertheless] waste is a necessary condition for society'.[74] What needs to be said therefore reaches beyond the temporal domain of specific cultures, and this is *that everything is eventually reduced to the condition of dirt.* That garbage looms everywhere, and in everything that becomes, once again, *humus.*

If we leave that to one side for a moment, what we might also say about traces of material disorder (for example, dirt, filth and dust) is that these become symbolic of garbage not simply because they represent displaced matter, but more precisely because of 'things' such as their actual formlessness (i.e., they may have been something once but are now nothing), and also because when the taint of garbage is attached to other things (whether in actuality or by association through language – for example, 'you are *filth*', 'you *dirty* bastard') it has the effect of reducing the value of the thing in question, and of stripping it of any descriptive characteristics that allow us to individuate it.[75] However, because the daily acts of cleaning, scrubbing and concealing that we routinely indulge in conspire to remove the dirt, to hold the garbaging of the self at bay, and to put some order over our affairs, our bodies (and so on), we must recognize the symbolism of garbage is perversely found in its opposite of order and cleanliness, in the objects and arrangements that temporarily *conceal* it – in the magical power of soap to 'remove all obstacles', and to clear a path to the future. Take, for example, Dominique Laporte's statement on the duplicity of the manufactured scents that are so commonplace in human cultures:

> Smells have no place in the constitutive triad of civilization: hygiene, order and beauty. In the empire of hygiene and order, odor will always be suspect. Even when exquisite, it will hint at hidden filth submerged in excessive perfume, its very sweetness redolent of intoxication and vice.[76]

It is the cosmetically applied surfaces that nevertheless become equated with life. Looking through catalogues of home furnishings, for example, it would seem that the perfect home is entirely devoid of any kind of debris, of anything that does not have a proper place, and that in fact the happy life is only attained by reaching some nirvana of blankness; by the erasure of moving, mutable, life in favour of the frozen ideal of the impossible and motionless snapshot of perfection. As Adrian Forty notes, the pursuit of cleanliness has reached into all kinds of environments:

In the decades since the 1930s, the aesthetic of cleanliness seems to have been accepted unquestioningly as the proper appearance of household goods of all kinds. Likewise the imagery of exaggerated hygiene appears in many other modern environments, such as trains, aeroplanes and public buildings.[77]

Compare such images then, to those that we don't usually see (certainly not as indications of a bright new future), those that would portray the inherent disorder of matter that is left uncontrolled. Household disorder symbolizes garbage in the simple sense that the evident excess of a space groaning with objects it can barely hold sees it take on qualities beyond the objects themselves (because these are difficult to distinguish from mere *stuff*). It becomes detached from its *ideal*, from what we are led to believe is its ostensible purpose, to become the monster that controls your life. It contains the stuff you trip over, it buries that document you have been looking for under another pile of 'stuff', and so on. Hence the emergence of a lifestyle psychology that (like the soap found in Mexico City) promotes the removal of obstacles to happiness through what is called 'dejunking'.[78] Dejunking aims to convince us that our present and future 'wellness' (as opposed to illness) rests on removing the clutter that clogs up our lives and chains us to the past. And here also the disorder extends to the minutiae of daily living, to the processes by which we decide how we present ourselves. Any hint of indecision (in the ideology of dejunking) indicates the presence of a disordering element and becomes symbolic of garbage ('I don't know what to wear'), and speaks of a lack of self-control. Here the person is paralysed, stuck in the swamp of doubt.

The recognition of this lack of control carries over into residual social categories, notably (in recent times) with the increasing visibility of so-called 'white trash' in the United States. On the one hand the language of 'trash' here refers to the vulgar ostentation of particular people who, no matter what their other achievements, never escape this judgement of inadequacy. An example is Elvis Presley. Whilst he may have been the 'king of rock'n'roll' he was also the so-called 'burger king', who remains forever white trash because even his great wealth and fame never pushed him to escape his lowly origins nor his lack of social refinement.[79] We see other aspects of white trash vulgarity paraded on television shows like *The Jerry Springer Show* (with episode titles like 'I'm Pregnant By My Brother', and where guests regularly resort to fisticuffs, as if participants in some bizarre latter-day carnival sideshow). The association of 'white trash' with such examples of socially unacceptable behaviour serves to reduce those it identifies to a position of social lowness, making it clear that to belong to this category of undesirables can be seen by others as 'a singular, shameful condition', according to John Hartigan. And whilst 'white trash' generally refers to the poor white (usually from the southern states of the USA) who exist as exceptions to community norms, in more specific terms it is applied as a term of disapprobation directed at 'grotesques' (seen anywhere):

> People continually asked me if I had visited the W family, a brood of about eleven parentless teenage and pre-adolescent children, most reputed to be 'retarded' – living in a sprawling shack surrounded by half-cannibalized car bodies with their indigestible innards chaotically strewn about.[80]

White trash are perceived to be potential contaminants in the sense that they could *bring the neighbourhood down* or *lower the tone*. So, these people are 'trash' not in virtue of some lowly occupation that ensures a proximity to garbage (as might be the case with any number of social menials – refuse collectors, cleaners and so on), but simply in terms of their failure to rise to a socially acceptable level of behaviour (of attaining a basic minimum of civility) that might include not having large numbers of parentless children, nor junk materials strewn across what should be a well-maintained lawn. They are symbolic of garbage because of the shambles that seems to control their lives, and because of the disorder they threaten to spread. This category of the uncontrollable might be contrasted with the less visible 'Knockers-Through' (social climbers who sought to improve their position by purchasing and restoring dilapidated housing in London), mentioned by Michael Thompson in his book *Rubbish Theory*, who suffered another kind of social exclusion:

> This tiny band who, with little money and much faith, began restoring rubbish houses in the late fifties and early sixties were ridiculed by the staid and established members of the middle class who regarded Hampstead, Highgate, and Golders Green as the only habitable atolls in the North London Sea of Plebs. Their attitude was reflected by bank managers, estate agents, mortgage-brokers, building societies and borough architects,

and so, as anyone who has ever attempted to buy a house will appreciate, a massive economic barricade was erected to keep the rubbish out.[81]

Beyond this we can see that the social values that bring respectability derive not simply from order, but from a kind of settlement; by resting on stability and consolidation as part of the bedrock of rational freedom and self-worth. Compare this, too, with David Matless's discussion in *Landscape and Englishness* of the so-called 'plotlands' (pieces of land sold to 'rootless' individuals and upon which various self-built shacks would be erected) that began to spring up in parts of England during the 1930s: 'Plotlands became symbols of speculation, deprivation, visual disorder and social marginality, transgressing the [countryside] preservationists' morality of settlement, hardly a place and beyond public authority.'[82] Notable in this regard was one Peter Abercrombie, a founder of the Council for the Protection of Rural England (CPRE), who declared that the shacks occupying these plotlands 'do not mellow with time, but have a knack of lingering on, patched and botched, into a decrepit and disreputable old age which becomes their perished soul as hoary mouldiness does rotten fruit'.[83]

And evidence that the incipient disorder of the various forms of social trash are antithetical to social stability (in their moral incontinence, their apparent directionlessness or disregard for the future) is perhaps found in the language of exclusion and disapprobation directed towards itinerants and vagabonds (the 'bums', 'gypsies', 'hobos', 'loiterers', 'floppers', 'moochers', and so on) who on the one hand exist on the margins of society (unlike the white trash, for example, who are perceived to contaminate from within), yet on the other become all the more horrifying for their separateness; in that they are seen to constitute that most horrifying of prospects, a mobile and rootless society, loosened from the solidity of commonly accepted values.[84]

This was a point not missed by others who utilized the disordering potential of movement to instigate highly particular forms of resistance to everyday life. France's infamous Lettrist International, for example, established an 'alternative travel agency', which sent various volunteer drifters on mystery tours through the normally avoided *quartiers* of Paris, at once making them feel like vagrants (without a plan; not knowing where they would end up), whilst reminding them, as Simon Sadler says, of 'that extraordinary sensation of being abroad even when at home'; one that surely contributes to our perception of real itinerants

Newspaper reaction to Carl Andre's *Equivalent VIII*, *Daily Mirror*, 16 February 1976.

as the uncanny counterparts of normal society.[85] Notably, one of the principal instigators of these movements, Guy Debord, produced a well-known map titled 'The Naked City' in which he had reduced Paris to a discontinuous amalgamation of scrap parts.[86]

Although its aims were explicitly political, the Lettrist International (and especially its successor the Situationist International) connected to a small constellation of twentieth-century avant-garde art movements that also provided the inspiration for the work of artists who imported garbage into the aesthetic realm. Indeed, the disorder of a great deal of contemporary art is founded on the fact that either objects are not what they seem to be (usually they are worthless tat), or (like garbage) they were one thing before, but stripped of a previous character become something else within a new context. And here the simple act of 'making' something *what it is not* becomes the act that makes a mockery of any sensible or *realistic* ways of organizing the object world.[87] This was summed up perfectly in the reaction to Carl Andre's *Equivalent VIII* (a rectangular form composed of two layers of 120 builder's bricks), bought by the publicly funded Tate Gallery in London in 1976, and greeted by the newspaper headline 'What a Load of Rubbish' (previous page). To reinforce what a waste of money this was for a pile of rubbish the newspaper ended the story with a footnote (or as they put it, a *Bricknote*): 'You can buy ordinary household bricks for between £40 and £50 a thousand. The 120 bricks the Tate bought would be enough to build a large fireproof moneybox.'[88] For reasons other than providing sensible building materials, one infers, they were simply a waste of money.

The shock value of this art – like the horror that greets the idea of a rootless society – lies in the fact that it makes a mockery of the things society generally values. The declaration that such gestures are rubbish is matched, if we don't know it, by the existence of the contested work of art itself (like Andre's *Equivalent VIII*), which having invaded the almost sacred spaces of the art world, declares the values of this world to be useless. That such work returns something once known in a different form makes our ways of understanding how the world goes together a little bit more useless, because it signals that such conventions have to change as the world changes, that we live in a world where all certainties are brought to an end. Of course, the fact that these artistic scandals usually end with the assimilation of the once contagious horror does not alter the fact that it is the ways of ordering that determine what is considered to be incoherent or disconnected in the first place. Like an organism that swallows a foreign body, it tries to throw it back out: to expel it as garbage.

ENDS (BEGINNINGS)

It is a well-known cliché that 'all good things come to an end'. But surely we could do better than this – more appropriate would be a statement like 'everything (good or bad) ends'. What we need to say clearly is that the language of garbage is a language of termini – of things cut off, things that we lose interest in, things that reach a point of no return. In the end, of course, there is ruin and death. Yet with all things garbage-related a transformation characterizes the perverse core of all we value because with the end comes the beginning.

This is nowhere more clearly the case than with our experience of the variety of consumer products; from food and household necessities, where brands are subjected to a relentless onslaught of re-birthing, repackaging, and transport around the aisles of the contemporary supermarket. Part of the reason for this ceaseless reinvention of the product domain is the importance of brand distinctiveness. A manufacturer's greatest fear is that a product may too easily be confused with some other similarly perceived variant of the same basic stuff (hence the well known 'cola wars' of the 1980s and their resulting new varieties of brand specific variations). The constant procession of 'best-ever' or 'new and improved' varieties suggests teams of underemployed scientists endlessly searching for the holy grail of everlasting product desirability (found, of course, only in its continual reinvention). This is the experience of a necessary part of everyday life (the purchasing of food and other household essentials) as a succession of *ends* – ends that are nonetheless concealed by the appearance of new versions and different products. Advertising works to ensure that the life of these objects is fixed to their desirability, and the images we are so familiar with in advertising aim, as Julian Stallabrass says, to stress the unique qualities that, 'mark the object as highly distinct from its surroundings . . . to stress its cleanliness, to light it in order to emphasize the clarity of its borders'.[89] As garbage, however, such objects are 'stripped of this mystification' and take on a 'doleful truthfulness, as though confessing [their truths]: it becomes a reminder that commodities, despite all their tricks, are just stuff; little combinations of plastics or metal or paper'.[90]

Head of Alexander III, photo, 1917.

The spectre of death is even more present within clothing fashions, where an entire year can be summed up by the calendar that comes to life in the new lines and shop displays (which appear as a reminder that another end approaches), but where the fashion media is on hand to helpfully act as guide in the new reality. But this is the false ending as a new dawn that works by separating (literally) the person from the old thing. Although things are always dying away in the world of fashion, the whole point of it is to reinvigorate life – the life of the fashion consumer – and thus, as Mark C. Taylor has written, desire can never be allowed to self-extinguish: 'to remain vital, desire must always desire desire. Through its wily de-signs, fashion conspires to extend life by perpetually engendering desire. To embrace fashion is to affirm life.'[91] Such false ends, nevertheless, just produce the garbage (the discarded and out-of-date) that we can easily imagine does not exist, blinded as we are by the replacement. Real large-scale endings at a social and political level, on the other hand, are always readily symbolized by garbage that is not so easy to conceal (see above). Amongst the rubble of often-violent upheavals lie the decapitated heads and broken limbs of great national heroes, the statues that once proclaimed their reign now the evidence of their demise. In the aftermath of the democratic revolutions in Eastern Europe (1989–90) the overthrow of the old regimes resulted in the uprooting, dethron-

Gennady Bodrov, *Heads of Lenin and Marx after the failed coup of August 1991*, 1991.

ing and eventual garbaging of the iconography of the old order. The familiarity of images of dethroned heads being carried away by helicopter, or paraded through streets tethered to impossibly small looking vehicles at this time might be explained by the zeal with which the communist regimes had embraced public monuments and heroic iconography as a way of erasing the past that had just been and gone before they assumed power. At the same time these *purgings* – what we can only conceive of as cleansing rituals – seem to be apparent wherever political activity results in violence, and so the destruction of monumental architecture both symbolizes the arrival of the new and signals the point of beginning (with the acts of destruction). Equally, ruins of the day-to-day life of the revolutionary Europe of 1989 and 1990 (household furnishings, now unfashionable clothes, obsolete products, and so on) had been cast aside to be replaced by newer and better counterparts from the West, leaving the uncanny remainders of the old to stand as nostalgic artefacts of departed innocence, as Svetlana Boym observed in the city of Berlin:

> As you approach Tacheles from Oranienburger Strasse, you are greeted by strange mechanical pets made of urban refuse, rusted pipes and wire, parts of old Trabants and streetcars. City trash, ruins, building materials, wires, remains of the old infrastructure

. . . all find their final refuge in Tacheles, which commemorates that transient moment when useful objects turn obsolete . . . this is the twilight-of-the-GDR trash that looks poignantly beautiful and personified into something childlike and sorrowful.[92]

East Berlin in 1989–90, like much of Eastern Europe, had undergone so many changes in its recent history that the impermanence of its streets and buildings, not to mention its shifting sense of identity, made it easy to see it as just another stage set to be erected upon the seemingly eternal ruins of the city. Ivan Klíma's *Love and Garbage*, set in the pre-revolutionary Czechoslovakia of the mid-1980s, seems to have been trying to make precisely this point; that in the end it will all change anyway, and that the only thing that is indestructible is garbage: 'In our country everything is being forever remade: beliefs, buildings and street names. Sometimes the progress of time is concealed and at others feigned.'[93]

The analogy of garbage and ends (and so, beginnings) is brilliantly realized in László Krasznahorkai's masterful novel of 1989, *The Melancholy of Resistance*, in which the order of a small Hungarian town is placed under threat by the arrival of a carnival that attracts a roving mob of otherwise idle men (once again, we observe the symbolism of the threatening rootless society). In the face of the challenge posed to civic order by their unwelcome presence the leaders of the town are shown to be ineffectual, doubly so because there are apparently sinister forces, temporarily dormant but, in the figures of the mob, waiting around for a sign from their enigmatic leader (who eventually sets them on a path of violent destruction). Of all the town's inhabitants one person sees it. This is the elderly Mr Ezster, a retired professor of music who spends his days hidden away, attempting to undo the harmonic universe of Andreas Werckmeister – both to reveal its artifice and to prove the underlying dissonance that music (the Werckmeister harmonies) cosmetically erases. Thus, when he is brought out into the town for the first time in months, the ruin that should have made apparent the extent of social inertia is everywhere clearly visible to his eyes:

> Everywhere he looked the roads and pavements were covered with a seamless, chinkless armour of detritus and this supernaturally glimmering river of waste trodden into a pulp and frozen into a solid mass by the piercing cold . . . as he continued

to appraise, as if from a considerable eminence, the monstrous labyrinth of filth, he grew ever more certain that, since his 'fellow human beings' had utterly failed to notice this flawless and monumental embodiment of doom, it was pointless talking about a 'sense of community' . . . Could this, he wondered, be a form of the last judgement? No trumpets, no riders of the apocalypse but mankind swallowed without fuss or ceremony by its own rubbish?[94]

Eventually an orgy of destruction is unleashed upon the town by the mob. And, as if to make clear the end that always comes, Krasznahorkai brilliantly deploys the analogy of the human body as the site of order that by extension reveals how the civic body, too, functions. The defensive forces within the physical organism of a human body that help to maintain it in good order, reach the beginning of the end with 'the unchained workers of decay' who are set to work reducing the no longer functioning body to simple matter in order to fully complete its return to the earth. All the simple constituents of the matter that made up the functioning body remain – but in parts – without the organization that once maintained them, and thus without

the clerk capable of making an inventory of all the constituents . . . the realm that existed once – and once only – had disappeared for ever, ground into infinitesimal pieces by the endless momentum of chaos . . . the chaos that consisted of an indifferent and unstoppable traffic between things.[95]

Between something and nothing; between whole and part; between the body as source of unique being and the universal matter of the garbaged self. This stateless condition of being one thing and then another (or even being at any time *neither one thing nor another*) symbolizes garbage. In an image from the fifteenth century that accompanied a wonderfully named poem – 'A Disputacione Betwyx the Body and Worms' – reflecting the universality of the description later found in Krasznahorkai's brilliant novel, two tombs are displayed one on top of the other in representation of the final journey that transports us from above ground to a co-mingling of the 'maggoty contents of the grave' with, and eventual consumption by, the earth below.[96] The text under the image does not equivocate about the outcome of this particular dispute:

An illustration to *A Disputacione Betwyx the Body and Worms*, a mid-15th century poem.

Take heed unto my figure here above
And see how sometimes I was fresh and gay
Now turned to a worm's meat and corruption
Both foul of earth and stinking slime and clay
Attend therefore to this disputacion written here
. . .
To see what thou art and hereafter shall be . . . [97]

2 Garbage and Knowledge

. . . materials that now lie in the dust may yet be worked up into a splendid construction
Immanuel Kant, Letter to Christian Garve, 7 August 1783

KNOWLEDGE: THE RECYCLABLE AND THE DISPOSABLE

'Garbage in, garbage out' is one of those expressions that is probably familiar to us all. Whilst it originated as a recognition that computer technology was limited in its processes by its humanly created origins (and the consequent difficulty in overcoming the errors or bad inputs provided by the computer user) the rise of the expression to the status of the proverbial is surely a recognition of its adaptability in any number of situations. *When things go wrong, or do not work out as expected*, it seems to say, *it can only be our fault, for the means themselves are perfectible.* It thus indicates, no doubt, a more general belief that what we produce – indeed, what we know and even believe about the world – cannot actually be separated from the parts that go together to make up some *object* (whether we take this to refer to an object of knowledge or a material thing). In the words of the information analysts, this simply means that 'Truly ambiguous, vague, or confused information remains so, unless it is further regimented.'[1]

As we have already seen, notions of ambiguity and confusion inform a symbolism of garbage because they actually signal a split in understanding, or a disconnection that leaves us unsure about what things are, or where they belong. It is this that marks them out as garbage. Whilst the requirement that information be disciplined extends in general to a notion like 'truth' it also informs ideas of aesthetic worth and, as we will see, technology. As such, this 'further regimentation' of knowledge represents the process of recycling and disposal. In the technical jargon of the world of computing 'garbage' symbolizes the boomerang effect of sloppy thinking, faulty programming or even bad information processing. To employ the architectural metaphor that will recur throughout this chapter, garbage symbolizes how easily a badly built structure will be at risk of collapse, because in computer programming the rules on which systems operate (their basic building blocks) can misinterpret your mistakes according to their own 'fuzzy' logic, which is not necessarily as discriminating as you might like it to be, as a philosopher of computing, Luciano Floridi, has noted:

> Examples of [fuzzy logic] are . . . sentences that are semantically, or syntactically ambiguous like 'when she met us she thought we were going to the pub', which a computer could interpret in thirteen different ways.

In other words, this fuzzy logic, which can to some extent cope with a level of imprecision in data inputs (if a certain range of errors has been anticipated in programming), still fails when information is truly ambiguous. Thus, garbage apparently still slips into the system if we mistake such fuzzy logic for a method of establishing what is accurate. So:

> A fuzzified logic, wrongly understood as a theory of degrees of truth, could only make them [unclear commands] *irremediably* ambiguous, vague or confused by isomorphically adapting itself to it. In database jargon this is sometimes called the GIGO rule: Garbage In Garbage Out.[2]

Fuzzy logic is then employed to make any system adaptable to complex inputs, to sift, sort and regiment any putative knowledge. It is applicable, as Floridi notes, whenever a 'system is difficult to model, e.g., because it is the result of the experience of a human being'.[3] In other words, the perfectible means are there: it's just we messy people tend to clog the works with our garbage.

The notion of disposal that underpins the common wisdom of GIGO is not entirely misplaced (although it does not tell the whole story). Everything a culture creates, whether beliefs, theories or material products, is fashioned into a particular form from some kind of undifferentiated source 'material' as the retained source of value. What goes unnoticed in these acts of assigning value is that the *garbage in* part of the equation is represented as the result of human error, as something that can be eradicated. An advertisement from 1979 selling

British manufacturer Rolls-Royce's technological superiority with the slogan *For Garbage Read Genius* exposes this misunderstanding of how knowledge works. If 'garbage in' does indeed equal 'garbage out', then the expression *garbage in, garbage out* says the same as their preferred variant 'genius in, genius out', with the crucial difference being the implication that Rolls-Royce is so efficient in its technological inventiveness that there is no waste. The product begins with genius and embodies more of the same, we are asked to believe. What is more accurate to say, as we shall see, is that 'genius' may well be used to describe the *output* of a technological process based upon the logic of computer programming but only after various unconnected elements (the once vague, confused or ambiguous) are brought into combination or regimented. These are the unconnected bits and fragments that on their own we might deem to be useless garbage, which are brought together to create something new. In this sense knowledge is always at once recycling itself, but also (and importantly) disposing of its waste products, which is to say, those parts that cannot in a particular instance be recycled. To the extent that the recycling and disposal of knowledge go unnoticed we should not be surprised. As I will suggest in what follows, the development of knowledge in Western culture seems inseparable from a cleansing or refining impulse; a will to order. The significance of this insight for our understanding of the centrality of 'garbage' in contemporary life will be apparent when we look, in particular, at the transformation of the world through the practical knowledge of that protean god of modern life, technology, which in the abstract represents the putting of nature into use.

The first important thing to note is that the path that takes us to 'garbage in, garbage out' is a very long one. If we take a daring plunge into the past we may see that the structures that provide the framework for the electronic processing of information in computing technology inherit a propensity for disposal that is also the primer for knowledge in a more general sense. From the philosophy of the Ancients and its concern with understanding how the world (or *kosmos*) must be constituted, to the critical focus on modes of knowing that is characteristic of modern philosophy from the seventeenth century onwards, a metaphor of good design seems to be in operation. As Jonathan Barnes notes in *Early Greek Philosophy*, the Presocratic philosophers chose the word *kosmos* to 'designate the universe'. *Kosmos* meant

For garbage read genius

GIGO of course is still alive and well and working for us, only now the acronym has a more acceptable meaning. Genius In, Genius Out.

In the early years of computing, computer cynics coined the acronym GIGO. It stands for Garbage In, Garbage Out.

Number crunching was then one of the few rewarding tasks for a computer – even at Rolls-Royce.

What we have done in the last decade has been to allocate to our computers increasing importance as a design and production tool. In the process, computer people have become fundamental to our lead in gas turbine technology.

You can see the outcome in aircraft, hovercraft, ships, oil rigs and power stations, for all of which Rolls-Royce provide the turbines. Also in nuclear submarines and electrical generation.

The result is an order book that takes Rolls-Royce into the 1990s, and ideas now on the drawing board that will surprise the 21st century.

A future that's as near certain as can be ... You don't need to be a computer genius to work out the significance of that.

Rolls-Royce Limited,
65 Buckingham Gate, London SW1.

ROLLS
ROYCE
ROLLS-ROYCE LIMITED
Come with us into the 21st century

For Garbage Read Genius, Rolls-Royce advertisement, 1979.

'to order', 'to arrange', 'to marshall' – it is used by Homer of Greek generals marshalling their troops for battle. Thus a *kosmos* is an orderly arrangement: the word *kosmos* in Greek meant not only an ordering but also an adornment (hence the English word 'cosmetic'), something which beautifies and is pleasant to contemplate.[4]

It is tempting to also read this 'designating' the universe as the activity of producing reality itself. Not in any simplistic or relativistic sense, but merely because of the way language must work to organize the understanding. The *kosmos*, so understood, in a way anticipates the Rolls-Royce definition of technological excellence; which is to say, it downplays, if not eliminates outright the possibility of systemic waste. A fragment from the writings of Theophrastus (Aristotle's successor as head of the Peripatetic school in Athens) is an early example of philosophy's explicit reliance on this duality of order and disorder, with the latter expressed in terms of rubbish or garbage. And here we note the predominance of one or the other condition indicates an absence or deficiency of the other. In the following passage it is reasonable to suppose that Theophrastus' comments are directed towards Platonism, or refer to the Platonic forms in suggesting that not to assume perfection in the 'first principles' amounts to doubting the possibility of perfection in the world of experience:

> They [the followers of Plato] would think it unreasonable if, while the whole heaven and each of its parts have order and reason in their shapes and powers and periods, there is no such thing in the first principles but [as Heraclitus says], the most beautiful world is like a heap of rubbish aimlessly piled up.[5]

Thus, if the *kosmos* is by definition well ordered, then there can be no waste within it (just stuff moved around), or else we might suppose that everything is really just a pile of rubbish. Heraclitus, alluded to in the above passage, stood opposed to Platonism, and famously held to a notion of change and impermanence that, according to the reading of Theophrastus, can render the idea of *kosmos* insufficient for an understanding of nature itself. The order the philosophers had seen in nature is distinct from what we would term natural necessity. As it appears to us, Heraclitus would say, 'the world and its furniture are in a state of perpetual flux'.[6] The suggestion that it would be nonsensical for philosophy to suppose that the world was not beautiful and orderly identified the root of a problem that still hangs over Western thinking today, and that is expressed in the idea of a separation between reason and nature. In the ancient cosmology the world is in some sense given (almost gifted), apparently existing independently of the human – or, indeed, the philosophical – understanding. This view is summed up very neatly in Jonathan Barnes's overview of the Presocratics. For them, he notes, 'the world was not a random collection of bits, its history was not an arbitrary series of events'.[7] And whilst it may not have been possible to see this world properly, according to the Ancients we may nevertheless find ways of perfecting our methods of seeing through the murk and dirt that may obscure the natural perfection of the world. In Plato, as Richard Padovan has argued, the world is put together (in the sense of contemporary usage), almost *cosmetically* as a work of art is, by the 'Demiurge' – a kind of universal craftsman who fashions this creation

> out of the raw material already present, like the clay used by a potter or the wood and stone used by the builder of a house . . . the Demiurge does not create the world out of nothing, but like a human designer or architect he merely rearranges it so as to bring it 'from disorder into order'. Neither the formless matter ('Necessity') nor the rational forms he imposes on it ('Reason') originate with him; he merely brings them together.[8]

Which is to say that this 'Demiurge' was a skilled recycler as well. The link between the ancient and modern philosophies seems to be cut in so far as what seems reasonable according to first principles in Plato (perfection) is set against a modern demand for factual evidence from the visible world, because just supposing good design was not enough. In other words, the belief in an orderly universe vanishes. And although we might read the Ancients as supposing that the finite universe is recycled into perfection, from around the seventeenth century, in particular, we have to see the history of modern philosophy as a history of garbage.

It is a history of disposal and tidying; of cutting off, chucking out, and of sweeping away the debris that lies on the territory of reason. And, much like the work that is undertaken to clear away our rubbish on a day-to-day level, the intellectual cleansing goes largely unnoticed: indeed, it vanishes to some extent under the presentation of an edifice of Reason as the perfectible, if not incorruptible, way of knowing, as something that stands apart from the mess and garbage of unclear thinking or broken beliefs. As Immanuel Kant wrote in 1781, the great benefit of freeing philosophy from the useless dead ends of its ancient inheritance was that 'it can with little expense' exempt us from 'a great deal of dogmatic rubbish', in place of which his revolutionary critique of pure reason would 'happily purge such delusions'.[9] Yet we do not see what lies in the wake of certainty because its trail litters the dead ends and back alleys of the structures that are given as a front or a surface: a certainty that nonetheless could not be presented without the creation of the rubble and excess of unnecessary parts (as we will see in the discussion of Kant, below). Of course, we also know that the products of reason – its great works, the important ideas and revolutionary theories these give expression to, represent the emergence of great edifices. But, if garbage is indeed so central to knowledge, how do we find a way into the domain of the leftover, the discarded – in other words, how can we see what knowledge uses up and throws away? One approach, which I will discuss in the next section, is to look off the page or, at least, in the margins, or, even, in what were for a long time known as *waste books.* In other words, we look amongst the half-formed ideas, unworkable hypotheses and dead ends of intellectual endeavour to the prototypical 'knowledge' that only appears as the litter of reason, the disposal of which misleads us into believing that there can be no 'garbage in'.

What we find here, as the leftovers of creation, indicates the successful cleansing of the exterior world, of (so-called) reality. The Western philosophical (or, metaphysical) tradition that gave birth to reason is, as is well known, caught up in this inability to fully integrate the interior and exterior aspects of experience (in the sense that we might say our beliefs represent the world out there), but in the history of the philosophical imagination the inherent *sensibility* of the world – its susceptibility to the courtly advance of reason – is taken as a primary condition of the activity of philosophy itself. And whilst Reason in its modern guise differs substantially from its Ancient predecessor, there is, nonetheless, a reliance at all times on a set of metaphors that speak of the activity of Reason in terms of sound building, good design, clean terrain and so on.

In an epistle to the reader that begins *An Essay Concerning Human Understanding,* published in 1690, John Locke modestly assigned himself a place in 'the commonwealth of learning' some way below 'master builders' and creators of 'mighty designs' such as Boyle and Newton, suggesting that for himself it was 'ambition enough to be employed as an under labourer in clearing ground a little, and removing some of the rubbish that lies in the way to knowledge'. An activity, moreover, that he saw to involve expelling 'frivolous use of uncouth, affected, or unintelligible terms, introduced into the sciences' as 'vague and insignificant forms of speech and abuse[s] of language'.[10] That Locke should have so clearly identified the chief value of knowledge in its usefulness (which is also to say in its removal of meaningless or erroneous knowledge) should be no surprise to us. At around the same time in England, the influence of the Royal Society (to which Locke was elected in 1668) was to spread a new enthusiasm for all manner of intellectual endeavours, and as Maurice Cranston wrote in his biography of Locke, 'the unformulated *ad hoc* empiricism of Newton and Boyle and the other Royal Society *virtuosi*' became a strong influence on Locke's intellectual development.[11]

This influence was found, for example, in a mania for experiments, which directed the Royal Society towards the position that experimentation was the basis of all knowledge and, according to its first historian Thomas Sprat, the goal of these empirical efforts would be to 'make faithful *Records,* of all the Works of *Nature,* or *Art*'.[12] The disposal of what was now useless under the aims of the new science – as if it was mere garbage – is clearly implied, yet it is not entirely new or unique, being reflected throughout the history of modern philosophy, and compels us to see Locke also within a tradition of philosophical scepticism. Examples of this tradition range from the ancient Greek, Sextus Empiricus (for whom philosophy was also a purgative, a way of expelling the waste) to Ludwig Wittgenstein in the twentieth century. In Sextus, it has been noted, we see in the metaphor of disposal the possibility of philosophical progress:

> Scepticism consists in *dissolving* pseudo-problems; philosophy is a means not a goal. In his main work he uses an image, which Wittgenstein made famous – Sextus was perhaps inspired by Plato's *Symposium*: the sceptic can use philosophical arguments as a ladder; when he has climbed up, he can *throw away* the ladder.[13]

In other words, philosophy was just the disposable means constituted by its defunct speculations and stratagems, and the activity of philosophizing itself unsurprisingly created its own leftovers. And for John Locke, as Rosalie Colie has written, the philosophical means worked towards a perfectible end, because whilst truth suffered 'in the world of opinionated human beings' it was nonetheless 'able to stand all assaying and to emerge as pure and unchangeable'.[14] How fitting it was that the words of the Roman philosopher Cicero (in the original Latin) graced the title-page of Locke's *Essay Concerning Human Understanding*: 'How much better it would have been to confess your ignorance rather than to sicken us by spouting all this rubbish, which cannot be pleasant even to yourself.'[15] And again, to emphasize that there is a continuity in the philosophical tradition in its attachment to disposal, this was echoed further along philosophy's development when Ludwig Wittgenstein famously ended his *Tractatus Logico-Philosophicus* by repeating the ladder metaphor of Sextus, and producing as his final words a sentence that would have pleased Cicero, who urged us to refrain from talking rubbish: 'What we cannot speak about, we must pass over in silence.'[16] And Locke's well-known under labouring claim – that he was merely sweeping away the rubbish to clear the way for greater men – was not unique and is, in fact, echoed in the writings (usually in letters or prefaces) of others around this time.[17] It is a sentiment that survives intact in David Hume's famous passage declaring the ancient metaphysical concerns of philosophy to be little more than garbage to be got rid of, which by this time (1748) must have been somewhat old hat within intellectual circles:

> If we take in our hand any volume of divinity or school metaphysics, for instance, let us ask, Does it contain any abstract reasoning concerning quantity or number? No. Does it contain any experimental reasoning concerning matter of fact and existence? No. Commit it then to the flames, for it can contain nothing but sophistry and illusion.[18]

It might be supposed that incineration just takes the disposal of waste – begun with the sweeping out of the old – to a new and more intense level. Where Hume seems consumed by a fervour that is matched by his desire to see all the useless junk of the past light up the sky, Locke's under-labourer claim seems overly modest considering the demolition he was set upon. Locke has also been read as using false modesty as a means of gently upbraiding the great master-builders of the scientific world for having, as Rosalie Colie observes, 'failed by themselves to clarify the grounds of science sufficiently so that an under-labourer of the sort Locke makes himself out to be, is still needed'.[19] The demolition and clearing away common in these times were all part of what Roy Porter described as a more general feature of the early Enlightenment in Britain, namely 'a demand for a clear-out and clean-up of the lumber house of the human mind', which had now been 'condemned as dark, dilapidated and dangerous', and, as such shaky structures inevitably become, now 'unfit for habitation'.[20] Yet, famous though Locke's *Essay* became as a kind of manifesto for demolition (and rebuilding), its apparent radicalism has affinities with other monumental works of philosophy and, indeed, one might equally look at figures such as Descartes or Plato to make the same point.[21]

So the garbage of knowledge is always present as a spectral double that is nevertheless pushed out of view by the need to clear the ground for the construction of beautiful and apparently flawless edifices. In the empiricist conception of science that emerged in the seventeenth century this job is undertaken through the objectification – the creation – of the material and conceptual worlds, with the philosophers, according to Simon Critchley, mere 'janitors in the Crystal Palace of the sciences'.[22] The job was to prepare the knowledge-mediators for scientific service – that is to say, to provide an inventory of the types, classes and so on, that could make *faithful records of nature* – and which might provide the built framework that would hold a structure together or, as Locke himself said, provide the design 'to raise an Edifice uniform, and consistent with itself'.[23] This need for order is expressed in a variety of ways but can be encapsulated and simplified by, on the one hand, a desire for permanence, and on the other, the concession that without garbage – without error and falsity – there is no knowledge. In the first case, the need to attain stability is summed up by Wittgenstein's comment that 'there must be objects, if the world is to have an unalterable form', a formulation that unsurprisingly – like Locke – calls for more vigilance in the use of language.[24] In the second case, a recognition of the 'raw material' of the garbage of knowledge as in Odo Marquard's observation that actually, 'sense is just the nonsense that we throw away'.[25]

The language of 'making objects', and the 'throwing away' of stuff, therefore, leads us back to the ancient Greek notion of the *kosmos* as the *well ordered*. And because the focus that philosophy placed on purging language of its aberrations and falsehoods in support of great Crystal Palaces, can we not suggest that this word *kosmos* now finds its truest expression in the meanings of its English derivative, *cosmetic*? As Dominique Laporte has written, 'if language is beautiful, it must be because a master bathes it – a master who cleans shit holes, sweeps offal, and expurgates city and speech to confer upon them order and beauty'.[26] Thus, where there is beauty there is also filth: the point is that discipline is required to retain the cosmetic appearance of purity. Moreover, it demands our submission. Laporte's *History of Shit* opens with the following extract from Paul Éluard's *Capitale de la douleur*:

> Language speaks and asks:
> why am I beautiful?
> Because my master bathes me

Here 'the master' signifies the importance of work, the avoidance of laziness, and the putting to use of knowledge. Thus, 'without a master, one cannot be cleaned. Purification, whether by fire or by the word, by baptism or by death, requires submission to the law.'[27] In other words, purity is never given, and the cosmetic makeover is therefore the refashioning of some thing or material according to an idea, end or, indeed, law.

WASTE BOOKS

In the Age of Reason the influence of the under-labourer Locke passes into the general wisdom of the times.[28] The clearing away of the rubbish is also directed towards the means of making knowledge most workable and efficient, because to neglect such means of self-improvement (one sees this in Locke's work on government and education as well) is equivalent to laying waste to one's own life. A journal entry of 8 February 1677 implies that Locke's modest aim of serving as an under-labourer to science, published in his *Essay Concerning Human Understanding* of 1690, had earlier been concerned (without the vivid metaphor) in terms of simply making our knowledge practically applicable. Thus whilst knowledge functions in apparent service of the master builders of science such as Newton and Boyle (as Locke claims in 1690), his earlier thoughts on the matter included less celebrated manufacturers, merchants and traders of early capitalism. As Locke noted, the purpose of knowledge was then:

For the use and advantage of men in this world viz To finde out new inventions of dispatch to shorten or ease our labours, or applying sagaciously together severall agents and patients to procure new and beneficiall productions whereby our stock of riches . . . may be increased or better preserved.[29]

Whilst the conditions for increasing the wealth of society awaited further improvement in the century that followed Locke's words, the connection between clear thinking and future prosperity is there to see.[30] If not quite expressing the late twentieth century's 'garbage in, garbage out', it at least suggested that we would be better off if we dispose of the useless or unnecessary. What, in the seventeenth century, the Royal Society historian Thomas Sprat was able to formulate as a desire to ensure knowledge would not be 'overpressed by a confus'd heap of vain and useless particulars', had by the beginning of the nine-teenth century been assimilated to the extent that an easy source of comedy could be found in playing out the incongruity of certain appli-cations of language and its use in the development of specialized knowledge within the increasingly rationalized world of commercial activity. Thus, at the beginning of Sir Walter Scott's novel of 1817, *Rob Roy*, we are introduced to the narrator and central figure of the story, Frank Osbaldistone, just as he is summoned home from France. We learn that he had spent time away from home – at his father's insis-tence – learning the rules of commerce, during which it was hoped that he might accumulate enough business acumen to be in a position to one day take over the family business. This was a hope dashed by his decline of the offer of a position in the family firm (the act that also precipitates his recall from France). The problem, we soon discover, is that Frank's failure to adhere to the efficient proscriptions of the com-mercial world become glaringly clear to his father in the actual form of his last letter home, which contains both his refusal of the offer and the worrying evidence of a slackness in his language that should have had no place in his commercially educated mind. His father produces this letter as evidence of a wasteful neglect of duty in preparing himself for his future in business, and confronts Frank:

This, Frank, is yours of the 21st ultimo, in which you advise me (reading from my letter), that in the most important business of forming a plan, and adopting a profession for life . . . that you have insuperable – ay, insuperable is the word – I wish, by the way, you would write a more distinct current hand – draw a score through the tops of your t's, and open the loops of your l's – insuperable objections to the arrangements which I have proposed to you. There is much more to the same effect, occupying four good pages of paper, which a little attention to perspicuity and distinctness of expression might have comprized within as many lines.[31]

Not only does Frank waste paper by getting caught up with the unnecessary details that occupy the 'four good pages', the more serious problem is that Frank has been 'infected' with the 'idle disease' – that is, an attraction to the ornamentation of unnecessary language that his father hated ('ay, insuperable is the word'), which is taken to its extreme as a language of nonsense in the despicable works of poetry. As the scene unfolds, Frank considers his position in this farrago of obligation and personal desire, reflecting that, 'it never occurred to me that it might be necessary . . . to submit to labour and limitations unpleasant to my temper'.[32]

After an amusing encounter some time later, during which Frank is quizzed on the 'mysteries of agio, tariffs, tare and tret', he declares himself unfit for a professional career in commerce. 'Nonsense,' his father replies, requesting his study journals to assess the evidence for himself. 'Have you kept your journal in the terms I desired?' 'Yes, sir.' Frank replied. On looking through the journal Frank's father reads aloud, in favourable tones, the contents which detailed the occurrence of various weights and measures important to their business, until he remarks to his head clerk: 'This is a kind of waste-book, Owen, in which all the transactions of the day, – emptions, orders, payments, receipts, acceptances, draughts, commissions, and advices, – are entered miscellaneously.' Owen, himself valued for his bookkeeping abilities, remarks on the function of the waste-book as the source material from which the proper and orderly accounts are later compiled (although he does not convey his real knowledge that Frank's father is mistaken) – 'I am glad Mr Francis [Frank] is so methodical,' he adds. Here, in these amusing scenes, is the demonstration that *no matter what comes out, garbage is in a sense what goes in*. The contents of the waste-book are of potential value, but they need to be cleansed in order that their value in the overall order of things is made apparent. It is this recognition of the necessity of waste that more adequately describes how knowledge is *built up* from recycled debris, rather than the common wisdom of the simply instrumental axiom 'garbage in, garbage out', which might lead us to believe that the production of knowledge includes no recycling, and no disposal.

It is interesting to note that in *Rob Roy* we can also find a demonstration of the relational quality of rubbish – that one person's trash is another's treasure. This is because Frank is undone by a piece of garbage, something within these waste-books that was not amenable to inclusion within the body of soon to be recycled and thus useful knowledge. Just before his father is convinced that Frank is on his way to becoming the man to fulfil his paternal hopes, able to take on the family business when the time came, his impression is undone when the litter of a 'blotted piece of paper fell from the book' to reveal the useless jottings of that idle disease, poetry. Frank's father picks up the paper and reads aloud, 'to the memory of Edward the Black Prince – What's all this? – Verses! – By Heaven, Frank, you are a greater blockhead than I supposed you!'[33] Whilst we note that the reversal of values and its part in Frank's undoing is the source of comedy here, consider what it tells us about the category of the disposable. By Frank the ledger is disdainfully referred to as 'business traffic' and 'commonplace lumber'; in other words, it is the language of commerce that is without value. His father, by contrast, sees clearly that in the miscellany of these waste-books (books that should nonetheless be purged of all ornamentation and superfluity) was actually contained the material that would later be transformed into the regimented ledgers that promised wealth and future security. Thus, the recycling and disposal of the miscellany is of crucial importance. It is the alchemical power of organization that transforms the base material into gold.[34] For Frank Osbaldistone, however, such under-labouring entailed the marshalling of his poetic curiosity to an extent unacceptable.

The thing is that curiosity moves. Driven by an ill-defined need to find, it is put into motion by the appeal of attaining a firm grasp on time and place. This can seem to be a contradictory motion that may abandon what is thought to be certain for even greater knowledge. Thus, curiosity moves, but seeks to be at rest; it proceeds from the imagination, yet is grounded in the concrete and physical and by the undeniable materiality of the spaces that locate us. In the history of knowledge the stir of curiosity is seen to be a source of fascination – it charms, lures and brings us into contact with the unknown and novel, but this presents certain dangers, and attachments to frivolous rubbish. Reason seems to need to be cold-headed, and as Frank Osbaldistone's father would have said, to avoid the enthusiasms of childhood. Indeed, the speculative imagination, it was thought, overheats because of its childlike inability to discriminate. In the words of Locke (as Lorraine Daston and Katherine Park note), such enthusiasm belongs to 'the conceits of a warmed or overweening brain'.[35] Such inflamed imaginations were also responsible for their part in producing the 'disorder' of knowledge created by a combination of newly available printing technology (around the middle of the fifteenth century) and insufficient means to submit it to control. Again, it is noted, before order there is only a mess to be cleaned up. This, as Peter Burke writes, represented the ruin of intellectual endeavours on a huge scale, where 'knowledge' was in danger of being degraded to the extent that, in sum, it would be no more than a kind of universal waste-book. One step in the organization of this matter was the wider institution of an alphabetical ordering that until the seventeenth century had not been the principal means of classification, but which, Burke tells us:

> Appears to have been adopted, originally at least, out of a sense of defeat by the forces of intellectual entropy at a time when new knowledge was coming into the system too fast to be digested or methodized.[36]

One thinks here, also, of Jacques Derrida's suggestion that the *logocentrism* of Western metaphysics (i.e., the privileging of the word, of speech, as the primary source of authenticity) conceives of writing, and its endless procession of printed artefacts, as the constitutive materials of an immense pile of waste:

> The history of metaphysics [is a system of logocentric repression, which] was organized in order to exclude or lower (to put outside or below), the body of the written trace as a didactic and technical metaphor, as servile matter or excrement.[37]

This, Derrida argues, is because 'the voice, producer of the first symbols, has a relationship of essential and immediate proximity with the mind', which makes for transparency, clarity, the omission of ambiguity. By contrast, writing, as this detached *product*, is subject to doubt; its existence invites ambiguity if not duplicity, where the voice by contrast promises authenticity.[38] Thus, we understand the great mess of disorganized texts following upon the growth of printing as such pieces of waste, and how their material excess prompts the organization of the expanding sphere of dubious (and potentially dangerous) knowledge. The scurrying around to erect defences produced by the threat of 'intellectual entropy' underlines as well the complex connections between two seemingly incompatible principles or origins of motion; namely, reason and curiosity, which now become understood as indices of the valuable and the worthless. As Derrida saw it, the closure of knowledge was an attempt to protect the future, because 'that which breaks absolutely' with what we know 'can only be proclaimed as, presented, as a sort of monstrosity'.[39]

To summarize in very general terms, the history of modern philosophy sees reason directed within certain constraints and towards what is perceptible (broadly, this is consistent with Locke and the empiricists) or to that which coheres in a sensible manner (we find this, pre-eminently, in Immanuel Kant). A less refined form of curiosity may arise from a similar instinct (a simple and practical need to know) yet be captured by some small wonder: a child, for example, may marvel at the apparent strangeness of shooting blades of grass, which seem to arrive on the surface of the ground as if from nowhere. But in the Age of Reason this kind of wonderment is practically useless; and indeed Locke, in his writings on education, almost regards the uneducated child as a walking embodiment of rubbish. The child has to be disciplined, brought under control; its curiosity directed away from the development of wasteful habits and idle entertainments.[40] Age and maturity are here contrasted with the yet to be developed child because they have been through a process of development, they are no longer in need of this sense of fascination, nor the unquestioning attachment to the novel or frivolous. Instead reason directs the mind towards *knowledge* – back along the paths of innumerable previous lives that constitute not only a route to the present, but also the *root*, or vital connection (where disconnection contrastingly produces garbage).[41]

The movement of curiosity, nevertheless, is what drives the rational scientific mind toward the limit of what is sensible precisely in order to consolidate our understanding of the world; with every hypothesis a speculative stab at the future, a determined, inquisitive gesture that forms a question mark. The problem is that the pursuit of knowledge places one in a kind of wasteland of indeterminacy – 'the immeasurable region of truth and error', which can result in much 'groping about' in order that the correct exit is found.[42] And here we can see the basic error in the maxim 'garbage in, garbage out' when applied to the working of knowledge, because *everything* that goes in has to be disentangled from the mess that constitutes speculative (or experimental) thinking, which in turn means that the *working out* of what is useful knowledge is also the disposal of what is useless – in other words we begin with garbage – it goes *in*, but is then worked out.

The building and cleansing metaphors of Locke and the empiricists also appear in the writing of Immanuel Kant, the father of all modern critical thought. Particularly interesting is the correspondence in which we see Kant working amongst the ruins, for example, in the following extract from a letter to Marcus Herz dated 21 February 1772, where Kant considers the necessity of doing more than merely destroying useless metaphysics:

> It appears that one doesn't obtain a hearing by stating only negative propositions. One must rebuild on the plot where one has torn down, or at least, if one has cleared away the brainstorms, one must make the pure insights of the understanding dogmatically intelligible and delineate their limits.[43]

It is crucial to note the kind of metaphors Kant brings into use here, and also in the *Critique of Pure Reason*. In the 'court' of critical reason 'it is not even necessary' to concern ourselves with the 'groundless illusions' of metaphysics, for we can 'dispose of the entire heap of these inexhaustible tricks' at once.[44] In Kant's letter to Herz he seems to strive for a *purity* that is only consequent upon a bout of *clearing away*. As we will see, Kant's importance to an understanding of the relationship between garbage and knowledge has two strands. First, there is the tearing down of unsound structures – a laying waste to the ground that supported the 'fruitless sophistries' of metaphysics; he was, in the words of Robert Pippin, the 'all-destroyer'.[45] Second, Kant's own positive rebuilding of the domain of reason is seen (especially in the philosophical correspondence) in terms of disposal. In other words the positive side of his system is found in the unlikely act of garbage expulsion (the ejection of the uncombinable remainder). This can be seen from the writing and thinking that begins the work of the critical philosophy some fifteen years before he finally published the revolutionary *Critique of Pure Reason*, and continues almost to his death, as he relentlessly attempted to gain acceptance for this, his greatest masterpiece. Thus, in 1797 – a few years before his death in 1804, and seventeen years after its first publication – Kant felt obligated to respond to a request for clarification of a point in the *Critique*, but was still cautious enough to warn his correspondent that his answers 'must be taken as mere raw suggestions', adding that he and his correspondent would be able to 'make the discussion more elegant after we have exchanged ideas on it again'.[46] The cleaning and polishing continued, in other words.

The transcendental reason of Immanuel Kant's philosophy (transcendental in that it was to move beyond subjectivity, yet be grounded in a form of reason all could acquire), which inaugurated the turn away from previous metaphysical speculation most fully, at once gave life to all subsequent speculation on our modes of knowledge, but in its conception sought merely a way to avoid making experience (which had produced all the speculations on wonders) the basis of reason. Instead, a 'mature and adult power' of reason needs to subject itself to criticism ('not to the facts of reason, but reason itself'):

> This is not the censorship but the *critique* of pure reason, whereby not merely limits but rather the determinate boundaries of it . . . are not merely suspected but proved from principles. Thus, scepticism is a resting place for human reason, which can reflect upon its dogmatic peregrination and make a survey of the region in which it finds itself in order to be able to choose its path in the future with greater certainty, but it is not a dwelling-place for permanent residence; for the latter can only be found in a complete certainty.[47]

To wander too far beyond reason's bounds – as metaphysics did – was to enter a metaphorical wasteland, as Kant noted: 'all paths have been tried in vain … they have become obscure, confused, useless'.[48] Complete certainty on the other hand, would quell such itinerant wanderings, amounting to an enclosing of knowledge that would separate and protect the grounds of its certainty from any encroachment emanating from the direction of the metaphysical wasteland with its 'confounded contagion'. Where Locke and others had utilized sceptical doubts to destroy and rebuild in order to clear a path for knowledge, they had still not eradicated the reliance on the subjective experience of the world; nor, in Locke's case, the offering of proofs for the existence of God and the immortality of the soul – both 'objects', according to Kant, that are beyond the bounds of possible experience.[49] In other words, Locke still had one foot in the wasteland. Thus, Kant would provide a more thoroughgoing cleansing of philosophy in order to give modern science properly secure foundations. As one of his notable contemporaries, J. H. Lambert, remarked in expressing his agreement with Kant's critical project, 'there is no denying it: whenever a science needs methodical *cleansing*, it is always metaphysics [that proves to be the problem]'.[50] Emboldened by the support of respectable contemporaries, Kant would flush out the waste by declaring the conditions of possible knowledge.[51] Writing at a time when he was still formulating his critical project, he observed:

> It must be possible to survey the field of pure reason, that is, of judgements that are independent of all empirical principles, since this lies a priori in ourselves and need not await any exposure from our experience. What we need in order to indicate the divisions, limits, and the whole content of that field, according to secure principles . . . [is] a critique, a discipline, a canon, an architectonic of pure reason.[52]

This was not merely the destruction of the dilapidated lumber house of metaphysics; it more importantly implied the existence of some kind of plan to raise a new edifice. A 'critique' does not merely signify the negative criticism of some thing, of beliefs or practices, for instance (as it seems to for the many who frequently claim to be 'critiquing' one thing or another these days, misusing 'critique' to refer to a criticism). Rather, in the sense employed by Kant, the critique cannot be separated from what he called the *architectonic*, which is to say the art of the system it *positively* proposes.[53] In other words, the critique is a creative act that separates the sound materials and building blocks from the garbage in order to build anew. As Karl Jaspers wrote, the critique 'differentiates and sets limits, and in doing so, *clears the way*'.[54] A critique is therefore also a system. One need only look at the table of contents of Kant's *Critique of Pure Reason* to see how he has laid out – 'cleansed' may be a more accurate term – the grounds of the possibility of knowledge: the organization itself stands as evidence of the disposal of garbage (as indeed it would for any such *critique*).

The significance of this decisive move towards Reason was that the domain of human thought, once purged of the fruitless activity of metaphysics (of that which reason cannot encompass) would be fully capable of falling under the directing influence of reason. But if the speculations (that is to say, 'certainties') of reason, in their temporal finitude, in a sense, wager on the future shape and conditions of time and space – on the context of experience, in other words – we might wonder how we understand what lies on the horizon of the finite and 'comprehensible' system reason makes? In elaborating the basis of possible experience, Ernst Cassirer wrote, Kant was also saying that 'every dividing line we draw presupposes in the very divisions it creates an original unity of that which is divided'.[55] It delivers knowledge that is 'valid because it is valid', and so we find Kant caught in 'vicious circles' in which 'the only way to justify universal validity is to pre-suppose it'.[56] Thus, the certainties of pure reason stand on the basis of the way it has divided reality, and in virtue of how it assimilates these certainties to itself. Put in blatantly simplified terms: the house is put in order by the disposal of garbage, but the determination of the value of the remaining edifice would seem to be unquestionable in the sense that the philosopher himself would be the sole arbiter of the sound-ness of the structure. Kant thus faced the problem of accounting for the structure of pure reason beyond the empirical world, the world of things. He responded to the problem by moving away from reflection upon 'objects as things known and given', to show instead how an 'object migrates into our cognitive faculty and is pictured in it', which is to say, he chooses to examine instead 'simply the assertion of knowl-edge', according to Cassirer.[57] And in this way we see that his system sets its focus on what remains after the destruction and subsequent clearing away.

In this decisive move, Kant effected a separation of reason from the misleading speculation over 'things-in-themselves' (his expression for that which we cannot know), a retreat into self-legitimating authority that leaves us pondering over how we could possibly begin to elaborate what escapes the art of reason in virtue of the fact that it is external to, and cannot be subsumed within, an ordered system? Surely, the exceptions become unspeakable? Was this just the same thing Wittgenstein (almost 150 years later) ended his *Tractatus* with – the disposal of doubt as some non-specific and non-combinable waste product that didn't even deserve a proper name – or, to repeat his words, 'what we cannot speak about we must pass over in silence'?

Ultimately, we are compelled to recognize the relationship between knowledge and garbage that, after Kant's *Critique of Pure Reason*, results in a more determined separation of the human (the will to order) from nature (natural necessity). The latter appears now as a derelict wasteland and potential rubbish tip. Yet, the prolonged birth of the *Critique* itself, as Kant's correspondence amply illustrates, provides an insight into the 'architectonic' of knowledge and demonstrates how nature's waste is tidied away, disposed of, in the working out of the system. The unrelated fragments and pointless ruminations will persist in other words as the excess of any intellectual endeavour – its *garbage* – until, or unless, they are recycled into useful knowledge. Now, after this point in the history of knowledge, the order of experience is firmly located with the faculty of reason. And whereas some of the Presocratic thinkers, like Heraclitus, had seen generation and decay as part of the ceaseless flow of existence, this was still viewed within an ordered universe of which the human was simply a differentiated element; reason did not adjudicate on what we could actually say about the world, as it did after Kant. It is only in the early modern world (particularly from the seventeenth century onwards) that the elaboration of the *conditions of possible knowledge* becomes a central concern of Western philosophy and so, eventually, the cause of reason's 'separation' from nature. Mark C. Taylor has expressed this rather neatly in terms of the contemporary language of networks and computing technology. Thus, with respect to the Kantian system, knowledge presupposed certain forms and grids which filter and organize experience, meaning that:

> The mind is programmed or, in different terms, hard-wired. Since all experience is mediated by this grid, reality as such or the thing-in-itself remains forever inaccessible. The real, in other words, has always already disappeared.[58]

Once again, whilst this separation had released the rational mind from the necessity of pursuing the labyrinths of metaphysical thought that produced such dead ends as, in Kant's words, 'the investigation of the existence of God, immortality, and so on', it was still a retreat into certainty.[59] Metaphysical thought was mere 'shadow boxing' – it took aim at a phantom and so, within the discourse of efficiency that reason promotes, it constitutes little more than a waste of time.[60] Ultimately, the Kantian revolution maintains a separation between our knowledge of reality, and reality itself (in so far as we can know that); that is to say, between what reason can gather together in its account of itself, and the disposed of elements of the so-called dream science of metaphysics, with its 'confounded contagion'.[61]

It is worth noting here that this development has important implications for a sociology of knowledge, as well, because everything in the subsequent history of thought seems to have developed as a consequence of this 'critical turn', which had the effect of forcing knowledge to provide the grounds for its own existence. Kant's stress on the importance of justifying how knowledge 'represents' the world, for example, indirectly provides the structure for contemporary discourses on a whole variety of social identities (which of course, are also statements also on our *knowledge* of the world), and these are more fully prefigured in the cosmopolitanism of his moral and political thought. In Julia Kristeva's terms Kant's political philosophy outlines a 'cosmopolitan concept of mankind finding its full accomplishment without foreigners but respecting the right of those that are different' and this is clarified through a notion of 'separation combined with union.' But whilst the contemporary politics of difference emerge from the Kantian system, it is the *critical* attitude as the primary component of the truth-seeking language of knowledge that is more relevant for our purposes. Here we would do well to recall that the legitimacy of the system is guaranteed by a kind of *clean break* that establishes the autonomy of reason. As part of such a disconnection, notions of 'similarity' and 'difference' tell us that all truths are true only contingently – that is, historically, and according to the judgements of the 'court of pure reason', which can effect ever more breaks to refine its domain. In this way the factual correspondence of knowledge with reality is an objectification that may become different from itself. Identity in this philosophical sense was therefore a principle of equivalence: a formal relation that provided a basis for certainty. But the logic of truth seeking entails a dual movement, aiming at separate (yet, nonetheless, intimately connected) ends: the foundations of knowledge have to be made good in order to guarantee the stability needed to support its continued outward expansion. As Kant wrote:

> This sort of investigation [i.e., in *The Critique*] will always remain difficult for it includes the *metaphysics of metaphysics*. Yet, I have a plan in mind according to which even *popularity* might be gained for this study, a plan that could not be carried out initially, however, for the foundations needed cleaning up.[62]

The truth-seeking gesture sees the philosopher mired in something of a mess of speculation to begin with, situated on a wasteland of uncultivated ground and surrounded by the not yet disposed of (or yet to be recycled) ideas; indeed, as Kant himself wrote, he was caught amongst the 'ruins of collapsed edifices' that would not 'even be very difficult' to rebuild.[63] Unsurprisingly, the work on the *Critique* was so prolonged (it took, according to some accounts, fifteen years) that the notes and drafts for the work produced their own excessive remainder. These, according to Ernst Cassirer, constitute 'a wealth of ideas, which even in comparison with the later, final expression of ideas in the *Critique of Pure Reason* have their own special and independent worth', but which, if approached from the point of view of seeking a continuity in exactness with the finished work, could only signal (in terms of the concepts and expressions used) 'a chaos of heterogeneous instances'.[64] These notes and drafts, in other words, were Kant's *waste books*, from which (as he claimed in a letter to a regular correspondent, Moses Mendelssohn) he hastily drew together the final work in several months (this after spending some twelve years, by his own account, in his 'dark workshop').[65] The effort that went into producing this, his greatest work, from the earliest days of its formulation necessitated 'exhausting academic work' (as Kant wrote to Lambert in 1770).[66] And from the time of its publication his letters show that he maintained an active role in attempting to have the work accepted as a 'reliable guidebook' to help readers find a way out of the 'labyrinth' of metaphysics.[67] Yet he did not judge his efforts to have been entirely successful, and towards the end of his life Kant wrote that he had seen before him 'the unpaid bill of my uncompleted philosophy'; that was, its failure in his lifetime to fully convince doubters of the legitimacy of the self-grounding philosophy of critical reason, as well as his belief that it should be applied universally. In a letter to one of his supporters, Christian Garve, he could take an ironic poke at his potential readership, whilst still somewhat distraught that all his cleaning and polishing, his long preparation of the foundations for this edifice, had failed to make the finished work presentable to his important contemporaries:

> For the time being, let us be called dunces, if only we can make progress with the insight, with whose development the public will of course not sympathize, at least until the work emerges from its dark workshop and, seen with all its *polish*, need not be ashamed of being judged . . . *Garve, Mendelssohn,* and *Tetens* are the only men I know through whose co-operation this subject could have been brought to a successful conclusion before too

long, even though centuries before have not seen it done. But these men are leery of cultivating a *wasteland* that, with all the care that has been lavished upon it, has always been unrewarding.[68]

Nonetheless, Kant remained confident in the aim of this endeavour; and in the belief that 'philosophy, both as regards its means and ends, is capable of completion'.[69] In this effort to secure the bounds of all possible knowledge, as well as in the method of completion that sustains the architectonic itself, reason is closed off to those things that have no place in the system.[70] Indeed, the activity of purging philosophy of metaphysics is only a clue to an important consequence of this way of conceptualizing the world (or speaking about our knowledge of it, as Kant might have preferred to say). The disposal and recycling that lies at the core of knowledge never actually finds a place in the elaboration of things like philosophical systems precisely because they have been *polished* prior to their public unveiling; they have been *worked out*. The thing is – as we have seen in the example of Kant – this 'working out' of the excess or unnecessary (the activity of disposing or recycling) comprises the very condition that allows anything to be given a place in the system. One has to look, as we have, in the waste books – the letters, fragments, footnotes and so on. From a philosophical or historical point of view, however, these probably appear largely marginal to the works they inform. We can only note that this is because history, as the reconstitution of the past from a specific point within some present, follows its own guiding *idea* – not the excessive remainder (that which we cannot speak of) that has been consigned to the garbage. How apt that Ludwig Feuerbach, writing in 1830, expressed a version of history's self-grounding that could just as well be extrapolated from our understanding of Kant:

> The only thing that has a history, is a thing that is itself the principle of its own alterations, that underlies all of its alterations as an omnipresent essential unity, and the alterations of which are therefore internal, immanent, determined by itself and identical with itself. The stone that travels from the hand of a beggar to that of a king, from America to Europe and from there to Asia, still does not have a history.[71]

Likewise, there is no place in the history of reason for its waste products.

History responds only to what these great intellectual products mean; it tells us how they work, of their part in some great chain as the latest creative achievement of the human imagination, perhaps. What we get, in other words, is the front. We never really see behind the exterior of these creations – we don't see the plumbing, or, unless we really look, the janitorial work that goes on. We are spared the wholesale trashing that propels knowledge to greater heights. What is the consequence of this? One reply to this question is to suggest that in the presentation of knowledge as this complete and self-sustaining system we do not glimpse the living process of knowledge creation, and are therefore blind to the generation and decay that underpins it. In other words, the ways of thinking of the human relation to the world that have been common to Western philosophy, especially in modernity, encourage a blindness to that which doesn't fit.

'TECHNOLOGY'

The currency of the illiterate wisdom of 'garbage in, garbage out' attains a high value within the contemporary economy of knowledge, its institutions, and public perceptions. In this, useful knowledge must attain a form of almost technical efficiency (and indeed, public accountability) that is seen to expurgate waste. This applies especially to those things that are deemed to be wasteful because they seem to be *of no value* because, as we are aware, garbage in equals garbage out. The poverty of such thinking is revealed in the absolute ignorance of how language and knowledge are means of sifting and tidying up that not only produce their own rubbish (as we have seen), but condition the way this very language – in its promulgation as knowledge, and its practical applicability as technology – puts the world to use (see opposite). To the Ancient Greeks something very like this was known as *techne*. Within the institutional framework of the contemporary economy of knowledge a notion like *techne* is quite in keeping with the guiding ethos of its administrators and paymasters because it values *not* the wasteful speculations of a curious mind (an Immanuel Kant), but instead refers to a practical knowledge that 'because it so often treats subjects of pressing concern and apparent usefulness' means that 'those who do possess it are well-regarded'.[72] Thus, if the utility of knowledge as expressed in *techne* was a source of distinction in the time of the ancients, should we be surprised that now it has become

Study team awarded massive grant to research 'the meaning of waste'

Academics find out how to get £1m for talking absolute rubbish

By **Graham Grant**
Education Reporter

ACADEMICS have been handed nearly £1million of taxpayers' money to study the meaning of 'rubbish'.

Reality: Roseanna Cunningham

Bill Aitken: 'Worthless research'

Garbage In, Garbage Out? The wisdom of the instrumental as reported in *The Daily Mail*, September 2003.

the model not only of how knowledge is put to use but of how it is produced? Accordingly we see *techne* combined within contemporary academic 'research' in the form of strategies for 'divvying-up' the world according to disciplinary boundaries in order to extract ever-more value, or more *outputs* (and thus, more garbage).[73]

The history of metaphysics (including Kant's own attempt to escape metaphysics) consists of such definite gestures of separation that in the act of disposal hope to sustain life. And so, the desire to eject the rubbish in the way through the refinement of knowledge creates more waste. In the words of Nietzsche, the metaphysical gesture displayed an 'extravagant pride' that resulted in what he saw as the logical rape of the *causa sui* (the self-caused cause) that defines such 'clean breaks':

> The desire to bear the whole and sole responsibility for one's actions, and to absolve God, world, ancestors, chance, society from responsibility for them, is nothing less than the desire to be precisely that *causa sui* and, with more than Münchhausen temerity, to pull oneself into existence out of the swamp of nothingness by one's own hair.[74]

But because we employ the metaphysical gesture of separation not only in organizing knowledge, but in our relationship with the material world – in our manipulation of matter – the divide between the valuable and the worthless does not only signal the triumph of reason and the self-rule of human autonomy, it also introduces the spectre of garbage as the universal condition that will once again drag us back *out of existence*, annihilate us, as we see when we look at knowledge in its practical applications, in its transformation or 'revealing' of the real. Reason and its subservient double, knowledge, give us the 'products' we want – things that we value and that, by and large, enrich our lives. Ye, we don't see the other side of this; a blindness that is not without its costs. The designation of a limit to possible experience inaugurates a revolution in the dissolution of old relations, outdated ways of thinking, and in the memorable phrase of Adorno and Horkheimer, 'excises the incommensurable'.[75] In a telling summation of Kant's critical project, Robert Pippin has written that:

> Reason, Kant frequently says, 'commands' nature and does not 'beg,' it 'legislates,' it even frames 'for itself with perfect spontaneity an order of its own according to ideas, to which it adapts the empirical conditions.'[76]

This is because nature, according to Kant, has no purpose of its own. It appears to be in a state of chaos, devoid of any intentional design.[77] The interesting point about this way of understanding Kant's philosophy is that it could almost stand as a summation of the relationship between technology and nature. In other words, what Mark C. Taylor calls the 'matrix' that acts as a grid to filter and organize experience, also transforms what is otherwise a kind of universal nothingness into use values. It also reminds us that our word *technology* derives from this Greek word *techne*, which meant something like the systematic *practice* of an art (as opposed to wisdom); such as the craft of an artisan, a tool maker and so on. And whilst wisdom was the province of the philosophers, *techne* was a form of knowledge that because it could be taught was available to all. As David Roochnik has written, *techne* is 'paradigmatic of knowledge that *gives us control*, that offers us stability'.[78] This brings us back once again to Kant who, as Pippin notes, wrote in his *Foundations of the Metaphysics of Morals*: 'Man now finds in himself a faculty by means of which he differentiates himself from all other things, indeed even from himself in so far as he is affected by objects, and that faculty is reason.'[79]

The combination of reason's differentiating capacity and the skill of manipulating natural materials ensure that human knowledge can develop specific foci in order to more efficiently seek such stability. The differentiation from 'all other things' that reason effects also describes the kind of separation that occurs between the human and the natural when the word 'technology' is understood in terms of its complicated etymology; where it means both the human art of manipulating nature as well as the differentiated processes, objects and products of knowledge having (to use the Kantian language) 'command' over nature. In the sense employed by the Ancients, *techne* is taken to be distinct from nature (*phusis*). More precisely it has been taken to refer to nature made in some 'human image'; it is, according to Heidegger, related to *episteme* (knowing) and both this and *techne* are in fact 'names for knowing'.[80] In Heidegger's terms, then, technology is understood as the ordering of nature for use, where *techne* means 'to be entirely at home in something, to understand and be expert in it. Such knowing provides an opening up. As an opening up it is a revealing.'[81] Thus, nature is a kind of resource whose capacity, Heidegger says, is 'orderable': 'nature reports itself in some way or other that is identifiable through calculation . . . it remains orderable as a system of information'.[82]

An aspect of Heidegger's rather complex elaboration of the essence of technology that is worth lingering on is the bringing together of older forms of technology and the technology of modern science as belonging to essentially the same order of *techne*. Thus, modern science, for all its exactness and productive capacity when set against earlier technologies, is just another form of *knowledge* that *technology puts to use*. In other words, Heidegger seems to be saying that nature is revealed as something *to us*. In the neologistic terms he brings into use in this essay, this is a 'revealing,' and this revealing 'that holds sway throughout modern technology is a challenging, which puts to nature the unreasonable demand that it supply energy that can be extracted and stored as such'.[83] Furthermore, the development of a technology that can effect such a transformation over nature ensures that we can take even greater steps to separate how we order nature from itself, and this too reveals a limitless potential for differentiated products of nature (which, in contemporary terms, might be consumables). Thus, in Heidegger's words:

> The energy concealed in nature is unlocked, what is unlocked is transferred, what is transferred is stored, what is stored up is, in turn, distributed, and what is distributed is switched about ever anew. Unlocking, transforming, storing, distributing, and switching about are ways of revealing.[84]

Given the beguiling abstraction of Heidegger's style, it is necessary at this point to provide and example in order to see what he might be saying. Consider the combination of knowledge and technological know-how that is 'stored up' in something like a kitchen appliance – say, a freezer or refrigerator. In the words of an advert for Union Carbide (which is actually selling their technological superiority) the forces of nature ordered for use – the 'extremes of heat and cold', 'vacuums and great pressures' – explain, as the advert says, *Why some things get better all the time* (opposite). Like many adverts of the time (this was at the dawn of the post-World War II prosperity years) it is keen to show how the benefits of science and technology add not only to the sustenance of life, but actually represent an improvement in human development. As well as the snippet of Aristotle at the top of this advert (notable for the way it coincidentally seals the link between past and present, as if cold storage was an afterthought of Aristotle's that Union Carbide had eventually got round to bringing to fruition), it reminds us that technology, of course, is essentially a (long drawn out) consequence of the development of philosophy since the Ancients. The text, as always in these artefacts, is particularly revealing:

> All the way from the farm to the table, modern means of food preservation protect foods against damaging molds, bacteria, insects. Chemical refrigerants preserve meat . . . nitrogen gas safeguards the purity of canned foods [and so on, until] Food preservation has become an industrial science – and well illustrates the fact that when man has better materials he can do better things.

And all the way *from* the table? This cleaned out version of life is, of course, aspirational. But whilst we keep in mind the general optimism of the post-war years, we cannot overlook the way that the efficiency of a technology that proclaims to cut out waste at every stage, in such declarations, presents one side of the tale: foods are 'protected', their lifespan is *prolonged* and kept *pure* against the claims of natural degradation, materials are used more efficiently, and so on. Garbage is here implied in the very language of protection and efficiency, but carefully avoids being elaborated because of the forward-looking language of perfectibility. What leaves the table, if not flushed away in the bathroom, might in the household have been dumped in General Electric's *Disposall.* We might wonder if the woman in the advert who is caught

"Wisdom must be intuitive reason combined with scientific knowledge"
—ARISTOTLE (DIALOGUES)

Why some things get better all the time

THE TEMPTING FOODS spread before the family of to-day are more nourishing and purer than ever before.

All the way from farm to table, *modern means of food preservation* protect foods against damaging molds, bacteria, insects—against loss of nutrients.

 Chemical refrigerants preserve meat . . . nitrogen gas safeguards the purity of canned foods . . . ethylene oxide and "dry ice" protect wheat before it is milled . . . stainless steel tanks prevent contamination of foods and beverages . . . and plastics line many food containers.

Food preservation has become an industrial science—and well illustrates the fact that when man has better materials he can do better things.

Producing better materials for the use of industry and the benefit of mankind is the work of UNION CARBIDE.

Basic knowledge and persistent research are required, particularly in the fields of science and engineering. Working with extremes of heat and cold, and with vacuums and great pressures, Units of UCC now separate or combine nearly one-half of the many elements of the earth.

UNION CARBIDE
AND CARBON CORPORATION

30 East 42nd Street   New York 17, N.Y.

Products of Divisions and Units include—
ALLOYS AND METALS · CHEMICALS · PLASTICS
ELECTRODES, CARBONS, AND BATTERIES
INDUSTRIAL GASES AND CARBIDE

Why Some Things Get Better All the Time, 1946, advertisement for the benefits of scientific knowledge, Union Carbide.

"GOOD-BY FOREVER" TO GARBAGE!

DISPOSALL

DISPOSALL MEANS
GOOD-BY TO GARBAGE
AUTOMATICALLY!

• New kitchen marvel, The General Electric Disposall,* shreds **all** food waste—washes it down the drain

Imagine! Your home rid of garbage forever. A cleaner, more healthful, more sanitary home!

Imagine! Countless footsteps saved each day—with food waste disposed of *immediately*, right in the sink, before it can become odorous, harmful, pesty garbage!

Just see—in these pictures—how simply, efficiently the Disposall works... once you've scraped all food waste, even rinds and bones, into the drain.

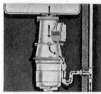

1. Out of sight, under the sink, the Disposall looks like this. A simple appliance that fits most any sink, it has a capacity ample for food waste from any one meal for an average family.

2. Protecting cover on sink drain is locked with twist to left, *once waste is scraped into drain opening.* Notice openings in the cover, for clean, flushing water to enter the Disposall as it works.

3. Turning on cold water automatically starts Disposall. Food waste is shredded into tiny particles, flushed into sewer or septic tank. No more garbage ... ever!

4. You'll agree with Disposall users who say: "It's my favorite kitchen appliance." "I would never give it up." "It saves me 32 minutes a day." "So sanitary!" "Perfect."

NOTE:

For the perfect laborsaving combination, the General Electric Disposall can be teamed up with a General Electric Dishwasher in a complete Electric Sink! General Electric Company, Bridgeport 2, Connecticut.

 **DISPOSALL**

General Electric's registered trade-mark for its food-waste appliance.

GENERAL ⊕ ELECTRIC

"Good-by Forever" to Garbage!, 1948, advertisement for General Electric's 'Disposall'.

saying *"Good-by Forever"* to Garbage! is not actually the same person who prepared the wonderful waste saving meal in the Union Carbide advert, but who seems to be missing. (After all, someone has to clean up the leftovers.) Here too we see the elevation of personal displacement, in the sense that one need handle the waste even less, into the near equivalent of a world without garbage. 'Disposall means good-by to garbage automatically' it tells us. And there is the added benefit of the previously wasted effort now saved by technology, now ready to be put to other uses because of the *'Countless footsteps saved each day – with food waste disposed of immediately,* right in the sink before it can become odorous, harmful, pesty garbage'.

To Heidegger and others, like Theodor Adorno and Max Horkheimer, disenchantment and ruin are written in the logic of modernity. This finds expression through technology because 'knowledge, which is power, knows no obstacles', according to Adorno and Horkheimer. 'Technology is the essence of this knowledge.'[85] Heidegger's pessimism is expressed towards the end of his essay on 'The Question Concerning Technology' in urging a return to some prior idea of *techne* as the kind of 'revealing' that brings forth truth and beauty – as opposed to what he termed 'Enframing', which, through modern science, 'pursues and entraps nature as a calculable coherence of forces'.[86]

Whilst the technological appropriation of nature is 'not simply a continuation of Platonic metaphysics', to quote Robert Pippin, it does result from the adaptation of knowledge, and its apparent perfectibility through a succession of separations (or 'clean breaks') that attempt to optimize knowledge. Certainly, it is a response to historical contingencies – as Robert Pippin says, 'crises, inventions, growing paradoxes of the old paradigms, and the gradual "delegitimation" of the old science'.[87] But it is also the separation and withdrawal that derives from the metaphysical understanding of the world (in the sense that metaphysics is always a separation and withdrawal), and is not simply co-extensive with something like capitalist production (as Pippin seems to suggest).[88] What we say here, then, is that every act of differentiation – every 'clean break' with the past, creates garbage; results in leftovers. This is not to say that ways and means are not found to re-use this garbage (as I have been arguing, this is what always happens), because nothing ever simply vanishes. Things – objects and ideas, for example – may fall out of use, be declared derelict and demolished, but what results from this just constitutes the material for new forms. In the facile 'garbage in, garbage out' vision of instrumentality we fail to see this (instead we only see that garbage 'disappears'), and the irony here could not be greater because of the extra garbage that the personal computer produces. Even here, however, we can detect an attempt to cosmetically alter the fact. Thus, where the Macintosh computer – which provided the basic model of the working environment for most subsequent computers – began with the 'trashcan' as the destination for unwanted files, in the Microsoft version ('Windows' which was charged with simply stealing the Macintosh idea) this is subtly altered to become a 'recycle bin' (complete with the environmentally friendly recycling symbol). While the trash from these virtual bins appears to be liberated to create space on the computer disk that can be re-used, as Slavoj Žižek noted, in reality it is practically impossible to erase and so constitutes 'the ultimate horror of the digital universe', which is that while things may be cancelled, or deleted, 'everything remains forever inscribed'.[89] The possibility of 'undeleting' files tells us that they don't really disappear, and so a 'simple PC contains a kind of "undead" spectral domain of deleted texts which nevertheless continue to lead a shadowy existence "between the two deaths," officially deleted but still there, waiting to be recovered'.[90]

In our ceaseless refinement, as we shall see, we yet manage to restore the dead in other forms as well.

3 Garbage Aesthetics

Minimal incoherent fragments:
the opposite of History, creator of ruins,
out of your ruins you have made creations.
Octavio Paz, 'Objects and Apparitions'

REFINEMENT

Refinement is an effect of differentiation, an act that selects and relates in experience the elements of a phenomenal world, turning the act into a creative making of the world. Thus, refinement is cause and consequence of judgement, the interaction that produces differentiation.

Often, it seems that a distillation of phenomenal experience separates a domain of aesthetic existence from the rational utility that otherwise orders the objects of the world: refinement organizes experience into the graceful and the gauche, the tasteful and the kitsch. Refinement separates, withdraws, and distils a sphere of value from the crudity of existence, which itself remains (in terms of our knowledge of it) inexact or random in its natural condition. The pull of attraction that guides us towards certain appearances, or to look at certain objects, makes little sense without some idea that in looking at the world we are guided by notions of familiarity and difference, and in this respect we cannot overlook the role knowledge plays in helping us to identify phenomena – to discern and thus refine a visual ordering of experience. To look at the world, to visualize the beauty or symmetry in things (or in their relations) is to see, to 'make', a mask-like appearance. And so, looking is also an act of revision, or editing. However, in 'discerning' the well-proportioned order that we give phenomena (which produces the aesthetic realm) we groom a finely nuanced existence that conceals the possible awareness that refinement also produces a necessary residue. In fact, the hidden by-product of refinement reveals, if seen, the discreteness of phenomena – it declares that the residual elements constitute a jumble of inexactness.

Reason, too, proceeds by refining knowledge, which is seen in the separation of phenomena into ever more particular elements which, in combination, constitute the world of appearance as we understand it. In modern physics the world of appearance is theoretically resolved – by an act of refinement, no less – into a world of discretely moving, yet hidden particulars; undermining the notion that the world of phenomena are related in the way our visual ordering privileges the regularity in appearance. We proceed, however, on the basis that what we picture in looking at the world does bear some resemblance to 'reality' – but this is only to the reality produced by the snapshot effect of looking, which filters phenomena into a meaningful visual and conceptual field. In modern society the plastic arts can be seen as a particular concentration of the activity that becomes manifest in a world-moulding, one that sees reason effectively derive the bounds of the sensible, thus separating it from the random; from nonsense. Artists, particularly those of the twentieth century, have taken refinement to the non-place of the residual, to the impoverished material world of objects that were distilled from a prior existential grooming; the aesthetic of representation is thus overturned by the artist who takes up residence in the very notion of plasticity. This is the realm of the impermanent, the protean, the fluid, the unpredictable and the confusing.

Nevertheless, we know that from coarse matter great riches are mined: that from the depths of the sea, for example, oil and its triumphant by-product, plastic, are withdrawn. It is fitting that plastic – the *garbage* of oil refinement – becomes the material of modern life par excellence; capable of assuming constantly renewed forms, it is the source of great value that, by analogy, describes at once the impermanence of much art from the twentieth century, and its origins in the crude, meaningless world of the discarded.

POETICS OF COINCIDENCE

'Spiders and salamanders' sit next to the obscurely labelled 'mouse materials', 'old fish marbles', and 'love letters: Jennifer Jones'. A snapshot (opposite) of the shelves in Joseph Cornell's workshop taken by Hans Namuth in 1969 reveals something of the curiosity that drove the artist to amass a vast storehouse of the banal and kitsch, items that

Hans Namuth, *Joseph Cornell's Workshop*, 1969.

were connected only in the imaginary world occupied by the artist. These curiosities were collected and brought together in his unusual and fascinating wooden box constructions, which gave life to the idiosyncratic order he would bring to the seemingly random assortment of items recovered from the shelves of his workshop. A look at some of the labels on other boxes in this photograph do little to convince the unsuspecting viewer that Cornell was not simply a kind of garbage collector, a magician of worthless and indistinguishable things who, in the works they made up, brought them vividly to life. 'Caravaggio, etc.' 'pegs' and 'best white boxes' enigmatically label the materials Cornell employed, and only partially help to unveil the world of this withdrawn, perhaps reluctant, artist.[1]

In his box constructions Joseph Cornell took the apparently random – objects that have no association except within the context in which they are presented – and brought them together to give a form to the associations of a sensibility captivated by the bits and scraps of products, magazines and other ephemera that, like garbage, would otherwise be ignored if left unconnected to this singular imagination. This is not to say that Cornell's work makes a radical departure from the centuries old tradition of *framing* a world (or some aspect of the world).[2] In fact, painting also traditionally gave form – or *made* – a world in the very act of framing; although perhaps in traditional terms this was less often with the conceptually or spatially unconnected objects Cornell favoured being combined within the bounded space of a single, unique, 'representation'. The mystery of this artist's work deepens because unlike Surrealism, with which Cornell has been associated, he did not deal with images of distorted perception in the same way as Dali or Magritte, or with 'objects' that could not be readily identified as something one might encounter during the course of any normal day.[3] The interesting aspect of these uncanny creations was that they actually did consist of the everyday – often the crushingly banal objects that form the small and overlooked aspects of, one suspects, a distant childhood where the past can be understood as the debris of a life that somehow continues as the ghost of the present. Thus, the work of Cornell gathers together the kind of objects that through the course of a life are usually either packed away or trashed.

The materials of these boxes (see opposite) in the grown-up world of utility are useless mementos belonging to a distant and irrecoverable past. The items that go into these works are all, nevertheless, things we can usually recognize – a child's marble, a discarded jar, a

Joseph Cornell, *Untitled*, c. 1950, box construction. Wadsworth Atheneum, Hartford, Connecticut.

seashell, the building blocks of a learning game – yet it is in the presentation of these items as part of the total work that they seem to lose any association they may have had individually, instead to be overtaken by the associations that arise in the mind of the viewer. The *Untitled* box illustrated, completed over several years in the mid-1950s, resonates to the muted sound of loss, or the thought of persons missing. Perhaps it is the ease with which one can see these parts as little more than garbage (things disconnected from a prior relationship; the toy separated from the child who played with it) that the sense of such a work can be transformed to reflect the universality of the experience of absence as a core aspect of the mature human condition? Perhaps Cornell's work prompts us to admit that we may lock away the past but that we cannot finally dispose of it because the immaterial traces of childlike associations persist?

As well as jarring with our sense of place in the world another particularly unusual aspect of Cornell's boxes of once-abandoned objects is that neither do the individuated items that make them up appear to belong together. A map of the moon forms the backdrop of a box that contains a clay pipe, the disembodied head of a child figure, a glass containing an egg and a representation of the Tower of Pisa with Saturn hovering over (*Soap Bubble Set*, 1936) – and there are a great many more similarly enigmatic creations in what Cornell left behind. The objects in combination here occur neither rationally nor naturally, the collections presented do not, therefore, represent anything one would expect to encounter beyond the realm of dreams and imagination. Whilst artists from the Renaissance until around the end of the nineteenth century had created objects that appeared 'orderly' or appeared to mimic nature, they were ultimately revealed to be manifestations of a humanly created order made apparent after reason had discovered an unruly and indeterminate nature that was not at all as uniform as conventional artistic representation might have led one to believe. What Cornell reveals to the world in these boxes is, by contrast, a self-created order, and thus the *coincidence* of the disconnected objects belonging together inside one of these boxes is only finally established as a consequence of the presence of a beholding eye, and by the suspension of reasonable expectations, which makes us complicit in a necessary descent into his fragmentary, nonsensical, underworld.

Although the viewer might be struck by the presentation of unlikely convergences, for Cornell these were far from accidental creations. Over many years, in fact, he collected these knick-knacks and clippings from magazines – fetishes – which were organized and recorded according to a staggeringly detailed, yet mysterious, working method that has since been recovered from the many 'dossiers' he left behind, as Lindsay Blair discovered. Even a selection of the labels Cornell pasted on his dossiers is revealing both for the radically subjective imagination at work and the pervading sense of displacement that the work captures: '*Journey Album; Museum Without Walls; Metaphysique d'Ephemera; Portrait Encasement; Center of a Labyrinth; Childhood Regained*', and so on.[4] With the peculiar precision of his working methods on the one hand, and the apparently arbitrary or 'unnatural' ordering of phenomena within the boxes (to the viewer) on the other, a gap opens up in our understanding between the perception of a seemingly coincidental assortment of items, and the subjective, cognitive power of artistic association. In this latter sense, Cornell's work follows closely the example of Marcel Duchamp who, along with a number of others, was responsible for legitimizing the appropriation of apparent rubbish within an aesthetic context. This was the result, generally speaking, of stripping objects of any prior value (the value may have been negative, considering the objects used were usually cheap or had been found), and also in the use of more or less recognizable objects in unusual contexts, a trick that reversed the conventional trajectory of manufactured objects (value to garbage) by reconstituting them in disguise, or as part of some coincidental relationship.[5]

And so too with the Cornell box constructions a gap is opened that separates art object and reality, artist and world, and it is into this gap that the artist moves in making the object public, and into which the viewer must move in order to make a connection. Cornell offers one example of a balance many artists in the twentieth century maintained between order and disorder, moving to and fro between the two conditions because of the necessity that the artist – in creating this gap between object and reality – to a significant extent loses power over the work of art. To find a public (something that Cornell at times gambled on only reluctantly) is, in other words, to relinquish the meaning of a painting – any work of art – and thus to accept that the work as presented to posterity, in its actual *existence*, does not represent some timeless truth, but is instead a partial and fragmentary act of creation. Plastic creation does not, then, enact a 'peeling back' of some veil of perception to reveal, in the object, a reality that has been there all along. What is more like the case is that the requirement of a viewer to make a work of art becomes a mark of the artist's residence in, finally, a world of contingency. The need for a public, when indulged, must be interpreted as the artist's acceptance that something fundamentally unfinished is released to posterity; otherwise art would constitute little more than a collection of private fancies.

Yet the history of modern art is a history of self-denial, not a history of acceptance. It is characterized by revolutions that turn away from the warm embrace of acceptance, and through a variety of iconoclastic or confrontational gestures, modern art sets the work of art against any potential viewer as a challenge. Marcel Duchamp's *Fountain* of 1917 – a reconfigured urinal declared art by the act of naming it – is the point of departure for so-called junk art and provides a good example of how a public is eventually brought round to accepting an object that had initially stood as an affront to the aesthetic hierarchy that regulated the art world. Duchamp's *Fountain* – in being far from *given* – can thus be seen to have evolved to the position it now occupies through a series of improbable coincidences – through its initial discovery (the scandal of its public display in 1917), then loss (when forgotten after the rise of Abstract Expressionism), and discovery again (the adoption of Duchamp as an influence by 'Neo-Dada' in the 1950s and 1960s). In other words this object had (and has) a 'life' way beyond its initial public unveiling, one that extends beyond what the temporally located, embodied eye, can, or could, see. Yet, even as one recognizes the contemporary acceptance of *Fountain* it still remains axiomatic that in spite of its iconic status no one can actually agree on something as apparently basic as *what it means* or *what it is*. This is because, as Octavio Paz has observed, the status of this object rests unusually in its function as a question mark suspended permanently over the notion of creation itself, and thus not without coincidence its 'meaning' is only found in the puzzlement it creates. Which is to say it works by forcing the beholder of such a 'creation' either to ignore it or to identify and draw meaning from the object world.[6] And in large part, this explains why such creations are so easily labelled 'nonsense' or 'rubbish' – they have no objective meaning.

By observing that a work of art is the product of two defining 'poles' Duchamp had accepted that this response would await *Fountain*. One pole is the artist, the maker of the material object, and the other the beholder who at some time and place unspecified *looks* at it and thus, in an act of almost Berkelian perceptiveness, confirms its existence.[7] In assaulting the traditional subject-object 'picture' version of realism (in which truth is apparently *given*, or unveiled), Duchamp suggested that these poles constitute a more or less indeterminate whole, that 'truth' emerges somewhere in the gap between the two poles, making the object neither one thing nor another, and hence nothing: a piece of garbage.[8] The two poles, he believed, were separated by a 'delay' that interrupts the eventual, defining, rendezvous of viewer meeting object. Which is to say that the viewer has a significant collaborative role to play; that the object is 'finished' by the viewer, thus creating a somewhat fleeting and insubstantial object that becomes, conceptually reminiscent of a Leibnizian *monad* – possessed of 'no parts [it] can neither be formed nor destroyed. [It] can neither begin nor end naturally, and consequently [it will] last as long as the universe.'[9] However, unlike monads, these objects 'die away' with each new viewer, are unmade, and so to the impartial eye can appear to be out of place within an aesthetic context. The physical object itself is merely a sign that has no real referent beyond what it is to the viewer – it is, objectively, a sign of a sign, if you like.[10] It degrades reality by not representing it.

With all art that uses leftover and found materials (generally, these are objects taken out of context, or placed in seemingly meaningless collages) the question of what is being looked at is caught up in establishing reliable signifiers, or finding fixed relations or properties, both within and between things: objects presented within a frame, the perspectival arrangement of space, and ultimately the relation of the arrangement to reality all lead to certain expectations. And in the well-ordered reality that we like to think we live in, it is easy for the degraded and worthless to be blocked out. Yet these are arguably the principle categories of 'stuff' that the artist continually dallies with,

As with the emergence of knowledge, the performance of artistic creation begins within a conceptual void – with loose associations, fragmentary ideas and the speculations of curiosity. It starts, in other words, with nothing whole, fixed or identifiable but with the formlessness of what we know as garbage. And importantly, art, like play, is at this stage of creation for nothing but itself, and it is from within such a void that the artist emerges with something. However, this void is not just some detached and empty otherness (say, the 'non-artistic' realm or the everyday), against which the subject is determined, but more specifically, as Hegel said, the void in this sense is actually 'an absolute otherness' *in which consciousness permanently dwells*: it is the negating power of self, originating within the subject. How might the Hegelian void be manifested, we could ask. One answer is that it is found in self-conscious acts of forgetting, in a cognitive power that dissolves known relations that once connected the subject to the world in some previous identification.[11] It is from this void, we suppose, that 'truth' emerges as the self-negating aspect of subjectivity. In terms of creativity, then, the artistic void should not be seen as equivalent to a nihilistic tendency; rather, what is barren and empty can only be the source of edification, not destruction (there is nothing of value to destroy). What we might take note of here is that the things we destroy (things that did have a value) are also made void; and the point is that all things, all objects, begin from nothing (garbage) and eventually return to nothing (garbage again). An example used by Jonathan Dollimore in a discussion of death brings out the dialectic relationship of creation and destruction: the ultimate negation of self is death, and the subject – in differentiating itself from the world – makes the power of death real because 'death holds out the promise of a release from the very individuality whose formation would have been unthinkable without it'.[12] That is, the individuation of self constitutes the creation of valuable life but at the same time makes death – the removal of this life – a spectre one cannot escape. In vacating the ground of a previous identity, in removing all categories in a transcendental reduction that temporarily excludes the world artistic creation delves into the void. Between reason and unreason, order and disorder, and ultimately between identity as similarity and identity as differentiation, it is only finally an act of differentiation – a break with the past – that ends the suspense, inaugurating the new and thus giving a finite reality to some object.

It is no surprise then that the legitimacy of accepted ways of looking becomes the target of the artist, nor that the art of the twentieth century itself became at times denial through plasticity. The point is also that our use of this term 'modern' to refer to a certain kind of art only makes sense as a category breaker, or when it is put up against what is already accepted, against tradition.[13] The 'modern' in art is an oppositional tendency that aims to destroy the past, and it just so happens that with painting we have one strain of modernism that outpaces others because the tradition of representationalism – in making pictures of the world, reality – has a more obvious relationship to questions of philosophical realism. This relation proves difficult to break – canvas and frame themselves make what we know to be a 'picture' and a picture is supposed to resemble something else in the world. In objects like Joseph Cornell's box constructions, the total force of his sensibility comes through as another attack on resemblance. Instead the frame is appropriated and declared the space for an order that the artist produces unseen, one that is only fully realized coincidentally by some poetic enactment that involves the convergence of artist and viewer. Many of Cornell's boxes are constructed on a grid, which in modern society we are given to associate with order. Yet within modern art, as Rosalind Krauss says, the grid 'is a way of abrogating the claim of natural objects to have an order peculiar to themselves'.[14] The viewer, in meeting with the object, likewise disorders the world of objects as known.

THE VISIBLE REMAINDER

The resurrection of dead matter seen in Cornell's works became a common theme that moved art in the twentieth century away from traditional painterly conventions. A reanimation of garbage takes place as the consequence of a world of increasing specificity, a world of *refinement*, in which we see a necessary residue in excess matter, which is removed from the valuable sphere of economic production. Cast aside like the lacquer that would accrue formlessly as a by-product of the marvellous technology that once etched a world of sound into the grooves of a piece of plastic, such visible remainders nonetheless stand as the evidence that something else is going on besides the conventional uses materials and products are put to.

The residual materials in question are normally taken to be totally devoid of value, representing only the leftover matter that never actually disappears, but instead, *temporarily* vanishes as a condition of a process that seeks in its refinement, to define what belongs and what must be trashed. This is the destructive, negative end of making, a reminder that all things made are eventually reduced to the same; that in 'death' identity becomes absolute. In 1997 the British artist Cornelia Parker, by happy coincidence, was in San Antonio, Texas, when she heard one day that a church had been struck by lightning, and transformed by the resulting fire to a heap of charcoal. After recovering debris from the scene of this natural destruction, she then created a fragmentary 'cube' from the charred pieces of wood, which were suspended using barely perceptible wire to create the form. Large fragments in the middle of the 'cube' give way to the smallest of visible pieces around the edgeless parameter of the object, which gives the impression of dissolution and, like the fragments of an explosion, disappears into the surrounding atmosphere in echo of the accidental creation of these pieces of matter. This installation is titled *Mass (Colder Darker Matter)* in reference to (and perhaps in commemoration of) the sacred house of God that once was the place of the Mass, the place in which the committed would receive the word. Now it was just cold dark matter, *mass* of an entirely different order; the *relic* of an object hanging together in a new form – this is the vulgar matter of life, now colder and darker because some natural intervention had profaned its once sacred function.[15] Fragments of matter, and indeed, matter transformed – crushed, melted, stretched, or recovered – appear throughout the work of Cornelia Parker.

In another installation, *Avoided Object* (1995), buried objects were located by a metal detector, then resurrected from beneath the ground of Düsseldorf in Germany, to eventually be suspended above the ground at a height corresponding to the depth at which they had been discovered. In the particularity of the form we are presented with here, this literal and metaphorical raising of dead matter takes a trend of the previous fifty or sixty years, and adds a degree of refinement that makes clear that where once the discarded objects of the modern world served the artist as the kind of way-finder that signalled a route out of self-expression, now any object, whether destroyed by the human hand, by natural processes or accidents could serve the artist as a means of engaging with the world.

By the 1990s, the history of twentieth-century art had seen painting so long removed from the centrality of oil and canvas as the principal media that a generation of artists (like Cornelia Parker, born in the second half of the century) did not need to find ways of escaping painting as traditionally understood; they had already developed in the anti-painting tradition that was still, nevertheless, a development of painting. In this respect, the found objects of Robert Rauschenberg, or the garbage-filled containers of the French artist Arman, precede the more formal compositions of Cornelia Parker, but establish the continuity between someone like Parker (and, indeed, another of her predecessors, Tony Cragg) and Marcel Duchamp in the idea that the frame was now banished, that there were no limits to the objects that might provide material for the artist.

Cornelia Parker, *Mass (Colder Darker Matter)*, 1997, charred remains of a church struck by lightning in San Antonio, Texas. Installation in the Frith Street Gallery, London.

The blurring of the distinction between artistic materials and object world was important because it forced a reassessment of the status of objects. In essence, the question these artists asked was 'what is an object?' Is to think of an object not always to think of particular kinds of object? And does this not usually bring to mind something physical, material and indeed useful? An object, in a material sense, is not only something that has a body, mass and form perhaps determined by its association with some function, it may be – like rock, dirt and other 'dead' or formless matter – a primary substance that is utilized in the creation of familiar objects of use; as sand, for example, is used in the making of glass, or wood pulp in the creation of paper products. Nevertheless, the metamorphosis in question begins to take its current form with the objects cast off by modern society. These were the objects that interested Robert Rauschenberg – the used up remnants of an industrial society that had continually to discard its useless junk in pursuit of a more refined, more functionally responsive and efficient world. What Rauschenberg saw was that once an object is deprived of the 'character' bestowed by functionality, it becomes something with a more fluid identity, and is thus difficult to fix in terms of what it now is. As such these objects were now malleable enough to perform in numerous different roles. The novelty of what Rauschenberg was doing is caught in a photograph (opposite) of the artist in a derelict New York lot in 1961 (at the height of his early fame). In this picture we see a dapper looking young man wearing polished shoes, and a smart, sensible overcoat. Rather incongruously, he is reading a newspaper as he sits – as if waiting to attend a business meeting – in a scene of apparent destruction. Here also we see the 'objects' of Rauschenberg's art: rubble, dirt, pieces of wood, a broken sink, discarded oil cans, perhaps a broken gas lamp. The mismatch between his appearance and that of his surroundings was reflected in the contextual reversal he completed by taking these objects of destruction into the civilized spaces of modern society, the museums and art galleries.

Rauschenberg shared the conviction of his friend and sometime collaborator John Cage, that 'no value judgements are possible because nothing is better than anything else', and he saw the taming of the artistic ego as a fundamental part of his desire to be an artist working in a way that reflected the world he lived in. Whilst conventional aesthetic refinement was avoided by utilizing a variety of found material, Rauschenberg was nevertheless aware that in the end he would still

Fred McDarrah, *Robert Rauschenberg in a Derelict Lot*, 1961.

have to choose certain objects over others. Nevertheless, in denying the hierarchical value of objects he merely wanted to, as he said, 'throw enough obstacles in the way . . . of personal taste'.[16]

And in most cases these 'obstacles' were pieces of garbage. The fact that Rauschenberg made such an impact when he did (the late 1950s and early 1960s) is unusual given that Marcel Duchamp – a spiritual forefather and collector of unusual material himself – had been living in New York on and off for nearly thirty years. The remarkable fact is that when Rauschenberg started out he had never seen any of Marcel Duchamp's notorious readymades – this was certainly true prior to his own notoriety. And the fact that he knew neither Duchamp nor his work reflected also the fact that Duchamp's reputation in the 1950s had been eclipsed by the emergence of Abstract Expressionism as the dominant school of painting in the United States (particularly in New York). Indeed, many artists would have never seen Duchamp's work before the 1960s except, perhaps, in photographic reproductions.[17]

The principal creative and aesthetic aims of the school of action painters who became associated with Abstract Expressionism was to permit the unconscious creative will to flow freely, spontaneously, in order to realize a connection with some unstated, perhaps unknown, source.[18] But for all that spontaneity was welcomed, Abstract Expressionism did not entertain the idea that found objects could be a crucial part of the process of creation; which is to say these painters placed great importance on the technical mechanics of painting, and on the attainment of an *immediacy* of inspiration that could apparently only result from a prior rigorous preparation combined with a mastery of the tools and techniques of painting. There was a sense, therefore, in which some, like Jackson Pollock, believed their role was as a medium; a receptor for the kind of truth that is received as part of an almost spiritual communion with the absolute.[19] Indeed, so total was the immersion sought after that the artist here is in some sense really unaware of what is taking place in the 'act' of painting. Jackson Pollock admitted as much when he suggested that his work was almost gifted to him, and that a painting therefore 'has a life of its own. I try to let it come through. It is only when I lose contact with the painting that the result is a mess.'[20] Rauschenberg, by contrast, felt that the urge to mine some foundational source (in the self-expression of the action painters) interfered with the limitless possibilities of artistic creation because although the activity of painting seemed spontaneous, the labours that prepared one to attain the mediumistic condition involved an excess of thought and preparation.

The limitation was not, in Rauschenberg's view, simply down to the use of traditional materials and techniques – he did work with the more traditional materials of paint and canvas himself, although rarely from the early 1950s onwards. When Rauschenberg did utilize the flat plane of the canvas, he would incorporate found items into a kind of collage, which he called 'combine painting' (so-called because it was neither painting nor sculpture but had elements of both).[21] Again, this was reminiscent of Marcel Duchamp, also a painter schooled in tradi-tional techniques and similarly concerned with escaping from what he had learned about what an artist should be: a desire that entailed the abandonment of the notion that there could only be certain materials of legitimate use for an artist. Thus, from the randomness of buying unlabelled cans of paint (a way of removing the aesthetic considera-tion of colour) to throwing 'obstacles' in the way of self-expression (in the use of found objects to create larger combines that broke the flat plane of the canvas and occupied three-dimensional space), Rauschenberg was also seeking the removal of the frame as a limiting and obstructive part of the painterly repertoire that pushed work into a particular set of expectations. What he wanted to do was to open his window to the world, to find a way of putting the world into his work rather than his mind into it, and in this regard he would seem to dif-

Robert Rauschenberg, *Untitled (Scatole Personali)*, c. 1952, box with dirt, stones and feathers.

fer significantly from Marcel Duchamp (who sought to infuse the work of art with ideas).[22] Rauschenberg had got very close to the objects that would soon come to dominate his work – the discarded matter of the urban environment – while working for a construction company in the early 1950s, and it did not take long for this acquaintance to produce artistic results.[23] As Calvin Tomkins explains, by 1953 Rauschenberg's first moves away from canvas saw him fascinated by the richness of the material garbage that was lying around New York City, and he was using materials such as 'rocks dug up on his block by Consolidated Edison workmen, pieces of lumber, scrap metal. In his bottomless curiosity to see "what is a picture and what isn't", he even tried making pictures out of dirt, which he packed into boxlike frames.'[24]

As Mary Lynn Kotz has written, these frames (see above) were:

Strange boxes, somewhat like those that Joseph Cornell was showing at the Egan Gallery, but much more primitive and fetishistic, filled with stones, nails, feathers, bits and pieces of glass . . . He took the boxes to the Galleria dell'Obleisco [in Italy], the only Roman gallery to show contemporary abstract art. Thinking them outrageously funny, the owner exhibited the objects as the latest 'modern art'. To Rauschenberg's amazement and the gallery owner's amusement some were sold. They called them 'Scatole: contemplative e feticci personali' (*Thought Pieces and Personal Fetishes*). In Florence, the Galleria d'Arte Contemporanea showed the work. A local critic wrote that the art was a 'psychological mess' and should be thrown into the Arno. Rauschenberg, who was about to leave for home obliged. 'It solved the packing problem,' he observed later.[25]

Like Joseph Cornell, Rauschenberg collected a vast storehouse of the random and banal, although the two artists perhaps differed in the sense that Cornell was a meticulous sorter and chronicler, whereas Rauschenberg had amassed his materials through a more indiscriminate method; or as Walter Hopps says, 'an ecumenical passion for collecting', which became his means of reordering experience.[26] The box construction *Coca Cola Plan* (1964) for example, brings Cornell's collections of ephemera to mind. Rauschenberg was aware of the ostensible similarity, but was equally keen to insist on a distinction:

> A big difference in our attitudes is that I dragged ordinary materials into the art world for a direct confrontation, and I felt Cornell incorporated highly select materials to celebrate their rarification [*sic*]. I love his work but I think that we live in different worlds.[27]

Rauschenberg allowed for the intrusion of accidents in other ways as well, particularly as part of a silk screening process that involved a potential for disordering any intentions he might have had simply because the medium entailed relinquishing a degree of control in the technical preparation of the screens, and the effects of this method could be difficult to foresee.[28]

But it was in the combines of the late 1950s that Rauschenberg more fully developed a way to frustrate the development of personal stylistic foundations – these pieces were formally ambiguous in the realization of some kind of mutant combination of painting and sculpture. He used many items and materials in the making of these: wood, glass, tin cans, stuffed chickens, a stuffed goat, broken furniture, splattered paint, pieces of concrete, buckets of cement, iron spikes, wire – the list could be endless because there was nothing he would not use. Between 1955 and 1959, Rauschenberg resurrected such discarded objects and incorporated them into more than sixty combines, of which the most well known are *Bed* (1955), a bedspread and pillows splattered with paint, which has been nailed to a rectangular surface and then hung, just like a traditionally framed canvas; *Monogram* (1955–9), perhaps his most famous combine, a stuffed goat purchased from a junk shop, smeared with paint and dirt and finished off with a car tyre placed around the body of the goat itself, which was then positioned atop a flat collage resting on the floor; and *Odalisk* (1958), which features a white rooster on top of a wooden box-like structure covered with childlike paint strokes and images of women torn from books and magazines. Other combines included found objects from the streets of New York, mainly (but anywhere would do): boards, bricks, chairs, ladders, bottles and so on.

For Robert Rauschenberg junk became an easier material to use because these 'dead' objects of *refuse* had no meaning apart from the negative undifferentiated one that declared their lack of worth – the total absence of distinction in the damaged or soiled objects – and making use of this garbage avoided the difficult question of suggesting a relationship between the object and the world through either stylistic conventions or representationalism. He had found that the position of modern painting could be summed up by the fact that the art had itself become too self-conscious: it was about form and material, yet – in the case of his contemporaries working as abstract painters – without really forcing a widespread search for an alternative. In the 1950s, instead, it was all about the paint and the canvas, and what could be achieved within the flat surface. He recalled that Josef Albers, one of his teachers and himself a notable abstract painter, tried to convince him of the freedoms of painterly abstraction; of the idea that, for example, one colour was no better than another. Yet, the liberation was still incomplete as far as Rauschenberg was concerned – even the simple issue of colour remained a potentially disabling one because it implied the need for a choice. The problem was that he 'couldn't decide to use one colour instead of another . . . I really wasn't interested in taste'.[29]

Rauschenberg took what Duchamp did in the readymade with the useful everyday object (objects that became junk when out of place) and made a comparable transformation with actual garbage, by removing it from a specific context. It is a curious historical fact that the respective origins of these objects – as junk, and as objects of value – follow through an initial transformation into 'art' in slightly different ways. The readymades are objects that, through the passage of time, begin, the more one observes them, to look sleek and unusually elegant. Rauschenberg's combines, by contrast, unfix our relationship to the object world in a subtly different manner; the gesture looks the same as Duchamp's, but by taking and re-contextualizing once useless remains (rather than utilitarian objects) we are still allowed to see the resemblance to junk. In fact, there is no doubt as to this relation – garbage is unmistakably recognizable as forever *foreign*; these objects are singular, but it is the uselessness of the parts that constitutes the entirety of their uniqueness.

THE OPPOSITE OF GARBAGE

There occurs in the work of Duchamp a destruction of identity on a clearly metaphysical level (in so far as he attempts to undo the potential unity of being), a result of his use of disguise to frustrate the reasonable expectations that a work of art represents something understandable or meaningful.[30] Identity is put into question in another sense as well in Duchamp's work, one that is important to our understanding of the profane nature of the materials artists like Robert Rauschenberg used. If the utility of objects signified the extent to which industrial society had attempted to make the material world more responsive to *need*, to make the stuff of the world more functional or efficient, Duchamp theoretically inverted the relation. With the ready-made, any evaluative – and thus aesthetic – context was denied not only because the objects were 'non-aesthetic', but also because they were often removed from any contextually given reference points; from associations of time and place that give all objects a functional definition, and thus from any cultural or social conditions that normally made things *recognizable.*

The transformations of the object we see in the readymade were a prime example of this. Mimetic forms of expression – landscapes, the still life, portraits – for instance, might have been said to apply a rather Lockean empirical spin on existence: that is, the portrait represented the internalization and re-presentation of a supposedly objective external reality gleaned from what Locke called 'primary qualities' (figure, mass, dimension and so on). Yet portrait painting may be at the extreme end of the limitations imposed by representationalism, leaving out much of the reality apparent beyond the frame of the canvas, and evident through other means.[31] It might be argued that, in conventional representational terms, some painting which passed as art was valued to the extent that it preserved a likeness to some objectively given phenomena, scenario, or person, with portraiture being the most obvious example of such a value.

On reflection, however, the portrait on canvas has a greater affinity with contemporary representational photography than with the tradition of artistic modernism, which has always sought to move beyond form. It is an act of identification that declares the objective and social value placed on *more of the same,* something that also, as Hillel Schwartz notes, easily becomes a trap for the artist:

> Ruth Henshaw Brown, who painted one hundred portraits a year and drew over a thousand profiles of New Englanders from 1828 to 1846, was directed to add new glasses to the face of Rev. Timothy Rogers, whose portrait she had done less than a year before. During a period of six years she was called upon several times to update the hair and dress of her painting of Lydia Burr. A losing battle, this finicky correctness, but it was strenuously fought, to the profit of artists who did fifty silhouettes or a dozen portraits a day.[32]

But if this kind of nineteenth-century representation did not speak of the fragmentary nature of modern life, in the twentieth century art moved towards the dissolution of the object, particularly when taken as an ideal or 'representational' form. And so, the days of art being accepted and understood principally as some kind of adornment or as an entertaining diversion for the viewer were now over. In general, modern art in the twentieth century dispensed with resemblances for a variety of historical and intellectual reasons, but Marcel Duchamp in particular wanted to explore the seeming impossibility of identification when 'objective reality' was perceived to deny the singularity of the individual experience; to get rid forever, as Octavio Paz wrote, of 'the possibility of recognizing or identifying any two things as being like each other'.[33] To strive for a place where the contents of the world, in other words, could not be ordered according to the concepts of reason, nor of reasonable values or expectations.

The enemy was the complacent acceptance of what was easily digested, pretty or decorative; it was to acquiesce in the easy and uncomplicated objectification given by popular acceptance. Perhaps the excesses of life – resulting from the mass production of goods – were making civilization lazy and flabby. Adornments spoke of decadence. Confection had replaced substance. But technological progress made it possible to rely upon consistency, a trend that continues into contemporary life where many of the objects we daily encounter are to be found exactly the same almost anywhere one goes. This 'shrinking' of the world (in terms of possible experiences, at least) has made surprises more exceptional. Novelty products, for example, may be surprising simply because they are deceptive in their appearance. As George Basalla noted, with the novelty item form actually contradicts expected function: 'saltshakers in the shape of lightbulbs, skillets converted into picture frames or clocks, ice tongs made to serve as paper towel holders', and so on.[34] This is the object world as a shadow of the utilitarian; it is the domain of 'kitsch', which is itself no more than a repository for garbage. In its German origin 'kitsch' was initially employed to designate degraded value.[35] Thus, when we take the everyday implements of modern living within their proper context they realize both a rational desire for order and control over life and, if you like, a functional 'transparency', which is to say the appearance gives no lie – *it does what it says on the label.*

There is a limitless supply of these objects and, not surprisingly, our ordinary language use settles their utilitarian basis, thus identifying the expectations that come from the names applied to them; ladders, refrigerators, vacuum cleaners, shovels, knives and forks, hat racks; these all have a definite, not to say objectively useful, purpose in helping us to organize our movements meaningfully, and in aiding our progress through the obstacles we face daily. Functional objects will also normally be labour-saving devices; for example, shovels and refrigerators in an important sense rationalize work (to prevent injury, or to increase leisure time). Yet we forget the technological genius that has gone into the creation of even the simplest of these everyday objects. A shovel, for instance, is a marvel of rational creation. What could be simpler than an implement for gathering up and removing the various obstacles we find – snow, dirt, or gravel? These objects represent progress and significantly stand in a relation of identity to their function, which we can see if we define such objects in terms of this functionality:

Chilling food = refrigeration
Removing creases = ironing
Lifting dirt from a carpet = vacuuming

The significance of functional objects to modern living is illustrated by the ease with which they soon come to be taken for granted. Duchamp was aware that in removing everyday functional objects from their intended use he was mocking the rationalization of modern life as well as the ordering tendencies of the aesthetic. During his life most of these transformed objects were never shown in galleries or museums, and were largely known only to Duchamp's friends. Many of the original readymades were lost, and most of them – at one time or another – were only to be found, after his rediscovery by the so-called Neo-Dadaists, in his New York apartment.

This apartment itself was a testament to idleness, to the unworthiness of work, from the first obvious sign to the visitor – the sight of a rope on entering through the front door, which extended from the inside door handle to a chair where Duchamp would sit and play chess, saving him from rising to greet his visitors. Duchamp's contempt for conventional household organization was evident in the absence of shiny, white and chrome surfaces, not to mention in the confusing arrangement of objects.[36] This disordered space represented something of an obstacle course to anyone but Duchamp (for whom, we might expect, it attained some curious order); it was the exact opposite of what a modern home should exemplify – comfort and ease of use – instead it was a disorientating funhouse full of randomly distributed objects that, to the uninformed eye, were simply junk. Here, the readymades were not installed for the aesthetic pleasure of guests, but were, rather, randomly distributed throughout the apartment without much sensible purpose. As Helen Molesworth noted in a description of a photograph of this scene, we see

> A coatrack nailed to the floor in front of a bicycle wheel atop a kitchen stool. There is a photograph in the background of which we spy the urinal suspended from a doorjamb; in the foreground a shovel dangles from the ceiling.[37]

One can imagine that Duchamp's frequent visitors would have had to be extremely careful to avoid accidents here, if only because little in this apartment met conventional expectations. If it was not clear what Duchamp was doing with the readymades at the time of their 'production' his apartment may have provided some insight into his unique relationship with the object world. It was there in his unusual conception of 'furniture', not to mention the odd way of ordering this particular living space. The transformation of everyday functional objects, to the extent that they cease to be functional any longer, subverts the reasonable expectations of the unquestioning mind: the readymade *gesture* thus casts doubt upon an unreflective assumption that the meaning of objects is only to be found in their everyday, or intended, use.

DEGRADED OBJECTS, RENEWED FORMS

There is an element of the contingent – of chance – to be seen in the symbolic power of these gestures, one which declares that the meaning we attach to the world is constituted through a continual *recycling of ideas and matter*, in the resurrection and re-ordering of all kinds of garbage that furnishes the actual physical 'being-ness' of existence. This was rooted in a belief that time, change, and the degradation or physical deterioration of life could be incorporated as a feature in the execution of a radically redefined plasticity that would then 'extend' from the object to the observer in recognition that there was no longer a privileged objective perspective which could determine a final set of properties for such a work of art. But the capacity for transformation also suggests that notions of value (existence) and garbage (non-existence) provide the language for the art of the transformed object. The fragmentary nature of experience in modern society is reflected by the incorporation of discrete and randomly associated objects in the works of assemblage and installation artists. There is a literal filling up of empty space – of the void – with reconstituted remains of once dis-tinct objects, in which the question for the artist moves (in the period covering the mid-to-late twentieth century) from one of how to utilize the flat surface of the canvas – a surface that is bound in three dimen-sional space by a frame that literally *masks off* the contents and sets the object apart from its environment – to one of how the language of art can be articulated within the language of everyday use. This was a question that has always been implicit in modernism, and that was found in the making of a reality that is itself not 'real' in anything but terms that demand the suspension of rational expectations.

Where artists like Duchamp, Rauschenberg and Cornell had pushed such a possible discourse to the fore by bringing found items within a more or less conventional frame – within boxes, projecting from the canvas, and so on – and thus into the actual space where art is still recognizable enough to be presented to the world (a space that by definition objectified and also legitimized it), it took an extreme development of the idea to really bring home the fundamentally alien

Arman, *Large Bourgeois Refuse*, 1960, rubbish accumulated into plastic container.

aspect of these objects made from garbage. It was the French artist Arman who took it to some kind of logical end by filling up a gallery with rubbish he found in the streets. The exhibition in question took place in 1960. Entitled *Full-Up,* it was a response to a previous exhibition by Yves Klein, *Le Vide (The Void),* in which the Iris Clert gallery in Paris had been cleansed of all objects, of all art, and then painted white by Klein. Some time later Arman filled up the space with his rubbish, including:

> 6 oyster shells, 3 cubic yards of used bulbs, . . . 200 pounds of old records, 48 walking canes, 7 coffee mills, . . . 5 bidets, 6 slices of bread, 3 flower pots, 180 bird cages, . . . 10 old hats, 12 pairs of shoes, 1 ice bucket, . . . 70 pounds of curtains, 5 hula hoops, 1 ashtray with ashes, . . . 1 cubic yard of metal shavings.[38]

Notable, too, was the public announcement of the exhibition, with 30,000 invitations sent out in the form of a sardine can filled with garbage, and inside which there was also a formal statement of intent: 'Iris Clert asks you to come contemplate in "the full" the total force of the real condensed into a critical mass.'[39]

The exhibition expanded what Arman was doing on a smaller scale, which was filling up containers with garbage; as in the 1960 piece *Large Bourgeois Refuse* (previous page). The force of garbage as an intrusive element in art thus exhausted by the totality of Arman's garbage invasion, artists later seemed to employ discarded objects, or other junk fragments in ways that began to realize known *forms* rather than to simply illustrate – for example – the degraded value of the material used in a work: the descent into abjection. We can see something of this development in *765 Paper Balls,* an installation from 1969 by the British artist John Hilliard, who in this piece anticipates some of the themes in Cornelia Parker's work, particularly in the implication that the matter of the world is eventually resolved into smaller elements, into garbage, which we see is just the same basic material in an unformed state, devoid of conventional objective properties. Hilliard's material takes the temporary form of small scrunched-up ball-like shapes that dangle with an eloquent lack of cohesion within the space of an empty room (opposite). Before he resurrected this material, it had, in a previous life, another form when it was constituted from pulp into a newspaper; a peculiarly poetic choice of material given that the newspaper delivers the facts of daily life before these too become

John Hilliard, *765 Paper Balls*, 1969, installation (detail).

overtaken by yet *newer* news. The newspaper, in a sense, signifies the ultimate recyclable material in its reference to the constant flux of events which can only be glimpsed momentarily as the new, events that are thus only worthy of a fleeting existence in reconstituted pulp. It all ends as rubbish, in other words.

These material fragments, like all used-up and discarded objects, are no longer identical with any useful purpose, yet they do not disappear when consigned to the garbage. In truth 'dead' matter is always taking another form, being 'reborn' as something else. In the garbage sculpture of Tony Cragg, for example, we are asked to consider that he is really doing little more than what painting and sculpture has always done, which is to fashion some recognizable form (a cube, the spires of a cathedral) from naturally occurring materials. The difference in the materials Cragg uses when compared with traditional sculpture is that pieces were originally *parts* of something else, yet composed as a whole they seem to have a shape that is assimilated within the finished form. What we see in his work depends on how we observe the object (it depends on what we look for; what we actually expect to see). The useful origin of the material of Cragg's various works in the 1970s and early 1980s would have been recognizable to us all as the implements of modern living (pieces of machinery, kitchen utensils, toys) yet as pieces of rubbish that he gathered up they had already been sentenced to death: declared worthless. Whilst such material still has shape, size, or bulk, it is rendered formless because at the level of the perception of everyday use the form (whatever it may have been) no longer matched the function. To recall an earlier example: a broken refrigerator no longer chills food; a defective vacuum cleaner no longer lifts dirt.

In some of Cragg's works these broken shards are more difficult to identify than in others. For example in *African Culture Myth* (1984) we see the silhouette of an African male – the form and line of the head is exquisitely but improbably realized by the positioning of jagged pieces of plastic, metal or clay; a plate, part of what is perhaps a tennis racket that looks as if a ravenous family pet has had a few bites of it, and so on. Elsewhere in the figure you might make out a mudflap (a rubber shield that usually covers the wheel of a vehicle), a tube, some rubber or plastic washers – but this detail eventually sinks into the form, and is replaced as an object of perception by the figure which merges in a completeness that seems impossible, but works with the assistance of the viewer.

While Cragg (like Rauschenberg and Cornell) allows the question of the identity of objects – in their wholes and parts – to linger before the gaze, his fragmented figures are perplexing because of the powerful effect of the fragment of a value that has been stripped of its properties. He points out the fact that we probably only identify with objects in our consumption of them, which of course is exactly what produces the shabby remains we throw away: 'We consume, populating our environment with more and more objects . . . with no chance of understanding the making processes because we specialize; specialize in the production, but not in the consumption.'[40]

And the failure to understand the making process is a kind of alienation from the life and death of matter, matter that is made object by the animating force of ideas and language that, in turn, determine the production of functional objects. The forms that Cragg presents

Tony Cragg, *Stack*, 1975, mixed media. Tate Modern, London.

are ways of appropriating the object world and giving it some new form that is wholly animated through the necessity of describing it in terms of ideas and language already known, that we recognize in terms of its physical properties. These could be simple forms; for instance, a large *cube* composed of broken pieces of rock, wood, carpet, books, newspapers (above); a constellation of decapitated *steeples* made from what looks like old car parts (*Minster*, 1987). What does this tell us about the way we populate the world with our creations? Well, language says 'cube' and 'steeple' but Cragg's objects signify the inadequacy of the language of forms (of what Locke called 'primary qualities' of figure, dimension and mass). And language may seem to fail us here because of the lack of purity or transparency in these *particular instances* of the forms described; that is to say in the terms of the degraded nature of the material itself; but to look at it this way would be mistaken.

The poverty is perhaps to be found in our language because what are 'cubes'? What are 'steeples'? They are nothing but names that have no content without particular referents. The visible remainders that here comprise the body of the objects in question directs us also to the continual renewal of objects (to death and regeneration), and to the indeterminate status of Cragg's curious sculptures themselves: these pieces seem to speculate on the resolution of a doubt within the mind of a viewer. Again, in an echo of Marcel Duchamp's readymade gesture, this is a kind of wager that is only resolved by overcoming the incompleteness of its suggestiveness. 'I'm simply proposing things', Cragg has said: 'I can be fascinated by a material or a new type of image in the same naïve way a child can be. It is better not to know anything than to make the stupid pretence of knowing everything.'[41]

Yet taking this 'lack of knowing' into the creative process obviously allows for the subversion of meanings attached (through language) to the world of objects at any given point in time; to the world as *named*. Tony Cragg summed up the universe of possibility that then becomes available in terms of a *modus operandi* that leaves the field of meaning boundless, and the potential sources of inspiration limitless:

> Simple processes – with materials no one else wants – ideas that interest me – images I like – made where people let me make them – rooms, walls, floors; the physical frame – emotional responses, intellectual responses – elegant works, ugly works, humorous works, beautiful works, decorative works – works in which I learnt from the materials – works like pictures – meanings I intended – meanings which surprise me – personal references, political references, cultural references, no references – as straightforward as I can make it.[42]

In *Four Plates* from 1976 we see four dinner plates placed in a line beginning with one plate in the manufactured form, succeeded as the image progressively expands to the fore by more fragmented plates, or rather the smashed pieces (because they have ceased to be plates) until we reach the point where, if the final plate were not identified by its physical relation to the complete plate within the frame of the picture, we would have no idea what it was.[43] Cragg here highlights the character of identity in conventional perception as one principally of resemblance, of (to use the philosophical jargon) the constant conjunction of contiguous phenomena (that is, we only know what a plate is by comparing it to a counterpart item stored as a visual memory). Once again, he directs us to another perspective on the matter, which is to say on *matter* itself as the resolution of a whole into parts that appears to point to some atomic flux that continues below the mask of the empirical *givenness* that presents the world of objects. And this is also the significant area he shares with the objects and installations of the chronologically later Cornelia Parker, in whose work 'dead' matter is resurrected into beguiling new forms.

The transformation of garbage in Parker's work is not restricted to giving new life to unwanted objects, but is also found in re-contextualizing fragments, in presenting partial perspectives, or even bending and stretching 'matter' until it is unrecognizable under the expectations of previous use and definition. 'As a child', she explained, 'I used to crush coins on a railway track. You couldn't spend your pocket money afterwards but you kept the metal slivers for their own sake, as an imaginary currency and as physical proof of the destructive powers of the world.'[44] In works like *Matter and What it Means* she presents an object of recognizable form, the form of a human body in this instance (although devoid of any actual human). An image of the installation shows two 'bodies' hovering over the ground: the forms were constituted by arranging a mass of crushed coins and suspending them from a ceiling (a device commonly used by the artist), whilst on the ground a layer of crushed coins covers the surface to resemble the shadow of a body, or maybe even to suggest the further disintegration of bodies (of objects in general) as the boundary between the two 'bodies' and what is underneath can be seen to fragment further into the elemental matter of nature. This is the body as a dried out being finally expired and returned to the earth. The implicit connection between garbage and self we see here is expressed more bluntly still in Tony Cragg's 1980 self-portrait *Harvest,* in which the figure of Cragg (a kind of garbage-shadow on the wall – the physical form once again created by scraps of discarded plastic) is bent over a pile of rubbish on the gallery floor. The figure, apparently, does not collect the fruit of the earth as in any standard understanding of the significance of *harvesting*, but instead *the visible remains* of the consumption of the 'fruits' of matter.[45] Identifying the human with the material of nature as of the same source, the relationship is a mutually sustaining one, but one that ends in decomposition.

4 Garbage Matters

where the consummations gather, where the disposal
flows out of form, where the last translations
cast away their immutable bits and scraps

A. R. Ammons, *Garbage*

MODERN LIFE IS RUBBISH

In 2001 a BBC news broadcast in the UK reported a strange fact. Refuse collectors in Nottingham had been issued with bullet-proof trousers as protection against the threat of HIV and hepatitis, because dirty syringes would regularly poke through garbage sacks and into contact with the unsuspecting refuse collectors. Could this have been, in a strangely exaggerated way, merely one more illustration of how far modern society had now gone in creating a host of uncontrollable forces? Was it simply an example of what Marx had noted with regard to the industrial societies of the nineteenth century, that 'with the mass of objects grows the alien powers to which man is subjected'?[1] It seems, on reflection, that there may be no simple answer to such a question. For example, whilst Marx identified the impersonal forces of industrialization with the division of production and its corrosive effect on an essential human capacity for creation he did so by noting that it resulted in an 'estrangement' that was made real in 'the form of sensuous, alien, useful objects'.[2] What he did not anticipate was that the alien powers we are now subjected to would not really be useful objects, but rather the nothingness of useless, formless and disgusting matter that is garbage.

One way of outlining what will emerge as a curious history of modern society is to insist that culture and society must be understood as differentiated aspects of nature, and as such, take the form of a *separation* from nature. In fact we are so used to thinking of society as an order distinct from nature (a legacy of the Ancients' distinction between *techne* and *phusis)* that we may be blind to the fact that life does not escape decaying *natural* processes or other disordering elements.[3] Nevertheless we can find fragments here and there littering the history of various aspects of modern society and in the history of technology, which take us towards the heart of this separation of society from nature and to how a fuller understanding of it may allow us to pursue the claim that modern life can be usefully understood in terms of rubbish. Take the following, quoted in Carlo Cippola's *Miasmas and Disease,* an ordinance of Florence Health Officers issued on 4 May 1622, which directed that towns within the state would now be required to remove all rubbish to places beyond human habitation:

> We order you immediately . . . to command that in all places under your jurisdiction everyone should remove and have removed from before their houses all the filth and rubbish which are to be found there . . . and all that which is in the squares and other public places should be removed by the representatives of the communities and carried outside the Towns, Villages and Castelli to places where they can do no harm.[4]

Set against a notion that the expansion of the object world produces an alien power, we might then look again at one aspect of modern society – consumption – that attracts much attention in contemporary social theory. However, while social and cultural theorists point to the overabundance of consumer products in modern life these are not usually viewed in terms of garbage, but variously as ways to understand the role of desire in the daily life of contemporary Western societies or how technological products of industrialization impact on the human imagination and so on.[5] Why, then, can garbage tell us anything about modernity? One way to answer this question is to highlight the way in which the central notions of order and identity – fundamental in modern society – can be characterized in terms of what Slavoj Žižek refers to as a *withdrawal* that in an act of self-definition creates an 'indivisible remainder' as a result of which there is established a social and cultural coherence, a connectedness, that we recognize as the valuable sphere of life.[6] This *remainder* might be productively thought of, and in a sense brought to life, as *garbage.* This notion of garbage extends in scope across a variety of such 'withdrawals'; from the excremental waste that first alienates the body from itself, to a number of psychological and material effects of modern existence, from the products of buried memory that on the one hand appear as elements of an uncanny and shadow existence, to – on the other – the multitudinous object world of (soon to be) garbaged consumer products.

For a long time the removal of the discarded excess of life was a practical problem that was met with a variety of ad hoc measures and improvisational solutions. Long into the development of modern society, for example, excrement and other household waste was simply expelled from the domestic space by dumping from windows – to remain where it fell until it could no longer be ignored.[7] Such rudimentary disposal methods form a link to the present in the sense that technologies of expulsion then and now must be understood in terms of how they affect social experience and the perception of time. Just as the Baudrillardian consumption of signs in modern society accelerates successive experiences to move the individual beyond his or her own past, so the arrival of the earliest mechanical means of getting rid of garbage allowed people to begin to abolish from immediate consciousness the decaying effects of time as represented by the unavoidable putrescence of life. In other words, the rationalization of garbage (the organization of social time in another guise) acts to conceal the extent of decay, one of the most obvious signs of which was, and still is, excrement. Although, as Dominique Laporte notes in his *History of Shit,* even by the late eighteenth century not everyone was convinced of the benefits of the mechanical banishment of this corporeal garbage, with no less a figure than Jeremy Bentham advancing a case for the profitable qualities of shit: 'It should be put to use as manure,' he observed.[8] Generally speaking, the basic imperative since the emergence of urban living has been to get rid of the stuff due to its capacity both for clogging up space and for clouding out the sensory environment with the oppressive force of a rank nature that easily takes on an alien aspect.[9] In his *Anatomy of Disgust,* William I. Miller notes the all-encompassing nature of this most elementary matter:

> Gestation and decay are all condensed into the primal odor of feces. Its stench expands to capture the odors of sex, desire, generation, and decay. It poisons us by smoking our flesh on the outside and recorrupts the inside by being inhaled as vapors.[10]

Whilst pinpointing standards of cleanliness that could be seen to be in any sense comparable to those we now know enjoins a detailed historical inquiry beyond the scope of this work, we can make the more general point that pre-modern living would have been dictated by the spectre and practicalities of decay – even if we simply cite the example of faeces. But is this enough to maintain that garbage creates a spur to order?

In his history of the toilet Lawrence Wright noted the guiding power of disgust, too, citing evidence that London's medieval latrines were barely tolerable by the turn of the fourteenth century, a situation resulting in complaints to the king that spoke clearly of the need for action. The response to such conditions amounted to little – there was no great technological advance, such as the invention of the first flushing toilet (some two hundred years later). This sense of technological inertia was not a peculiarly local problem and may indeed have represented an unwillingness to tackle the waste problem with new solutions. As Dominique Laporte has suggested, sixteenth-century ordinances on the disposal of household waste in France were actually *backward looking*, constituting an attempt to revive the Roman sewers in early modern Paris. Nevertheless, these examples of a developing waste problem concur to some extent with Norbert Elias's claim that a 'civilizing process' dates also from the sixteenth century; although Elias (in contrast to Laporte) made no mention of the gradual privatization of either excrement or menses, to use two examples of obviously prevalent wastes.[11] The difficulty in dating the development of standards in hygiene is intimately connected to the external nature of waste in relation to identity formations, to the fact that what precisely we value and remember as worthwhile in life is what we *take away* as we leave behind what then becomes 'garbage'. That personal identity – as Harvie Ferguson has recently written – must be understood to establish both a corporeal and psychological separateness. This in no small way helps to explain the fact that technological developments in hygiene were driven largely by reactive measures to meet the overpowering effect of waste, as opposed to any strictly formalized planning.[12] A point not missed by Manuel DeLanda, who argues that, contrary to our contemporary illusions of the power of reason to effect progress, the urban formations of modern society followed discontinuous or 'nonlinear' patterns of development. One consequence of this was that:

By the thirteenth century London had already generated a specialized bureaucracy for handling the flow of water into the city; but management of the flow of waste out of the city did not come about until the nineteenth century, even though the English capital had recurrent sewage crises since the 1370s. It was not until the river Thames's capacity to transport waste reached its limits, causing an odor that made parliamentary sessions impossible to conduct, that the problem was confronted.[13]

Another outcome of the close (yet discontinuous) relation between material decay and progress that on reflection becomes clear is that where the reality of excremental waste is a feature of daily life this can quite accurately indicate the absence of structures and beliefs common to modernity. On the one hand this means simply the absence of a rationalized system of waste removal, but in more complex terms it signals the low importance attached to a notion of personal identity as corporeal individuation.[14] The latter idea is important and somewhat complicated. For example, the effect of a sense of individuality on habits of cleanliness and in establishing a 'privatized' space brings us to a recognizable present where bodies are separated one from another as a matter of social and personal development from an early age. Yet the apparent modernist individualism of such a way of living should not prevent us from speculating on whether or not the notion of individuated identity, characteristically a feature of Western philosophy from around the seventeenth century, may curiously have been one unlikely consequence of the overpowering effects of waste in medieval towns and cities prior to its subsequent elaboration in the work of Descartes and others. Can we say, in other words, that garbage gives added impetus to certain ways of abstract thinking as well as to ways of organizing society?

Crucial to our understanding is to recognize that what we now know as garbage is, as I argue here, traceable to the privatization of human wastes, and that where evidence of the social recognition of waste appears in public ordinances it is conditional upon, and lays the basis for, a corresponding private responsibility. In fact the beginning of the privatization of waste in pre-modern towns and cities (found, for example, in the eventual abandonment of communal latrines) predates modern philosophical notions of individuality by several hundred years. This makes it very difficult to establish whether people were more disgusted with the waste of others because there was an already developed and spreading sense of the individuation of human existence, or whether in fact it was because bodily separation had asserted itself as some kind of *ur*-act in the foundation of modern individuality and as a response to the conditions found in our ancestors being thrown together in towns and cities with what amounted to a crowd of strangers.

Whatever the answer may be there is one significant point to make, and that is that society nevertheless develops at later times *as a response to this alienated waste* – to garbage.[15] But to return to the question of how garbage came to assume an oppressive or alien power we need to look more closely at some *techniques* of waste – at the ways in which social and historical developments in understanding the powerful nature of degeneration and decay effected a gradual separation of the human body from (its own) nature. Lawrence Wright mentions developments that suggest that the 'privatization' of waste in medieval England may be dated as early as the twelfth century, pointing out that even 'among the lower orders there were some private latrines'. Indeed, he notes some quite detailed housing ordinances of 1189 requiring that 'garderobe pits, if not walled, must be at least 5½ ft from the party line [i.e. the line that defines ownership of property]; if walled, 2½ ft'.[16]

This so-called 'garderobe' was usually built 'within ample thickness of the walls [of the house], each with its own vertical shaft below a stone or wooden seat', and often situated above a watercourse running below the house, which could accelerate the speed of the waste removal.[17] We might note also that the designation 'garderobe' (in common currency the word meant a private room or, indeed, a *wardrobe*) itself had associations with individuality and privacy, and perhaps hints at the repugnance people must have felt at the idea of contact with the bodily waste of others (if not the shame that evidence of their own hidden doings could bring upon them). Interestingly, there is no clear separation here of the sense of the garderobe as a more or less secure and excluded space (where the wardrobe hides the clothing that coincidentally covers the now profane body) and the sense of the word in which the private room itself becomes the cloak of individuality, and hence in another variant 'the privy' (a word that is still known, and to a lesser extent used, today).

In fact 'privy' was just one of many euphemisms used in England at this time that point to bodily waste taboos, as did other 'coy evasions' such as *necessariam* or *necessary house*, terms that covered the bare fact of the very unavoidable nature of dealing with human waste matter in a language suitable to respect and privacy.[18] The suggestion that the medieval world had already seen the beginning of a privatized waste process – certainly by the thirteenth century – is not only attested to by the existence of the previously mentioned public ordinances, but also in evidence that medieval England operated a form of market in waste disposal work. Wright mentions contractual documents showing that men who were employed to clean privies were extremely well paid which, from the point of view of a contemporary understanding at least, might indicate a scarcity of labour for such tasks. One such account of work carried out at Newgate Prison in 1281 states that men were paid *three times* the normal rate, suggesting that there were not many takers for this work in the absence of large financial inducements.[19]

Despite early evidence of a division of labour in waste processes, technological developments *per se* were still a long way short of the privatization of waste we know now, and indeed even these examples may have been the exception to the rule, as it was clear that there was still widespread use of communal latrines in the twelfth and thirteenth centuries. The noxious power of human and other waste should then be located with the rise of urban living and the absence of opportunities to simply go elsewhere and escape it, a situation evident in complaints made in 1300 to the King and Parliament about the 'putrid exhalations' of the Fleet River in London, which like many rivers at the time had latrines built over it as the most efficient means of removing waste. The problems with such ad hoc technologies at this time were becoming both difficult to avoid and difficult to come to terms with. Lawrence Wright recounted that Sherbourne Lane, a place once remembered fondly in the local imagination as a desirable dwelling place located next to a 'long bourne of sweet water', had through time come to be known by a designation that suitably – unmistakably – identified the qualitative change in living conditions; locals referred to it by the more appropriate appellation of 'Shiteburn Lane'.[20]

By the late nineteenth and early twentieth centuries the widespread arrival of domestic plumbing in Britain (in the form of bathroom closets containing a toilet, bath and sink with running hot water) was one of the most important consequences of the ever more complex nature of the separation and specialization of productive work. It was only through the multiplication of various personal and nonpersonal tasks (whether originally private or communal) that modern society was able to industrialize production processes by a division of labour and so develop a level of social rationalization that reached beyond the creation and consumption of mere necessities and through which society has 'propelled' itself forward into the world of abundance that characterizes consumer society.[21] Such progress had the *necessary* effect of depersonalizing the waste process (other essential processes similarly rationalized include more obviously food production), meaning that apparently separate developmental processes within modern society were entirely complementary. The end result of this supposedly virtuous cycle is that without the organization of garbage disposal, specific kinds of industrial production become impossible, and vice versa. The most often overlooked, or avoided, consequence of the development of modern society as a system of social rationalization cannot be disentangled from the fact that specialist production and public bureaucracy ensures that we are already one step removed from the consequences of our own waste in that we need never see it.[22] As we will discover, in the most technologically developed societies this has evolved to the point where the progressive obsolescence of consumer products makes the old and used-up so commonplace that we show no concern about dispensing with the remains.

It is not without coincidence that the word 'flushing' contains a peculiarly modern aspect; that it throws up associations with novelty and motion, not to say the very 'fluidity' of modern life. As Zygmunt Bauman observes, there are good reasons for considering fluidity and 'liquidity' as 'fitting metaphors when we wish to grasp the nature of the present'. As 'fluids' are 'light' or 'travel easily' they are clearly distinct from notions like 'rigidity' and 'solidity' that are more readily applicable to the unchanging past.[23] Although waste technologies at once alter the experience of time as *the physical presence of decaying matter* and so make it easier to forget age and degeneration, the liquidation of the past clearly prepares the way for the reinvigoration of the present. Here we might consider the matter we expel only to be broken down eventually by the force of the water that also propels it from our lives – indeed the removal of this dead matter is also the obliteration of (physical and psychological) obstacles to future movement. Thus, the notion of the *liquidity* of the present describes the de-materialization of the object world, not to mention the practical ease with which we can apply the technological flush. Obviously this marks a corresponding psychological shift in the human relationship with the world, where 'flushing' becomes analogous to the more widespread removal of a prior historical necessity to be mindful that was itself determined by an inability to escape time.

In modern society our removal from human waste, in particular, takes the form of a gradual progression that has accelerated in contemporary experience to the point where examples of the latest technology in public toilets appear to the user as if totally untouched, in the sort of pristine condition that seems to have the dual purpose of allowing one to feel free of the malign sensory effects of the disgusting and alien, while at the same time rather bizarrely calling into question the regular function of the equipment. Is it a toilet, or an information booth? This all points to an uneasiness with being reminded that other people defecate, and more specifically, to the fact that they may even do so in the same place as we do. Ralph Lewin, in his book *Merde*, notes that these latest innovations attain their unique effect of total newness through the integration of a variety of technological means and urban camouflage to present the appearance that every use is possibly the first-ever use. From the outside these conspicuous looking cylinders, visible all round and often plastered with advertisements, bring the public toilet into open space (where in the past public toilets would have been located underground or at least made inconspicuous), although there is nothing as simple as an open door inviting any passer-by who needs to answer the call of nature – only by the insertion of a coin is the function of the object revealed. Once inside a disposable plastic covering 'fresh-seals' the toilet bowl itself, a feature that can be 'renewed automatically by pressing a button', and then completed by operating an accompanying device for the 'irradiation of the toilet seat with ultraviolet light'.[24] This latest 'fashion' in finding an accommodation for the *necessariam* in a busy world merely illustrates the latest development in our removal from personal responsibility for garbage. Just compare these technologically advanced irradiating privies of the twenty-first century with a notion of 'going out for a walk with a spade' as Lewin says men in the trenches during wartime would when 'nature called', indicating no less of a sensitivity to the communal effects of defecation that is suggestive of a privation (why else would one go *out,* and with a spade?). It goes without saying that should our automated means of disposal ever break down, we would soon be well aware of the fact.[25] A brilliant illustration of this occurs in José Saramago's novel *Blindness,* where we see the population of a city stricken by an inexplicable and infectious blindness that leads to their confinement and separation from the rest of society. With this separation, and with the loss of sight, comes the inevitable problem of not being able to control the human waste that under other circumstances we are 'blind' to, that has been rationalized out of experience, but which – under conditions of actual sensory blindness – can be imagined to have the most devastating effects for the maintenance of order.

We remain blind to the reality of waste because modern society has almost perfected the means to forget – not only because we are largely ignorant of the productive tasks undertaken by others, but because within this individuated existence we may easily resort to any of a bewildering array of alternatives to 'reality': mind-altering drugs, tourism, cinema, literature, and so on. Under these historical conditions memory becomes an easy source for subjective doubt, the imaginary graveyard of progress that buries the past as if it was simply useless rubbish.[26] Thus the expanding sphere of garbage in modern society is overtaken by an impulse to live in the present, and indeed is a marker of the forward motion of life that creates the space for a continual renegotiation of the terms in which we may identify with the world (obviously in order that this movement does not run out of control). A certain duplicity in contemporary modes of living is also seen in absent-minded consumption – this, the obverse of the waste process, is realized in the production of ever more novelties – a self-sustaining accommodation of self and society that institutes a relentless movement of desire to and fro, effectively creating an economy of ignorance. Another aspect of this may be glimpsed in the corresponding development of the control of movement within the topography of modern cities. Compare the rather distant historical image of an advance flag-bearer who marches before a sluggish motor vehicle (as a warning to unsuspecting pedestrians – and where a person moves *faster on foot* than the vehicle, we can guess that people were still so unfamiliar with the sight as to have no expectation of the approach of such a danger) with the fast – indeed, spurting – movement of contemporary motor vehicles under the regulated control of traffic signals. Here a whole host of successive decisions once requiring our active involvement are removed from daily life.

Yet the gradual erosion of what has gone before is most obviously illustrated at the seemingly insubstantial level of fashion. As a socio-historical category fashion is normally thought of in terms of relatively large time frames, and indeed all eras might easily be marked by the idea of a dominant style of dress. Yet the fact that this is the consequence of memory alone becomes clear when we remember that life is contrastingly always *life as lived in the present*. Consider the evangelical fervour of advertising, which begs us to cast off once cherished but inevitably faded objects as part of some half-formed dream of a glittering future where everything always seems to be bright, clean and refreshing. Gilles Lipovetsky has noted how the consumption of products thrives on an 'order of *autonomous* phenomena, responding only to the play of human desires, whims and wishes', signalling, perhaps, an age where the lack of objective meaning has created a void, to which the only response is found in a subjective identification with the object world through consumption.[27] The act of purchase, indeed, is the consummation of desire, which gives way, in the words of Jean Baudrillard, under the 'systematic organization of ambience', which marks what he calls the consummate stage of modern society.[28] The subject of such a world bears the mark of a strangely schizophrenic subjectivity, always at the mercy of a future seduction that comes to form in a modification of the Cartesian *cogito* (hence its being one thing or another): now we exist as we consume.

The contemporary obsession with novelty is the source of an astonishing diversity of consumer products all demanding attention, and all claiming a uniqueness that must not be denied, but that may nevertheless be the effect of some kind of confidence trick. Take soap, for example, as the perfect illustration of the diversification and duplicity of the product world: once sold as off-cuts from large indistinguishable blocks that were wrapped in simple paper as a minor concession to a crude form of product differentiation and only later, gradually, differentiated more subtly by specific manufacturer branding.[29] The manufacturers Procter & Gamble saw the limitless potential of simple detergent technology and the way it made itself available for use in the creation of a whole range of ostensibly unique products. Thus shampoos, liquid detergents, dishwasher detergents and household cleaners came to occupy whole aisles of a typical supermarket. These were all new products whose purposes were once fulfilled by plain old soap.[30] More broadly, then, we might take fashion to transcend the basic materiality of things in their undifferentiated condition, especially in the way fashion can proclaim an almost spiritual world of superabundance. Fashion is, according to Mark C. Taylor, 'profound in its superficiality' because it functions as the highest contemporary realization of modern society as a mask of games; but this is a fleeting, not to say earthy, spirituality that has more of the quality of a ritual dance – an approach to some liminal condition – rather than any sense of completeness, as Taylor observes in his remark that 'the profundity of fashion does not involve depth but reflects the infinite complexity of a play of surfaces that knows no end'.[31]

In the end the consumption process thrives only on the creation (the expectation) of a demand that is found by tapping into the modern psyche's orientation towards the new.[32] But it is here also that the relationship between modern life and garbage becomes clear: once desire has been awoken, rarely, if ever, are we prompted to consider one crucial aspect of the life of the seemingly limitless alluring objects; never is the consumer reminded of the necessity of the eventual degradation inherent in the product world, nor for that matter conscious of the fickle operations of the temporary affections that are entertained by desire. What we see and believe is instead mediated by concealment of the seemingly necessary end of such a desire, which as Walter Benjamin saw, characterizes fashion as a 'provocation of death', always becoming 'something new, something different' as the deadly end closes in.[33] Nevertheless these are the insights of the detached observer that largely bypass the consumer of modern society. Used-up products can only be imagined as objects devalued or no longer desirable that, crucially, contradict the fact that the specific value of a new object is contained not in any ostensible use-value, but in the desire that craves it (indeed, this is in one way what objectifies it – desire is objectified in the products as well as the products themselves existing as objects *of* desire). It is worth noting that this may have little to do with the rational order of an object world that claims *to be* based on use. So the consumer object is in a sense also spiritualized – it assumes, if you like, an alchemical power beyond its functionality.[34]

Still, we need to contrast this subjectivity of desire with the finite properties of particular objects – to eventual decay, uselessness, and exhausted potential. Thus, memory of the past is also memory of the inevitable exhaustion that could be dangerously projected into the present and future, thus destroying the vision of newness that advertising has become so successful in creating. And one consequence of the failure of memory to intervene in this way, and bring desire back down to earth, is that aside from the most ardent *neophobes* (for whom every new social trend or fashion is also the sign of impending social decay), modern society remains largely ignorant, often wilfully so, of the inevitable end that the once cherished and shiny new objects of consumer society will find. But, as we have seen, ignorance is crucial to identity, and by this I mean that 'ignorance' must be understood as the primitive 'stuff' from which knowledge separates itself (as in the

Heideggerian notion of *techne*), and so in a sense knowledge constitutes an ordering of the unsorted – sense reorganizes nonsense; value reorganizes garbage as a *way of knowing* the material world.[35] Those sceptical *neophobes*, in recognizing that progress is accompanied by the inevitably hazardous side effects see, in a sense, beyond the surface gloss of modern life to a degeneration that looms all around and that is constituted as a property of everything. The social amnesia that is a consequence of product consumption rests, we can see, on the objective and rational means by which we consume and dispose, and these in turn rest on the separation and specialization of knowledge and production, by the division of productive tasks that developed as part of the earliest industrial processes. This rational process can be summed up in three words: forget, consume and destroy – and on closer examination it is clear that these terms are actually equivalents: to destroy is to consume, to forget is to leave behind (also to destroy), and to consume is to banish need (also, in a sense, to be capable of forgetting).

The mutability of the material world is identified primarily through our awareness of its many objects. Where the stuff of the world is determined to be 'objective' it is because the properties or qualities of certain objects can be *known*. However, the 'empire of fashion' establishes an alternative order that contributes to the degeneration of the apparently unalterable objective world that knowledge leads us *also to depend on*. Somewhat paradoxically, Lipovetsky notes, the spectre of degeneration emanates directly from scientific progress and the logic of competition where 'supply and demand revolve around novelty', ensuring that:

> Obsolescence is accelerating: specialists in marketing and innovation can assure us that within ten years 80 percent to 90 percent of our current products will be outmoded; they will appear in new forms with new packaging.[36]

The accuracy of such forecasts may be approximate, but can be understood to symbolize the inevitable expansion of the sphere of consumption driven through cycles that multiply new objects at a rapid rate. The concentration of time and effort that goes into the division of production effects an acceleration not only of consumption itself but, more generally, establishes the basis for the development of alternative means of self-creation as well. That is to say, in consumer society subjective identities replace objective determinations of value as the principal domain of experience, and so whilst the world is (objectively) defined in terms of its objects these do not have an unalterable form, nor, indeed, are they any longer easy to define in terms of 'properties'.[37]

In psychological terms this suggests the emergence of an inherent instability that assumes a central role in the modern sensibility; one that is fully signalled by the social veneration of speed and efficiency, and given form in an ever more baffling array of products (that is, objects that are technologically complex and in need of an ever increasing army of service experts) that may give expression to a certain anxiety about the capacity of the object world to satisfy subjective desire. When progress is understood as the historical consequence of an increasing technological perfection that raises our expectations then it can no longer simply satisfy appetites – it also provokes a competing desire for more new experiences (and thus more objects). And where desire expands it is only to create a gap that will be filled up eventually with garbage. But as we have seen, the corollary of this progress is a kind of social amnesia that creates a vast (non-)category of the residual that we know as 'garbage': the true 'nothingness' of modern existence. Only when experience drags us back to the ultimate profanity of the depersonalization of modern life with the occasional reminder – the glaringly visible garbage heap, the stench of a blocked toilet, the random litter cast about by the wind – of the actual indestructibility of garbage, is it sufficient enough to make us stop, to perhaps reflect on how easily that modern life could see the apparently unalterable object world reduced to a formless accumulation of garbage.

At this point it is useful to be reminded that one definition of the verb 'to consume' is actually 'to destroy or expend': to annihilate the good or valuable.[38] And as value seems to be subjectively determined in contemporary life, consumer objects are usually committed to the void in advance of their eventual material deterioration. It would thus seem that this development, particularly since the middle of the twentieth century, contributes to the imaginative construction of garbage as a deathly spectre looming over the object world that always has to be outpaced. In psychological terms degeneration presents a clear contrast between the relative value of *novelty* and *utility* in which the consumer is seen to adjudicate (in the act of consumption) on matters relating to his or her own self-actualization. Thus, in consumption we *buy the self* rather than simply buying a product. Under such circumstances we each, as Gilles Lipovetsky so perceptively puts it, 'become a permanent decisionmaking center, an open and mobile subject viewed through the kaleidoscope of merchandize'.[39]

Fashion is then built upon a schizophrenic impulse in the sense that it reveals both an inability to settle one's mind on some particular object for any length of time, yet also because it presents a problem in resolving the tension that gives rise to future desire, specifically because this desire needs to be continually renewed. Within such uncertain conditions consumer products can be like magical charms that offer the possibility of self-renewal. Certain kinds of consumption may, indeed, express the longing for some quasi-eternal aspect of experience that is also manifest in the desire to avoid death. As Mark C. Taylor puts it: 'Forever committed to the new, the duplicity of fashion is destined to trace the passing away that does not pass away'.[40] Here, too, we see the specific genius of fashion (by which I mean the attachment to novelty) as the motive power of consumption: contempt of the old demands the disappearance of the now offensive object, which always leaves space for a replacement.

From such a perspective products are simply garbage in waiting, temporarily refashioned into a useful or desirable form out of some primary matter to meet any of a countless number of ideas that are usually symbolic of the opposite of death or decay – youth, beauty, machismo, athleticism, sex, and so on. Can desire ever be fulfilled under conditions where the want itself is what ultimately confers death on the object? And if the act of throwing away declares not only the end of a subjectively determined usefulness but also, and crucially, the failure of an object to any longer stand in a relation of identity to some particular, fleeting, desire or other, is the creation of garbage in modern society then not the result of a *positive affirmation* of the self? Any positive answer to these questions leads us to conclude that modernity is inconceivable without an expansion of garbage.

Whilst the actual stuff that is garbage may remain relatively inconspicuous, our general susceptibility towards the ephemeral, and thus to obsolescence, grows unbounded; the evolution of modern expectations can be characterized by qualitative leaps – we want *more*, we want it *better*, and it has to be delivered *faster,* a situation recognized in the earliest days of mass consumption when General Motors in the United States felt able to claim that their 'big job' was to: 'Hasten obsolescence. In 1934 the average car ownership span was 5 years; now it is 2 years. When it is one year, we will have a perfect score.'[41]

The possibility of establishing such a compressed temporal succession of desire is most clearly summed up by the seasonal nature of
ready-to-wear clothing. We might say that the restlessness of fashion
approximates a kind of Heraclitean motion in which all limits are cast
aside, where previously fixed forms are undone, and we are then able –
with little real effort – to remove the unwanted. Removal is a crucial
aspect of the organization of the object world inasmuch as garbage is
equated with *externality* both in material and psychological terms. It
disappears *outside* into a different 'space' – a space that is beyond self-
perception and out of sight. And such is the location, where, unsurprisingly, it easily becomes invisible. Once outside of the safety zones
of the domestic household the objects that become garbage are seen
only as dead matter, with an additional twist added by the fact that
these objects are no longer the concern of the individual consumer.
Eventually garbage (as the residual, the unwanted, the excess) blends
into the conceptual background that constitutes modern society –
found in the fact that value becomes apparent only after an act of differentiation – and in physical or simple material terms becomes another
feature of 'normality' (so long as it remains *outside*), because:

> Unlike the evidence of many another problem, be it a social one,
> such as poverty, or an aesthetic one, such as bad architecture,
> the evidence of specific pieces of household garbage disappears
> from one day to the next. The garbage that is taken out is even-
> tually left at the curb or in the alley, and very soon it is gone. All
> of this garbage is quickly replaced by other garbage. Garbage
> passes under our eyes virtually unnoticed, the continual turnover
> inhibiting perception.[42]

Is it any surprise that garbage may be largely inconsequential to most
of us? That garbage points us to the primacy of a subjective declaration of uselessness is well illustrated – paradoxically – by the unseen
and unimagined uses it may be put to, as, for example, the source of
dirt on some previously private life. Such uses of garbage only arise
because garbage is placed beyond subjective control (to be taken care
of as part of the social organization of waste). We are blinded to the
enduring reality of garbage by the fact that we subjectively determine
the properties of the objects that constitute garbage in a separate
experiential sphere (in the consummation of desire). But once the
limits the consumer unwittingly places on the object are 'removed',

the finite and temporal nature of the object is also destroyed. It is then that the threat of garbage becomes real in a peculiarly modern way because, if unsorted, it simply gets in the way. It is the nothing that becomes an uncanny something. Garbage contradicts a principal idea of modernity in that it questions the belief that we control our lives, and that *we* banish *our own* past in a positive statement of self-determination.

ENRICHINGLY, IN WITH DEBRIS

Until relatively recently the understanding of 'muckraking' had not changed much from an association with 'scavenging', 'foraging' or 'ragpicking' that originates with John Bunyan's seventeenth-century tale *The Pilgrim's Progress,* in which the 'man with the Muck-rake' is presented as an emblem of absorption in earthly pursuits, an image of material rootedness as against spirituality.[43] However by the late nineteenth century this term had come to mean something quite different, to refer to persons who 'fished around in troubled waters', suggesting that there was some value to be found in the private discrepancies of others (should they become known). And it was later still (in 1910, according to the *Oxford English Dictionary,* 2nd edn, 1989) that the verb 'to muck-rake' was first utilized to refer to the now familiar practice of subjecting powerful persons or institutions to allegations of corruption or other illegal or scandalous behaviour.

More recently, however, the term 'muckraker' also takes in a number of less cavalier (and more methodical) people and organizations who are interested in using garbage to reconstruct or present a picture – a view – of, variously, consumer behaviour, celebrity and political lives, or even enemies of the state. In considering the variety of these muckrakers, we can determine a field of activity that goes from so-called 'garbology' (the study of garbage) to 'dumpster diving' (the use of garbage to 'get the dirt' on someone). It seems apparent that the changing contours of this field produce a particularly interesting topography of value beginning some time after World War II, when people in Western societies, in particular, seemed to develop some kind of awareness that discarded material objects might also conceal some other, unseen, non-material properties or powers; that garbage might actually reveal an alternative 'truth' about how things really were – how lives, in particular, are actually lived. The growing awareness of the

Neat and clean, a suburban development in Palm City, Florida.

hidden powers of garbage is also, and importantly, contemporaneous with the expansion of commodity production and consumption, and with a significant increase in the leftovers of social and economic progress. This relates in a separate (yet similar) way to prototypical knowledge economies, which in the twentieth century realize an astounding increase in waste created by bureaucratic and rational institutions from roughly the middle of the century onwards.

There is a vision of contemporary life – particularly suburban life – as being characteristically neat, safe and clean, from the implied domestic comfort of the world promised by consumer product advertising to the calm, ordered and largely indistinguishable streets and homes constructed from factory-produced components. The bland uniformity of such suburban landscapes (see previous page) is nevertheless painted as the illustration of a lifestyle that one might aspire to. Set against such a vision, however, garbage takes on a transforming power that undermines any supposedly reasonable expectations that the world persists in a state of relative harmony and order. The image of garbage cans that for years lined up outside these homes on collection day merely reinforced the belief that urban planners had come close to creating a domestic utopia removed from the dirt, grime and disorder of the city. But unknown secrets lurked within those shiny corrugated metal garbage cans, and their plastic descendants.

In the 1970s, a group of researchers at the University of Arizona came together as the Garbage Project, believing that within our discarded wastes lay the truth about consumer society, and that *garbology* (the use of archaeological methods to examine the buried remains of consumer society) was the ideal science to look at a society that created vast mountains and deep tomb-like pits of this waste, now rendered largely invisible by the twin effect of the conditions of industrial modernity and the expanding suburban utopia. In an interesting choice of terms these researchers claimed that their intention was to look at human life (that is, consumption) 'from the back end'.[44] The metaphorical 'behind' of what is up front, or normally seen, is particularly apt because garbage (like shit) is identifiably the product of a particular person who consumes (digests) and then throws away (excretes), and so what goes in the 'front end' ultimately disappears unseen, but transformed into matter of another kind now stripped of the features that once made it desirable.

Whilst all garbage obsessives encountered here see a value in waste, the Garbage Project researchers are perhaps distinguished by

GARBAGE ITEM CODE LIST

The Garbage Project
University of Arizona

BEEF* 001
OTHER MEAT (not bacon)* 002
CHICKEN 003
OTHER POULTRY 004
FISH
  (fresh, frozen, canned, dried)* 005
CRUSTACEANS & MOLLUSKS
  (shrimp, clams, etc.) 006
T.V.P. TYPE FOODS* 007
UNKNOWN MEAT 008

CHEESE (including cottage cheese) .. 010
MILK* 011
ICE CREAM
  (also ice milk, sherbet)* 012
OTHER DAIRY (not butter)........ 013
EGGS (regular, powdered, liquid)* .. 014
BEANS (not green beans)* 015
NUTS 016
PEANUT BUTTER 017
FATS: Saturated* 018
  Unsaturated* 019
  Bacon, saltpork* 020
  Meat trimming 021
CORN (also corn meal and masa)* .. 022
FLOUR (also pancake mix)* 023
RICE* 024
OTHER GRAIN (barley,
  wheat germ, etc.) 025
NOODLES (pasta) 026
WHITE BREAD 027
DARK BREAD 028
TORTILLAS* 029
DRY CEREALS:
  Regular...................... 030
  High Sugar (first ingredient only) .. 031
COOKED CEREALS
  (instant or regular) 032
CRACKERS...................... 033
CHIPS (also pretzels) 034

UNKNOWN PRODUCE* 040
FRESH VEGETABLES* 041
CANNED VEGETABLES
  (dehydrated also)* 042
FROZEN VEGETABLES* 043
POTATO PEEL* 044
FRESH FRUIT* 045
CANNED FRUIT
  (dehydrated also)* 046
FROZEN FRUIT* 047
FRUIT PEEL* 048
RELISH, PICKLES, OLIVES* 049

SYRUP, HONEY, JELLIES,
  MOLASSES 051
PASTRIES (cookies, cakes
  and mix, pies, etc.)* 052
SUGAR* 053
ARTIFICIAL SWEETENERS 054
CANDY* 055
SALT* 056
SPICES & FLAVORINGS
  (catsup, mustard, pepper, etc.)* .. 057
BAKING ADDITIVES
  (yeast, baking powder, etc.) 060
POPSICLES 060
PUDDING 061
GELATIN 062
INSTANT BREAKFAST 063
DIPS (for chips)................. 064

NON-DAIRY CREAMERS &
  WHIPS 065
HEALTH FOODS* 066
SLOPS* 069
REGULAR COFFEE
  (instant or ground)* 070
DECAF COFFEE 071
EXOTIC COFFEE* 072
TEA* 073
CHOCOLATE DRINK MIX OR
  TOPPING 074
FRUIT OR VEG JUICE
  (canned or bottled) 075
FRUIT JUICE CONCENTRATE 076
FRUIT DRINK, pdr or lqud
  (Tang, Koolaid, Hi-C)* 077
DIET SODA 078
REGULAR SODA 079
COCKTAIL MIX (carbonated)...... 080
COCKTAIL MIX
  (non-carb. liquid) 081
COCKTAIL MIX (powdered)....... 082
PREMIXED COCKTAILS
  (alcoholic) 083
SPIRITS (booze) 084
WINE (still & sparkling) 085
BEER* 086
BABY FOOD & JUICE* 087
BABY CEREAL (pablum) 088
BABY FORMULA (liquid)* 089
BABY FORMULA (powdered)* 090
PET FOOD (dry) 091
PET FOOD
  (canned or moist) 092
TV DINNERS (also pot pies) 094
TAKE OUT MEALS 095
SOUPS* 096
GRAVY & SPECIALTY
  SAUCES* 097
PREPARED MEALS
  (canned or packaged)* 098
VITAMIN PILLS AND
  SUPPLEMENTS
  (commercial)* 100
PRESCRIBED DRUGS
  (prescribed vitamins) 101
ASPIRIN* 102
COMMERCIAL STIMULANTS AND
  DEPRESSANTS* 103
COMMERCIAL REMEDIES* 104
ILLICIT DRUGS* 105
COMMERCIAL DRUG
  PARAPHENALIA 106
ILLICIT DRUG PARAPHENALIA .. 107
CONTRACEPTIVES:
  MALE 108
  FEMALE 109
BABY SUPPLIES
  (diapers, etc.)* 111
INJURY ORIENTED
  (iodine, bandaids, etc.) 112
PERSONAL SANITATION* 113
COSMETICS* 114
CIGARETTES (butts)............. 123
CIGARETTES (pack)* 124
CIGARETTES (carton)* 125
CIGARS 126
PIPE, CHEWING TOBACCO,
  LOOSE TOBACCO 127

ROLLING PAPERS
  (also smoking items) 128
HOUSEHOLD & LAUNDRY
  CLEANERS* 131
HOUSEHOLD CLEANING
  TOOLS (not detergents)......... 132
HOUSEHOLD MAINT. ITEMS
  (paint, wood, etc.) 133
COOKING & SERVING AIDS 134
TISSUE CONTAINER 135
TOILET PAPER CONTAINER 136
NAPKIN CONTAINER 137
PAPER TOWEL CONTAINER 138
PLASTIC WRAP CONTAINER 139
BAGS (paper or plastic)* 140
BAG CONTAINER 141
ALUMINUM FOIL SHEETS 142
ALUMINUM FOIL PACKAGE 143
WAX PAPER PACKAGE 144

MECHANICAL APPLIANCE
  (tools)....................... 147
ELECTRICAL APPLIANCE AND
  ITEMS 148
AUTO SUPPLIES 149
FURNITURE................... 150
CLOTHING: CHILD* 151
  ADULT* 152
CLOTHING CARE ITEMS
  (shoe polish, thread) 153
DRY CLEANING
  (laundry also) 154
PET MAINTENANCE (litter)...... 155
PET TOYS 156
GATE RECEIPTS (tickets)......... 157
HOBBY RELATED ITEMS....... 158
PHOTO SUPPLIES............... 159
HOLIDAY VALUE (non-food)* 160
DECORATIONS (non holiday) 161
PLANT AND YARD MAINT 162
STATIONERY SUPPLIES 163
JEWELRY 164

CHILD SCHOOL RELATED
  PAPERS* 171
CHILD EDUC. BOOKS
  (non-fiction) 172
CHILD EDUC. GAMES (toys) 173
CHILD AMUSEMENT READING .. 174
CHILD AMUSEMENT TOYS
  (games) 175
ADULT BOOKS (non-fiction) 176
ADULT BOOKS (fiction).......... 177
ADULT AMUSEMENT GAMES ... 178

LOCAL NEWSPAPERS* 181
NEWSPAPERS
  (other city, national)* 182
ORGANIZATIONAL NEWSPAPERS
  OR MAGAZINES
  (also religion)* 183
GENERAL INTEREST
  MAGAZINES*................. 184
SPECIAL INTEREST MAGAZINE
  OR NEWSPAPER* 185
ENTERTAINMENT GUIDE
  (TV Guide, etc.)............... 186
MISCELLANEOUS ITEMS
  (specify on back of sheet)* 190

* See Special Notes

Garbage Item Code List, Garbage Project, 1992.

an adherence to the scientific principles that govern the collection of archaeological data, and in an important sense they are more than merely muckrakers. Like the good scientists they claim to be they operate with hypotheses and act according to acceptable practices for the collection of evidence. As their 'Garbage Item Code List' shows (see previous page), the researchers had a table logging the discarded wastes they found according to 190 categories, which – importantly – identified the waste materials in terms of what they previously were. The point here was to 'transform raw garbage into data'.[45] Such methods also produced some other interesting means of sorting garbage, including an extensive beer can 'pull-tab typology' for distinguishing a brand of ring-pull once separated from its parent can, and a map of the spatial distribution of garbage in public places, which allowed the Project to predict the probable location of various kinds of garbage ranging from broken glass to clothes and sexual objects.[46] Discarded sexual objects (sex toys) and other associated paraphernalia (magazines) were rarely found amongst household rubbish, but frequently found in public garbage cans (or near public waste ground), discoveries that demonstrate a normal awareness of the fact that nothing really ever disappears when it is discarded. Pornography, it seems, might be the only discarded stuff that is blessed with such special attention over its disposal – an indication of the power garbage has to compromise one's carefully constructed identity.

Beyond the methods of sorting and collating 'raw garbage' what we may see is that the reappropriation of garbage compromises our ability to set the *inside* of our lives apart from the *outside* world. In other words, garbage represents also the psychological 'underneath' that, if still unburied or unsorted, returns to connect us to the past we thought we had trashed. Landfill digging, by contrast, pushes the garbologist towards a more banal encounter with waste material, where the conversion of garbage (which is, at a deep level, we must remember, *the cut-off, the discarded* and so on) entails its restoration to a previous identity (as a particular kind of clothing, food or other material), which is nonetheless only reconstituted in its association with other such findings. This glosses over the difficulty of thinking in terms of garbage emanating from a non-existent 'back end'. Within a fluid economy of values (indicated by the circumstances under which one person can value something that another discards) people create garbage at highly individual times, and for extremely personal reasons. Once the garbage is scientifically ordered it loses some of its psychological power because the consumer trends that it seeks to generalize do not reassert the original meaning of these 'things', inasmuch as *that* could only have been the outcome of the prior consuming passion of the individual. What we find with meticulously ordered garbage does not tell us much about the confrontation between the self and the potential disordering experience of its own garbage.

Nevertheless, one important aspect of garbage archaeology is that it demonstrates the ease with which a rational re-sorting of 'data' can objectify ('make' or 're-make') a world, a particular 'reality'. The analyses of landfill garbage, for example, seem to show that people have a somewhat schizophrenic relationship to the objects they first consume and later expel. Thus, remains of food products were resurrected to produce a reality at odds with the one the subjects of one study clearly believed they occupied. The message is clear – whilst you may forget what you eat, drink and consume in other ways, the garbage does not lie. What it does is poke a hole through the thin veneer of self-actualization that is formed in the act of purchase. The table below tells two competing stories – the one memory tells self (under reported), and the one garbage tells the outside world (over reported).

UNDER REPORTED (%)		OVER REPORTED (%)	
Sugar	94	Cottage Cheese	311
Chips/Popcorn	81	Liver	200
Candy	80	Tuna	184
Bacon	80	Vegetable Soup	94
Ice Cream	63	Corn Bread	72
Ham/lunch meats	57	Skim milk	57
Sausage	56	High-fiber cereal	55

Source: Rathje and Murphy, *Rubbish! The Archaeology of Garbage*
(New York, 1992)

The faltering memory illustrated in the overestimation of healthy food consumption demonstrates not only our blindness to the evidence of garbage, but perhaps the way that the satisfaction of appetite is not as easily reckoned as all those things we are reminded are good for us. Those foodstuffs that are objectively determined to be 'bad' for us (sugar and candy, ice cream) are conveniently banished from memory in subjective reports of what has been consumed. We might suggest a fairly obvious reason for this: 'healthy' products are probably always purchased as the outcome of a deliberative process, whereas 'unhealthy' or comfort foods are likely 'impulsively' or even guiltily snatched.

The Arizona garbologists viewed landfilling as the unconscious contemporary equivalent of the ancient Egyptian practice of burying the dead in a manner designed to prevent decomposition. Whilst the mummification of garbage is not what is intended by burying our garbage in large holes in the ground, the fact is that the lining of the holes with thick plastic to prevent leakage ensures that decomposition may take many decades to begin. The separation and exclusion of garbage in this way – ostensibly the result of accumulated acts of banishment – curiously ensures its longevity. Landfill sites are the time capsules of contemporary society, 'treasure trove[s]' full of 'wonderful things', according to Rathje and Murphy.[47] The archaeological study of the garbage of consumer society only confirms a truth that was already evident to those who bothered looking – that no matter ever really disappears; but also that by means of entombment and preservation it does not greatly change form either, it is still possible to recognize it as what it was.

In a more general sense landfill muckraking – the foraging and retrieval of supposedly dead matter – realizes the gap between self and world that now opens before us as a result of the indestructibility of these once beloved but now trashed objects. In terms of uncovering the unknown possibilities 'attached' to garbage we must not overlook the slightly shadowy figures who can only be said to be 'fishing around in troubled waters'. To a greater extent than the academic endeavours of the Arizona garbologists, it is the outlaw figure that comes to understand the very personal and subjective qualities of garbage, and thus conveys its significance in revealing some truth about how we create and maintain the self through exclusion. From journalistic muckrakers of the early twentieth century (who first earned the dubious epithet) to present-day celebrity dumpster divers, this kind of figure succeeds in getting closer to underlining the importance of objects and garbage to a sense of self in modern society because the specific threat garbage carries is in the unwelcome (though not illegal) interference in the affairs of others. Whilst we may accept that scientists could have a legitimate interest in garbage, it does not prevent the formation of an idea that messing about in other people's garbage is somehow abnormal.

In common with the archaeologists of the Garbage Project, the renegade muckraker shares some important beliefs, and among these would be the view that ultimately we are our leftovers, and that garbage – far from being spent or used-up – presents an alternative version of 'reality' and does not entail, as the verb 'to consume' suggests, the exhaustion of possibility. Thus, the ease with which a trash obsessive can intervene in the life of others simply by paying attention to the rubbish that is commonly forgotten once disposed of, can have devastating consequences. It is axiomatic that we live in an age of *transactions* – of negotiations, exchange, purchase, and so on – that constitute the framework for any kind of social existence in contemporary society. In other words, a mediated series of experiences conjoins the more or less anonymous parties in these relations and at each stage of such an existence, inevitably, is garbage.[48]

In terms of commodity production this gives birth to what Marx recognized as alienation, the disconnection consequent upon a transfer of human 'qualities' into the discretely and rationally produced object-as-commodity. Consumption, we should recall, is mediated by formal and objective rules and structures (opening/closing times, the checkout queue, the menu), which might be viewed as the flipside of the producer's alienation; where capitalist production takes something from you, the mediators in the consumption process may become obstacles to getting what you need. This undeniably helps to discriminate the precise forms of our consumption but in the process objectifies our relationship to the world, both in terms of satisfaction (self-creation) and disappointment ('alienation').[49]

On this basis it is not too difficult to think that just as we 'pick up' the bits of the world we like and 'integrate' them to become as one with ourselves, we must undoubtedly discard other bits of ourselves, which are left all over the place. These 'leavings' may be difficult to grasp as substantial 'things' (in the way that we can grasp the reality of the physical objects we discard), and indeed may even be insubstantial 'things': a stray comment here, an ill-considered opinion or a minor indiscretion there. But like material objects, verbal incontinence produces its own garbage; it creates its own objects because when exposed to the external world, it can take on a life independent of its original purpose. This is also the 'place' from where the garbologist can re-arrange a life from the broken fragments left behind. If the value of the seemingly insignificant information contemporary life generates (bills, receipts to be retained, official communications) cannot be anticipated what does this mean for our disposal practices? The volume of personal material waste creates a need for ever more cunning technologies to 'de-materialize' the leftovers that might be resurrected

Has Someone Taken Over Your Good Name?, 2003, information leaflet, US Postal Service.

by anyone keen enough to take an interest in garbage, or even to 'steal' your identity, an increasing risk as the details of our lives are continually reduplicated through technology. As one expert noted: 'Most people don't give much thought to what they're discarding at home: phone bills, credit card statements, medical prescription bottles, bank statements, work-related materials . . . the amount of information you can learn about a target is astounding.'[50]

The hidden potential in the waste of contemporary society is symbolized by the triumphant paper shredder (see over). The corporate waste company Allegheny Industries suggests that shredding is the way 'to keep your unwanted and obsolete records from being read by the wrong people'; 'simply *throwing things away* cannot possibly provide the security you need'. 'Wastebaskets and trash bins are easy to search, and crumpled papers are easy to read.' In Don DeLillo's *Underworld,* a tale in which the subjective arrangement of the past has as its objective counterpart the waste management industries of modern society, there is, appropriately, a display at a waste industry convention that features the latest of these technological innovations – it is a 'confidential shredder called the Watergate'.[51] The name 'Watergate' itself of course, resonates to the sound of intrigue, of unknown indiscretions, if not the Machiavellian deeds such a device will conceal in virtue of its power of changing the physical form of waste.

Such technologies reduce the guarded reality of deceit and dissimilation to a collection of puzzle parts. Alas, like the shiny porcelain surfaces that only reveal the presence of dirt, this shredded remainder points to the absence of the secrets (indiscretions, dirty deeds) it was employed to conceal. As Mark C. Taylor has noted, a puzzle may simply present itself as a need for detection, simply because we occupy a reality that is a surface that conceals infinite layers below.[52] This garbage – as another layer of our reality – is something else that looks like it could be worked out; made to yield up its secrets. 'If depth is but another surface, nothing is profound,' Taylor notes, but 'this does not mean everything is superficial; to the contrary, in the absence of depth everything becomes endlessly complex'. Something that soon became apparent to a self-styled garbologist named A. J. Weberman.

There's An Allegheny Shredder To Meet Your Needs

In today's competitive business world, your company's most valuable asset is information—in the form of financial records, personnel files, payroll data, customer lists, contracts, marketing plans, computer disks, etc. Most companies protect their information during

its active and storage phases. However, when this information is no longer required, it is often discarded carelessly.

The problem is that if your company's information were to fall into the wrong hands, the result could be anything from embarrassment to catastrophic loss of revenue.

Simply "throwing things away" cannot possibly provide the security you need. Wastebaskets and trash bins are easy to search, and crumpled papers are easy to read. With the recent emergence of "dumpster diving," rifling through trash is an easy way for anyone to obtain your company's confidential information.

Shredding is the most reliable way to keep your unwanted and obsolete records from being read by the wrong people.

Today, thousands of banks, insurance companies, hospitals, government agencies, and other organizations—including the majority of the Fortune 1000—rely on Allegheny paper shredders for cost-effective destruction of their confidential materials.

Allegheny offers the widest range of paper shredders available—from office models to high volume shredding systems that can destroy up to 10 tons of paper per hour.

As the industry leader, Allegheny offers more than just equipment. We offer <u>solutions</u>. We can assist you in setting up a complete document destruction program —developing the most efficient means of collecting your confidential materials, processing them through the shredding system, and recycling the shredded paper for a profit.

There's an Allegheny Shredder to Meet Your Needs, 2000, information leaflet, Allegheny Industries.

Weberman, who lived in New York and attained notoriety during the 1960s, claimed to have been the founder of 'non-governmental garbology'.[53] The fact that he made a point of emphasizing his distance from authority (note the description 'non-governmental'), thus creating an anti-establishment position, was another way of pointing to the less obvious fact about muckraking, and that is that government secret services were keen garbologists themselves. Edgar J. Hoover, the director of the FBI at the time, had authorized so-called 'trash covers', a method of gathering evidence on targets also commonly known in espionage circles as simply 'trashing' or 'dumpster diving'. As with A. J. Weberman, it wasn't any old rubbish the government men were interested in. In fact, both 'official' (i.e., government) and renegade garbologists were concerned with obtaining the 'dirt' on particular individuals, the incriminating stuff that would be found in the trashcan leftovers that were later used to reveal the private details of someone's life.

For his part Weberman claims to have started with the innocuous idea that by 'scanning' the garbage of his idol Bob Dylan for personal titbits, he might be able to understand the singer's (at the time) increasingly surreal songs. He was no less baffled by the detached public persona Dylan seemed to develop after he had achieved fame, which to a fan like Weberman stood in apparent contrast to his prior involvement with the more literal worthy sentiments and political activities of the 1960s 'folk movement' in the United States. Weberman formed the opinion that Dylan had (as a consequence of this transformation) betrayed 'his public', and that the Bob Dylan public persona was not the same as the private individual; that the rather normal husband and father he was off-stage contradicted his public persona (the anti-establishment rebel). Weberman was therefore motivated by a kind of partially expressed anxiety over the exact identity of this person, and the belief that perhaps the singer had not only assumed a different name to that given at birth (as he indeed had – his birth name was Robert Zimmerman) but also lived a different life altogether to the one suggested by his image, that he was in fact an 'act' in the widest sense (and not only as a performer) of being a phoney. As Weberman wrote in his memoir:

> In 1971 I'd started the Dylan Liberation Front (D.L.F.) . . . to remind Dylan about his failure to contribute money or energy

to anti-war and civil rights organizations, and his lack of support for political prisoners despite the fact that he'd built his career singing songs about their struggles.[54]

Accordingly, given these aims, Weberman and various other protestors would congregate outside Dylan's New York apartment chanting 'FREE BOB DYLAN!' 'Free Bob Dylan from himself.'[55]

The case of A. J. Weberman vs Bob Dylan presents an interesting example of how garbage allows the distinctions between inside and outside, public and private to become blurred. In fact, the realm of garbage is where inside and outside clash. Tired of people trying to attach great significance to the words of his songs at this time, Dylan had withdrawn into a more private realm, and began to avoid engaging with an audience that was keen to have him as a spokesman for an alternative culture (an audience consisting of possessive 'fans' like Weberman). This kind of objectification was summed up by the unwillingness of both his audience and other notables in the folk movement, such as Pete Seeger, to accept his evident changes. It is said that Seeger tried to sabotage the famous performance at the Newport folk festival in 1965 when Dylan 'went electric' with a live band, by taking an axe to the electricity power cables. Whether true or not, the kind of resistance summed up by such tales, and in the gestures of protesting fans, capture the sense of Dylan's difficulty in asserting ownership over his own life. Fans like Weberman went as far as to present him with petitions suggesting he return to 'folk' music (and to the broad political concerns of the folk movement). By attempting to 'own' him in this way (to determine his identity) they were also denying that he – as an artist – could submit himself to the uncertainties of the creative process, with all the attendant transformations that may entail. In effect their desire to objectify him could only be realized by 'destroying' his creativity at a specific point in time – by 'consuming' endlessly the version of his product that they preferred: Dylan had actually been made acceptable as a commodity by his protest stance and his adherence to the anti-materialistic way of life espoused by the folk movement. Aware that such a role might bind his creative instincts, Bob Dylan's 'nonsensical' lyrics and rather obscure public utterances of the time were one obvious strategy (and make more sense taken as such) to escape the objectification of those who sought deep meaning in his words, limiting his status to that of a 'protest singer'.[56] At the same time little did he know that his trash could provide the meaningseekers with an alternative way to objectify him – precisely by reversing his persona from hero to villain, with the aid of his garbage. On first discovering that he had been made a target, Dylan responded by 'putting extra dogshit in his garbage'.[57] Later he would meet Weberman in the first of many attempts to get him to stop his trash trawling, an encounter recorded in a recent biography of Dylan:

> Bob told Weberman that he might write a song about *him*.
> 'Well, I could use the publicity.'
> 'Yeah, well, that's one reason why I wouldn't do it, but I got a good song if I ever wanted to do one.'
> 'What's it called?'
> 'It's called *Pig*.'
> 'I'm a pig, eh?'
> 'Yeah.'
> 'Ah, bullshit, I'm a pig, man.'
> . . . 'You go through garbage like a pig.'[58]

The confrontation between Dylan and his tormentor exemplifies the realization that there was a way to reach within the bounds of the carefully constructed and largely private self – and that garbage could be a route to some idea that there was a more objective 'truth' about a person. This is seen in the birth of a larger public interest in the private lives of celebrities. Indeed, the notion of celebrity itself (of being 'celebrated' for being famous – for public activities that must always only be a part of what a person is, or does) not only creates our contemporary icons, but also stands as a tacit acknowledgement that trash now rules almost universally – that the banal minutiae of gossip and froth provides some dubious connection with the 'real' lives of (perhaps) otherwise unremarkable people is no more than a recognition that the reality of garbage is found not only in the material, but also in the suffocating cloak of celebrity lifestyle 'facts'. That is not to say that actual material garbage is not of interest (when it clearly is), because in the case of the rich and powerful (perhaps as distinct from mere celebrities) the remainders of a hidden private life, thoughtlessly discarded, are now eminently reusable in previously unforeseen ways. This much was seen in the UK during the 1990s when a latter-day Weberman known as Benji the Binman was responsible for a series of scandals that ruined the careers of a number of politicians and celebrities.

Whilst Weberman may barely occupy a footnote in any history of modern culture, he stands as an exemplar of a changing attitude toward garbage in modern society. In his occasionally amusing memoir, *My Life in Garbology,* he made an interesting observation about his own significance when recalling his initial muckraking impulse, which relates specifically to the contemporary difficulty in maintaining a separation between the private and the public spheres (when we depend so much on the rational structures of society to order our lives). 'As I eyed the home of the reclusive poet', he recalls, 'I wondered what went down behind the door that Dylan had slammed in my face. Just then I noticed Dylan's shiny new steel garbage can and said to myself, "Now, there's something that was *inside* and it's *outside* now".'[59]

And this realization of the boundary having been broached is the symbolic affirmation of a change that alters the significance of the boundary itself: now the domain of exclusion does not simply exist as a place of banishment (determined by one who creates garbage), but one of danger (determined by some other who uses garbage). In other words, once what was inside is expelled it is no longer subject to control, indeed, the necessity of the release effectively creates the uncontrollable circumstances, because once *outside* it does not simply go away; rather, it invites re-appropriation. Garbage is like death. It is, as a character in Ivan Klíma's *Love and Garbage* remarks, indestructible.[60] It never disappears. Upon reflection we may come to realize this with the certainty of a fact, but as with the mortal end we cannot actually foresee its arrival, and so what is thrown away in a positive act (the act of self-creation) can compromise the self simply because the final form or use of this garbage remains unknown under normal conditions of disposal. Garbage is both a threat to us and a gift to posterity. In pursuit of such unlikely bequests Weberman continued to steal the garbage of Bob Dylan for many years, and for much of that time Dylan continued to try and mollify him, and even offered him a job as a driver, according to one of his biographers. 'You can hang around me and see that I am clean,' Dylan reportedly told him.[61] Appropriately for such an uncivil operator, a final street encounter whilst rifling bins was reputed to have temporarily put an end to Weberman's interest in Dylan. Catching him amongst the discarded diapers, chicken bones and newspapers of his garbage, Dylan allegedly gave him a beating for all the trouble he had caused, and – Weberman reports – for behaving like 'a pig'. It did not end there, however, with Bob Dylan's wife tossing in the appropriate observation that, 'compared to Bob, you are filth'.[62]

Thereafter, Weberman's muckraking was channelled in different directions, and amongst others subjected to his infamous 'garbanalysis' were John Mitchell (Attorney General in the Nixon administration), Arthur Schlesinger ('a Harvard brains-truster for John F. Kennedy'), and the vice president to Richard Nixon, Spiro Agnew. Weberman's notoriety was such that he even made it into those renowned chronicles of trash culture, *The Andy Warhol Diaries*. In an entry for 22 February 1981, the artist noted how he ran into 'Alan J. Weberman', 'The King of Garbology', on his way home:

> I knew who he was because he handed me a resume with all his garbage credits on it. He said he'd just been through Roy Cohn's garbage and Gloria Vanderbilt's . . . I was scared that he would see where I lived so I went in the other direction.[63]

Unsurprisingly the famous 'garbanalysis' touted by Weberman as the method for understanding his targets seemed to result in very little of substance beyond serving up the private life of some unfortunate public figure for all to see (usually in likenesses made from garbage) and in the end the threat he once posed was dissipated by his own status as a kind of anti-celebrity. In the end garbology, as practised by Weberman, was reduced to the level of a circus sideshow.

For the most part Weberman indulged in a pseudo-ideological battle against the traditional left-liberal hate-figures of the time, often seeming to invite the kind of violent response that might lead to the most sensational news headlines. In fact publicity for his deeds was essential, and Weberman often made sure reporters accompanied him on his trash foraging expeditions.[64] Thus, whilst fearful of another target, Norman Mailer (much more noted then for his 'pugilism' than the physically slighter Dylan), Weberman still felt that it was worth raking through the garbage cans left outside his apartment because of the guaranteed publicity. But unexpectedly, given his reputation, Mailer did not lose his temper when he sighted Weberman, nor did he seem overly concerned with the sight of a stranger in his garbage. As Weberman noted: 'Mailer looked at me standing in the rubbish, poking round with a pocket flashlight, and walked on. From the look on his face he must have thought I was a government agent.'[65] In a way Weberman's perception of how Norman Mailer probably viewed him revealed as much about the similarities between himself and the G-Men as any differences. Both sought to use garbage – the leftover fragments – and to make something different with it. The covert trash covers of the FBI had the more serious aim of feeding the cold war paranoia of Edgar J. Hoover, and contributing to the widespread fear of 'reds under the beds' (the 'foreign bodies' that threatened to infect the system), not the titillation of celebrity news headlines.

In the political climate fostered by figures such as the FBI chief, to be 'on the inside' was to be safe, essentially patriotic – a non-contaminant – and by extension perhaps, to be aware that there were traitors, or outsiders, within one's midst. The Bureau not only went through the trash of those considered a threat to American values, it 'intercepted their mail, broke into their homes and offices, and planted illegal microphones and wiretaps'.[66] In the paranoia surrounding life during the Cold War upstanding American citizens were supposed to conform to some objective ideal of 'the American way of life' (a demand that persisted for longer and on a far greater number of levels amongst their Eastern European and Soviet counterparts). The danger of non-conformity from within, of communists in America, suggested an acute awareness of how easily order could be infected by an unwelcome parasite that disorder could gnaw away from within. What was outside, the despised and feared, had to be guarded against lest it find a way in to contaminate the body politic. Here, the historical precedents are obvious. As Niccolò Machiavelli would have recognized, Hoover was merely living up to the reality that in political affairs – in defence of the state, particularly – there was dirty work to be done, but crucially the point was not to deny or neglect this fact, but rather to wear clean gloves, to cover up as a means of avoiding dirty hands.[67] In terms of the maintenance of the body politic, the view of security agencies was that activities like 'dumpster diving' provide one way of inspecting, and hopefully preserving, this body.

A fear of disorder – and a corresponding desire to maintain order – is implied in the very notion of 'official secrecy', which by the twentieth century had created a whole economy of subterfuge. This more or less lived off the indeterminate matter of trash (whether material objects found in trash cans, or in the 'distorted' objects and beliefs of unwelcome ideologies), and from the fact that the separation of the valuable from the unwanted creates this garbage as a kind of gift. The fear of disorder also thrived in the awareness that once a level of control is assumed, to maintain it becomes a necessity, and state security imperatives both reveal and conceal an expanding 'sphere' of uncontrollable and random garbage. This is summed up in the uneasiness that arises

Tourist sunbathing next to a rubbish heap, 1973.

when borders and distinctions of almost any kind are blurred, where the detachment of parts of the self creates a momentary doubt, as they pass from things we once identified with to the unsorted and devalued matter that constitutes garbage. A consciousness of this transport of identity is necessarily *self*-consciousness, however, which is to say, a realization that bits of you have been more or less 'chopped off'. To doubt is (in this case of disposal) to ponder on the wisdom of throwing out and on the contrary implications of retention, which can be equally debilitating to a sense of self.

Here, as an illustration of the precarious status of the self, is one of the most enduring tensions within contemporary experience: the capacity to assert an identity (to exercise the power of will over our own lives) is compromised, paradoxically, by the very act of doing so, by consuming things, by simply living. This is precisely because our identity is so inseparable from what we consume, but even more because what we consume never really disappears. Instead, it returns eternally, in new forms. The strange fact that through some unseen process garbage becomes something else is only incidentally to do with us, and actually more to do with chance. And chance, by some act of poesis, is merely the rubbish of reason.

5 Garbage and the Uncanny

> The better orientated in his environment a person is, the less
> readily will he get the impression of something uncanny in
> regard to the objects and events in it.
> Sigmund Freud, 'The Uncanny'

DUPLI-CITY: A TRACE INSCRIBES THE VOID

The city is life and garbage is death. In the modern West the city dweller
becomes accustomed to a place within the urban environment that is
characterized by the familiar. We think of streets and houses, public
spaces and commercial zones, traffic signs and transport hubs, and what
we are reminded of are what Kevin Lynch called our 'way-finders'.[1]

The topography of the city represents an ideal of order, and is
actually impossible to conceive of as anything but a consequence and
form of order that overcomes spectres of degeneration; hence the ease
with which the dystopian can be suggested by representing the city as
an urban wasteland. But perhaps just as importantly the city has
another life that reflects the selective nature of individual memory, and
it seems impossible to think of the city one lives in without bringing to
mind these physical or geographical attributes (the 'way-finders') that
stand as markers for the daily activities that inspire our various movements to and fro. From these we can readily obtain a mental impression of our own habitat and indeed become better orientated within
this environment. But whilst self-selecting memory can constitute its
own particular order, it is less easy to bring to mind the intangible
traces of the many thousands of other lives that create the more or less
imperceptible depth beneath the surface we visualize and create, and
that memory therefore sustains.

As well as memory and topography, the city we observe also
conceals a multitude of unknown qualities and activities that make

everyday city living more or less variable according to one's desires (or perhaps one's luck). Whatever you desire you may find here, just as any misfortunes that befall you will surely illustrate the 'spatial interruptions, fractures and lags' that constitute the *unknown* city.[2] The interconnecting routes that flow in and out of one another at nodal points on a grid, for example, are characteristically fluid. They represent the city as a state of controlled flux that can soon become the shadow counterpart of the city that gives life. These 'non-spaces' as Marc Augé calls them, take the form of 'dense networks of means of transport', for example, where the whole can in some sense remain intact, yet be dissolved into 'solitary individuality', and caught up in 'the fleeting, the temporary, the ephemeral'.[3] It is perhaps at times like this that we are at risk of losing the sense of order or orientation within the urban environment; times, as we might suggest after Freud, that the uncanny may make itself felt.[4]

But this is to get ahead of the story. We need first to understand how the city has come to function almost as a gigantic stage set on which any number of personal dramas may be played out. In this sense, the city is the *tabula rasa* of modernity: the blank slate of imagination that functions as the site of erasure and inscription. The question then arises – how does it come to be haunted by garbage?

In Ed Ruscha's 1967 collection of aerial photographs of Los Angeles (published as *Thirty-Four Parking Lots in Los Angeles*) we can obtain a glimpse (see overleaf) of the ideal form of order so common to the imagination of modern city dwellers (if not to their actual lives).[5] This is the bird's eye view of the totalizing city that expands beyond individual experience (as which it may exist merely as a vehicle for need and desire), in which the cityscapes, leaving aside the grids, resemble the empty blankness of an architectural model. While in times past the arts of memory reconstituted the public sphere on the basis of monuments and landmarks, as Anthony Vidler notes, modernist cities are established just as much on the basis of a forgetting that, in the work of Le Corbusier,

> takes the form of erasure, literal and figural, of the city itself, in favor of a tabula rasa that reinstalled nature as a foundation for a dispersed urbanism and made its monuments out of the functions of modern life – the bureaucratic skyscrapers.[6]

The abstract effect of this theoretical blankness is doubled by the fact

Ed Ruscha, photo of Wilshire Boulevard, from Ruscha's book *Thirty-Four Parking Lots in Los Angeles* (1967).

that almost all the images we see in Ruscha's *Parking Lots* project show cityscapes seemingly devoid of significant human traces (which are, just the same, implied). Such a representation depicts the city as the product and culmination of the Enlightenment; it is transparent, as Vidler says, 'of the self to the other' and 'of all selves to society'.[7] For example, we may see the grids of the various parking lots as the temporary resting place for a ceaseless rectilinear motion, projected through darting highways that always (like the ideas of the Enlightenment) strive towards some goal, some good or other. Like progress in the abstract, the city of imagination is defined by its destinations.

What these may be remains unspecified, so all that is left is the idea of forward motion: movement as progress, as desire, and as the avoidance of death. The city thus understood becomes an arrangement of (not always mutually convergent) strategies for negotiation, and the means toward the maintenance of human relations.

Of course no one lives in an Ed Ruscha photograph – in the blank, abstract and merely formal landscape of a city, that is – because such apparent voids are inscribed by traces, by the evidence of lives lived that cut across the ideal grids that can be both liberating and confining.[8] As Nicholas Royle writes, 'the uncanny has to do with a strangeness of framing and borders, an experience of liminality'.[9] These ideal forms, when taken alongside the sifting and ordering propensity of subjective memory and imagination, cast the unwanted or the unknown into the shadows that conceal the residues of our making. The phantoms of past and present are given their place alongside the debris of material existence and the garbage of self-creation. We live, in other words, a shadow existence in these cities, where life is not as neat and tidy as the abstract ideal or self-selecting memory suggests. The shadow city can be summed up by reference to a never-ending war. In this, the twilight activities of refuse collectors seem to reconstitute daily the mutating features of the spectral and unfamiliar aspect of the cityscape we either cannot see or choose to ignore, but which is subsequently cast as the ghostly foe of Enlightenment and civilization.

It is likely that we rarely see the full effects of garbage because our personal involvement in the mucky details of its disposal is replaced by the objective and impersonal direction of municipal government in the form of the cleansing department. In the garbage war, the refuse workers are cast as the unlikely storm troopers for progress, saviours of the city and of modern society. Not only does this fact go unrecognized but, just as significantly, their very existence ensures that the spectre of garbage is kept at bay. Ask yourself, when do you ever see those shadow cities of the dead – the garbage dumps, sewage plants, and landfills – that are not only removed from the places where their contents are presumed to offer no threat, but that end up as barely perceptible hinterlands to the idealized city? For most of us the truth is that we are more likely to whiz past these sites in transit between destinations, and this may constitute the only time we come close to seeing them. In his recent book *London Orbital*, Iain Sinclair describes the unseen territory through which the M25 motorway cuts the clean lines that signify our blindness to all this: 'The M25 . . . increasingly functioned as an asteroid belt for London's rubble, the unwanted mess of the building boom, the destruction of tower blocks, the frenzied creation of loft-living units along every waterway . . . .'[10]

We have arrived at this situation because the sheer amount of garbage – the human wastes, rubbish, putrid leftovers of the kitchen, the mud – eventually became so intolerable that the city had to fight back, and fought back so successfully that garbage has now been pushed into these half-existing zones that no one ever sees. In the Britain of the seventeenth and eighteenth century the general rule seems to have been that even if public agencies had been willing to do something to combat the worst effects of rapid urban growth, it was on such a scale as to make it practically unmanageable. For example, it was only in the late eighteenth and early nineteenth centuries that streets in newly developed urban areas began to be paved (allowing a degree of control over the filth). Prior to such improvements there was a 'disjunction between old and new property, and between rich and poor residents' when it came to the kind of environment they had to put up with – meaning that money was the best way to escape the grime and rubbish.[11] In *The Wastes of Civilization*, J. C. Wylie paints a picture of an environment of unremitting filth and garbage extending right up to the middle of the nineteenth century, noting that the increase in wealth that brought people into towns and cities also:

> brought more rubbish, and with arrangements for disposing of it no more adequate than those of a medieval town, the fop of the eighteenth century, with his red-heeled shoes, had to tread ever more delicately than his counterpart of earlier ages, when he contemplated the wretch in the pillory being pelted with dead cats and turnips.[12]

One thing we might have expected to find as part of the attire of such red-heeled fops was a pair of protective overshoes known as 'pattens'. These were like early versions of the platform shoes we know from the twentieth century, but which fastened over the shoes to provide a mobile and miniature bridge over the filth of the street. Archaeological research on the banks of the river Thames in London has suggested that these pattens were worn from around the twelfth century, becoming more common in London (and evidence suggests, other cities across Europe) from around the fifteenth century. In terms of personal comfort these overshoes would have been an important means of raising oneself above the filth, especially as it was uncommon for refuse collectors to visit anywhere apart from the back lanes and alleys of the towns and cities. In the main thoroughfares the garbage was simply left to rot in the street. One historian notes that conditions were worsening well into the middle of the nineteenth century, with urban growth creating a 'physically and morally dangerous environment, one in which filth and destitution combined to create a breeding

Detail from Jan van Eyck, *Giovanni Arnolfini and his Wife*, 1434, oil on oak. National Gallery, London.

ground for disorder and disease'.[13] In 1855 Michael Faraday, one of the great scientists of the Victorian era, wrote to *The Times* complaining of the state of the river Thames, noting that 'the whole of the river was an opaque brown fluid'. In true scientific fashion he devised an experiment to test whether or not his senses might have been deceiving him as to its opacity, and then carried it out at many points along the river, as he reported in the same letter:

> I tore up some white cards into pieces, moistened them so as to
> make them sink easily below the surface, and then dropped some
> of these pieces into the water . . . before they had sunk an inch
> below the surface they were indistinguishable though the sun shone
> brightly at the time; and when the pieces fell edgeways the lower
> part was hidden from sight before the upper part was under water.

In anticipation of the 'great stink' of three years later, which was to drive MPs from Westminster and lead to the suspension of Parliament because of the stench coming from the adjacent river Thames, he continued, 'the smell was very bad, and common to the whole of the water; it was the same as that which now comes up from the gully-holes in the streets; the whole river was for the time a real sewer'.[14]

Thus, the unwritten history of these exclusion zones of the present – the dumps, sewage works, and landfills – begins with urban growth, and with the inhospitable nature of the human environment. And where the modern garbage war may now include the accoutrements of a more conventional war (for example, in the use of bullet-proof work wear as protection against discarded syringes), now, as in the early modern towns and cities, garbage is a ghostly foe, a shadow of our supposedly cleansed reality, where its method of disposal (today, semi-automatic routines of binning and ejecting) ensures that it no longer really comes to light. Instead, it vanishes into a spectral reality that is uncanny.

One might suggest that the life of the city and of city government as we now know it, begins with the recognition of garbage. J. C. Wylie notes that whilst the first Sanitary Act in Britain was passed by Parliament in 1338, it nonetheless left the responsibility for disposal with private individuals, who were entrusted to 'remove from the back streets and lanes of all towns all swine and all dirt, filth and branches of trees and to cause the streets and lanes to be kept clean for the future'.[15] Well into the middle of the nineteenth century in Britain, Wylie adds, there were still disagreements over who was responsible for the cleaning of the streets. As in medieval times, 'all manner of liquid and solid filth was thrown into the streets'.[16] In cities where tenement dwellings are common there are still those who remember the last days of this kind of disposal with the so-called *midden* as incontrovertible evidence of the potential filthiness of city life. These middens were the potentially noxious refuse-heaps that could be found in the backcourts of buildings that housed dozens of people, consisting of wastes dumped from upper level windows. Although a thing of the past now, one can still see in many forms of urban housing the network of service roads, back courts and alleys where the midden would have been found, and that now exist primarily for the removal of waste from the more domesticated rubbish bins serviced by city refuse workers. These networks form a kind of shadow topography of the supposedly 'real' city out in front where the traffic of daily life sets into observable motion. It is only the stealthily effective garbage collectors who visit this shadow city. They can be seen early in the day, a mobile, roving, gang of human termites, boring through the dead matter of a thousand lives.

Finding efficient means of banishing garbage also became a necessity because the populous cities realized a change in the way people related to their immediate environment – in the ways they could now live – because a city no longer made easy the kind of existence where it was easy simply to move out of the way of our wastes – they were to be found at every turn in the new, populous, urban world. City living embeds its inhabitants within what today we would call 'networks' – it makes them interdependent – to the extent that abandoning the city for an itinerant life would be a huge risk. In their book *Rubbish! The Archaeology of Garbage,* Rathje and Murphy suggest that we can see a contrast between city dwelling (in general, the condition of living under the 'protection' of some kind of government or authority) and itinerancy. A community that is premised on mobility fits uneasily within modern society because it contradicts the settled nature of modern life in general (and not simply urban life). Mobility in this sense can only be accommodated if there are actually new spaces to move into, as these are needed to compensate for the lack of central organization over life (or where such organization is encountered, an unwillingness to adhere to its demands). Rathje and Murphy note that garbage helps us understand this to some extent, because one of the reasons why itinerant people need to move is because the volume of garbage eventually becomes an obstacle to even temporary settlement.[17]

By contrast with a desire to be rootless, everything that constitutes a normal life in modern society emphasizes the importance of stability and order as protection against the vagaries of such an unsettled and apparently chaotic existence. Across a spectrum of social life that encompasses everything from political rights to product consumption, our physical stability becomes a *condition* of life in contemporary urban societies (things like voting, banking, and credit consumerism, all become difficult, perhaps impossible, if one seems to be unsettled or homeless). Here, John Locke makes another appearance in this story. His notion of property as a condition of freedom (set out in the *Two Treatises on Government*) not only values solidity and self-control, but in terms of its historical implications, comes to symbolize the way that city living potentially extends the reach of such freedom. In this kind of freedom the self is loosened from the grip of nature – from the inconveniences that may once have required one to move because the stench and decay of existence became too much to bear – only to be secured in life by a different kind of stability, by the taming of movement. The forms and physical objectivity of bricks and mortar, houses and pavements, and so on create an expectation of order that transfers over time from a relationship between the self and the physical and material (in the ownership of property) to a social and psychological orientation (an idea of personal stability) that is, effectively, an abstraction from the real. A life where the products of nature provide a source material for what we might call the various 'furnishings' of life; this stuff that can be disposed of just as easily as it can be purchased.

While the nascent bureaucracies of early towns and cities slowly began to realize the risks to health posed by varieties of garbage, the cities of consumer society contrastingly seem to gain life from the creation of ever more *stuff*. Now the vitality of the city depends precisely on maintaining a far more precarious balance within the person of the consuming individual, who must on the one hand develop a 'healthy' desire for more products (or the economy will suffer) and yet must also seek protection against psycho-physical debilitation (perhaps as a result of over-consuming) by controlling these same desires. In other words, the consumer is engaged in a constant internal psychological battle. The ideal modern citizen would realize a walking contradiction; become a kind of 'psychic refuse collector', taking care to spend and trash with equal enthusiasm and regularity, like a mechanical, pleasure-seeking product mulcher.

It is at this point that the present must be detached from the past, and that the modern affair with disposability expands into all spheres of life. That disposal is now concerned with the psychology of personal stability (with being at home in a more subjective environment) is recognized in the awareness that the past is old stuff, and like depleted and worn out objects, it just clogs up our lives. Nietzsche remarked on this spectre of the past as the 'liability' of personal history – its dangling attachment to our present freedom constitutes an uncanny presence. Whilst it is unlikely that Nietzsche would have recognized the disposability of modern life as something entirely desirable, his observation that the inability to detach the past leaves one 'damned to see becoming everywhere' seems particularly apt, for it describes the reality that garbage is *everywhere becoming*. Indeed, what the modern self seeks to avoid is just this fact, because it would constitute a situation where self-belief is impossible; where 'we see everything flow apart in turbulent particles'.[18] Such is the spectre of garbage.

But no matter how desirable escaping the past may be, nothing points to the fact that it is a simple matter. For the past, too, is a shadow that tracks us, that threatens to recombine with a reluctant mind and body to deny it the freedom to selectively reconfigure life (and thus the world) in order that forward movement is not impeded. And so the past must also be seen as garbage too – what is past is spent, banished, used up and made void, yet it possesses the threat of the uncanny which, according to Freud, is perceived in terms of eerily familiar things – objects, images, dreams and so on – that resist any of our attempts to effect a separation from them. These odds and ends that we attempt to detach from ourselves may constitute an unwelcome presence because 'in reality', as Freud noted, the uncanny is 'nothing new or alien, but something which is familiar and old'.[19]

Like memory, the garbage of the object world is no less the consequence of a system of organization. The difference here is that social organization rationalizes consumption and therefore also its wastes – beginning in this case with the earliest cities and ending with the great global cities of contemporary capitalism that offer any product from any place imaginable entirely disconnected in time and space from its production (indeed, surely extended even further with cyber shopping). *The great thing about the city*, we always say, *is that you can get anything.* Whilst we may see litter and dirt on the streets, or poking out from overstuffed garbage cans, we don't see the beginning and the end of it all. In the city we *really* can forget garbage – indeed are urged to do so – because the individual responsibility for garbage has, of necessity, been destroyed. Destroyed as a condition of progress. An interesting result of ruminating on garbage is that it takes one back to the most basic fact of life, to the human body as the primary and original site of physical organization. Unsurprisingly, as Anthony Vidler writes, the idea of a body is central in the development of how a city should be constituted; the notion of the body was 'the original ordering device mustered for every traditional city . . . the original paradigm of order for urbanism as for architecture . . . the body provided the organic tissue, so to speak, by which the city might be recognized, memorized, and thereby lived'.[20] If the uncanny comes to light when we no longer feel at home in our environment, we note also that the psyche itself must now be understood to *inhabit* the human body (which explains why prosthetic limbs and automata are associated with the uncanny as well). The relationship between the psyche and the corporeal body is one of knowing; we possess what the anthropologist Marcel Mauss called 'Techniques of the Body' that both orientate us within our social environment and constitute ways of maintaining the self. Mauss spoke of things such as bodily movements (walking, carrying oneself, marching and so on) as examples of such techniques, but also what we might refer to as regulating activities, such as spitting, washing, 'soaping' and so on. Within such a taxonomy of body techniques one could easily make space for disposal as a modification of what Mauss termed 'hygiene in the needs of nature' (but left blank for the reader to fill in). 'There is no technique and no transmission in the absence of tradition,' he notes, and in this sense we can see that the technique par excellence of the modern body is an extension of hygienic techniques.[21] It is the one that re-orientates the body in its relationship with the environment, namely disposal.

And rather curiously we sum up the disposal of care with the peremptory exclamation 'I don't give a shit'. My point is that this can only be understood by reference to the spectre of garbage; which is to say, in the light of a shadow history of progress that culminates in some sense with city living – with urbanization. The equally curious thing is that while the body may have served, in Vidler's words, as the original paradigm of order for urbanism, the wasting functions of the body were clearly not recognized in terms of their necessity for order – pre-modern towns and cities rose on top of the garbage (literally so, in some cases). And the cities of modernity in their ideal forms of blankness and transparency erase, by their very success, the traces of such wasting through their capacity for subjective assimilation, as 'wayfinders' or aids to memory. Only under such conditions of erasure and disposal is 'shit' so easily dismissed. The metaphoric function of the word now rests in the effectiveness with which it can be ejected from our presence in the objective reality we now inhabit.

Materially, garbage represents the shadow *object* world, the leftover of a life, a world, or a dream, created by the voracious speculations of commodity production and consumption. It is thereafter impossible to conceptualize the city without the ghostly presence of *the something that becomes nothing* – the litter, the droppings. The city is where we come to worship at the great cathedrals of consumption, and in this universe of a million products unlimited desire can be tapped with great ease. *Something for everyone* is what the city cries out. Yet, whilst the world may float on this desire the scattered rubbish that uncontrollably creeps from its grave cast around by the wind or kicked by the casual and unknowing passer-by (as stuff that had apparently been declared dead and disposed of) is sufficient to reveal the uncanny nature of human existence in modern society. It is, in Julia Kristeva's terms, representative of the *abject*. Being neither subject nor object, this category of the *abject* has: 'Only one quality of the object –

that of being opposed to the *I* . . . what is *abject* . . . the jettisoned object, is radically excluded and draws me toward the place where meaning collapses.'[22]

What is banished, excluded and made separate may result in a 'massive and sudden emergence of uncanniness', which, according to Kristeva, one encounters as if it were a detached limb – it 'now harries me as radically separate'. But only as a result of its bringing to presence can it annihilate. If left unacknowledged 'on the edge of non-existence and hallucination' the abject becomes the 'primer' of culture.[23] And this is the role of garbage. Internalized, consumer products sustain and protect one within this boundary because they are not simply pieces of matter (the abject) – they have positive properties, and are the objects of desire and utility. Simple matter, by contrast, does not exist in the magical realm of what Karl Marx would have recognized as commodity fetishism, because *its stuff* has become (as a result of disposal) undifferentiated. It has no ostensible use and can only be seen as something akin to an obstacle or, indeed, a source of dread and disgust.[24] In Bruce Robinson's 1986 film, *Withnail and I*, we witness the palpable force of dead matter as conveyed through the entirely filthy living conditions of the film's two indolent central characters. The story takes place in the London of the late 1960s and follows the fate of two unemployed actors whose booze- and dope-fuelled existence sinks to extreme lows on account of their determination to remain true to their vocation as actors. In a celebrated scene, the two are seen standing in the kitchen doorway arguing over the use of their dwindling coffee supply:

'Why don't you use a cup like any other human being?'

'Why don't you wash up occasionally like any other human being?'

'How dare you? How dare you! How dare you call me inhumane?'

'I didn't call you inhumane. You merely imagined it. Calm down.'

'Right you fucker. I'm going to do the washing up!'

'No, no, you can't. It's impossible, I swear to you. I've looked into it. Listen to me, listen to me. There are things in there, there's a tea bag growing . . . you don't understand. I think there may be something alive.'

'What do you mean? A rat?'

'It's possible, it's possible.'

'Then the fucker will rue the day.'

He rushes to the sink and is immediately repelled by the horrific reality that confronts him . . .

'Oh Christ Almighty. Sinew in nicotine base. Keep back, keep back. The entire sink's gone rotten. I don't know what's in here.'

'There's something floating up.'

'What is it? What have you found?'

'Matter.'

' . . . Matter?'

The thing is that matter *goes on*. It never really disappears, but instead takes on different forms. What looks like a glistening and desirable object at one time eventually ends up in a pile of crap. This is the fate of all things. Even burning the stuff doesn't make it go away – it just dissolves it into an atmosphere that sends it back down with the rain. In fact, there is nowhere for our unwanted matter to go unless we export it to the heavens, but even then the debris from space travel falls back to earth eventually (thousands of pieces of it every year). In general terms, however, the development of civilization removes us from encounters with the abject. Instead, we leave garbage to be dealt with by others.

SPECTRAL ENCOUNTERS

Somewhere or other it usually happens in the morning. Perhaps even the middle of the night. In an interminable but barely noticed struggle an equally anonymous legion of combatants face their enemy. It is neither a human, nor really a foreign, foe. This persistent, spectral threat has no face. No violent words or overt threats accompany it – but it just keeps on coming. Like the tides this is a force of nature that never disappears for long. It is our garbage. Would it be entirely ludicrous to suggest that refuse collectors have a profound insight into the essential degradation and decay that defines a natural propensity beyond human time and that would exist outside of any social order? There is no history of the refuse collectors who have nonetheless always been engaged in this struggle against ruin. Still, we might take the melancholic street-sweeper of Ivan Klíma's *Love and Garbage* to symbolize an intimate acquaintance with transience, as he reflects that the ceaseless traffic of society gives only an *illusion* of freedom, of apparently unfettered movement because, in fact, 'all that increases is the needless movement of things, words, garbage and violence'. Rather 'because nothing can vanish from the face of the planet, the fruits of our activity do not liberate us, but bury us'.[25] For the rest of us the existence of this other world from which we are kept apart has, as we will see, the effect of making foreign to us all this *stuff*. Garbage – which emanates from the essentially human as its detached remainder – becomes, as a consequence, uncanny.

The social significance of refuse collectors, like garbage itself, largely eludes our attention. Like the wastes and mess they look after they are degraded because, according to Michael Walzer, their relationship to dirt, waste and garbage 'makes them the object of disdain and avoidance'; we 'impose . . . patterns of behaviour, routines of distancing, that place them in a kind of pale: deferential movements, peremptory commands, refusals of recognition'.[26] If garbage can become uncanny it is because, as Freud wrote, the experience of our environment forces us to repress that which unsettles, the refuse collectors are the token of this repression, the 'un' in uncanny that makes the familiar foreign.[27] But in this repression is hidden the awareness that they represent only the suppressed consciousness that human waste might one day overwhelm us.

Here there is an interesting observation to be made about the relationship between the word *unheimlich* (which in literal translation means 'unhomely') and the Scots word 'canny' (from which we derive the negative 'uncanny', which is the standard rendering of *unheimlich* into English). Canniness in some sense encapsulates a *knowing* and so it is also our ignorance of ruin, decay, and so on, that renders garbage *uncanny,* unfamiliar or unhomely. That is because society (or the powers of social order, at least) in taking care of waste disposal, dissolves our knowledge of the world and sees it dispersed to specific parts of the social organism (if we can call it that).[28] If, as Heidegger says, technology is a way of knowing that distils our knowledge of nature for instrumental purposes, the refuse collector – as a token of this technology as well – reveals that our knowing (as we saw in the case of Kant's transcendental deduction) stands also for an *un*knowing, the disposal of that which we (or reason) cannot know. Thus, the uncanny is prefigured throughout Western metaphysics which, as we have seen, is always a device for separating and withdrawing 'knowledge', or being confined behind a self-imposed boundary.[29] The shadowy figure of the refuse collector stands for this withdrawal and, as such, takes the form of a permission to forget.[30] Thanks to arrangements that place these figures – masters of disposal – in a sense, at *our* disposal, we are excused the worry of exactly how to get rid of our garbage.

The separation of the self from the full implications of the waste process produces another effect that has long-range implications, however. It also removes us to a great extent from the regulating function of disgust (which is knocked out of proportion) that would be induced were this stinking matter not in the hands of the authorities. This leaves us with absurd attitudes to all kinds of filth and waste, where the thought of placing a hand down a cleanly flushed toilet to recover something of value that has been dropped in, for example, becomes hopelessly complicated. The garbage of bodily wastes and putrid discharges carry the taint of death: it is the dead matter that has been ejected into an alien temporality beyond our own control that raises the gorge. The invisibility of the essential drudgery of disposal and the never-ending return of the refuse collectors and cleaners conceals also the essence of garbage, and this is that its inherent lack of value not only destines its exclusion from the material world of value, but the cleansing of our consciousness. Is it not the case that for the most part we view cleaning and disposal as a negligible activity, something that is not anticipated with any sense of enthusiasm? Do we not resent this claim of the material world that reduces us again to being simply a part of it? The problem is that the rational disposal of waste (that is to say, the system in its totality) represents garbage as an accumulated and indistinguishable mass of stuff that is no longer identifiably any*thing*, least of all anything that we think is, or was, our own, because it is the concern of the people (such as the refuse collectors and cleaners) who are appointed to take care of it.

In Klíma's *Love and Garbage* the unnamed narrator who temporarily pushes a broom on the Prague streets to combat his inability to write, remarks on how he is forced by his employers to wear a 'garishly coloured jacket' – in other words, the standard high visibility vest worn by people who work next to traffic – but, he adds, not for his own safety. It was, rather, a symbol designed 'to make sure everyone recognized me from afar and gave me a wide berth' because he swept the streets.[31] As if this item of clothing on its own had the power to signal his residence amongst the unclean, or even worse became the cause of his invisibility beneath what it symbolized. This, as well as the brush and cart, mark him out as part of the world of refuse. The indistinctness of the stuff is reflected in the way that those associated with it blend into the background. A point not without its own humour, as Andrew Davies noted in his discussion of police methods employed in Greater Manchester early in the twentieth century to infiltrate illegal betting pitches; a situation where the most effective way of avoiding suspicion, of being present to catch the offenders in the act whilst remaining anonymous, was to adopt the disguise of '*midden-men* or refuse collectors'.[32]

The social meniality of the street-sweeper (indeed, we may say this of almost any other industrial or domestic cleaners) is given purely by their placement within an economy of aspirational or meritocratic values that emerge as one enters adult life. In Klíma's novel the degradation of the street-sweepers is mirrored in the recognition of the eclipse of childhood optimism and the perception of a world where everyone does an interesting job, and where even people who clean the streets may be cast as superheroes. Unable to comprehend this about-turn in values that emerges in the light of adult reality, the narrator recalls that as a child he was once he was so impressed on observing a Prague street-sweeper at work, that he had imagined that the duties of job must have constituted 'one of the most important jobs a man can have', but now he knew that this was not so; the street-sweepers were people of no importance.[33] He himself was now also a 'nobody': 'simply a person who swept the streets, a person hardly noticed'.[34] He notes later, in resignation to this reality, that 'those who cleansed the world of garbage or rats were never shown any respect', and recounts a story that, for him, confirmed his belief that the street-sweepers or refuse collectors had, in virtue of proximity to garbage, always assumed the role or position at the absolute bottom of social respectability:

> A few days ago I read about a jilted stucco worker who, exactly two hundred years ago, in St George's church, had slashed the face, mouth and shoulders of his lover, for which he was gaoled, and taken to the place of executing, but was reprieved and instead sentenced to clean the streets of Prague for three years.[35]

But within the rationalization of modern society the association of people with garbage moves beyond the properly occupational hierarchies of Western economies (which, in any case, makes for a degree

Captain Clean. The 'leader of the fight to clean up Glasgow . . . who will enlist an army of schoolchildren in the fight against litter and filth', 1979, illustration for anti-litter campaign.

of respectability) to encompass a radical otherness as seen from the viewpoint of modern 'normality'. This is already prefigured as the alien within the industrial landscape of the nineteenth century, for example, particularly in Marx's category of the 'lumpen proletariat': those who have not only sunk to the bottom of the social order, but in Marx's terms are totally useless (certainly in terms of any revolutionary potential) and are thus 'the social scum, that positively rotting mass thrown off by the lowest layers of old society'.[36] This dangerous class, he wrote, forms in all towns 'a mass quite distinct from the industrial proletariat. It is a recruiting ground for thieves and criminals of all sorts, living off the garbage of society.'[37] In *The Eighteenth Brumaire of Louis Bonaparte* Marx calls them 'the refuse of all classes, the ruined and adventitious offshoots of the bourgeoisie, vagabonds, discharged soldiers, discharged jailbirds . . . pickpockets, brothel keepers, rag pickers, beggars', and so on.[38]

These were the very people encountered at around the same time in well-known investigations by Victorian social reformers such as Henry Mayhew and Edwin Chadwick. Mayhew, in his extensive surveys published in 1861 as *London Labour and the London Poor*, encounters the strangeness of the Victorian underworld as a kind of shadow of the real world he inhabits, the world of thrift, stability and solid Christian virtues. Just as accounts of uncanniness rest on blurring the line between what belongs and what is foreign, Mayhew's astonishment lies in the fact that such a class of 'foreigners' actually formed a double of respectable society within the city of London. This is set up by his opening description of an inherent split within the human race, which is divided into two 'distinct and broadly marked races, the wanderer and the settlers – the vagabond and the citizen'. This splitting of the world in two is, on its own, noteworthy because it makes what is essentially common foreign, and thus any understanding of it can only be expressed in terms of these differences. 'Each civilised tribe' he notes, contains a potentially dangerous 'wandering horde intermingled with, and in a measure, preying upon it'.[39] Amongst the less threatening of these were people who lived, by one means or another, on the rubbish of society (trading in damaged goods, for example) or who worked as scavengers, dustmen, flushermen and so on, as well as the more dangerous – 'who partake more or less of the purely vagabond, doing nothing whatsoever for their living, but moving from place to place preying upon the earnings of the more industrious portion of the community'. These were 'the pickpockets – the beggars – the prostitutes – the street-sellers – the street-performers', and so on.[40]

The element of shock displayed in such accounts is reflected in the present when we are very occasionally reminded that there still exist such people, living in communities that survive on nothing else but garbage. A newspaper report in 2001 – under the heading 'Life and Death on a Rubbish Dump' – retold the events surrounding a disaster in one of these 'garbage communities'. Payatas, on the outskirts of Manila (the capital city of the Philippines) was said to support up to 100,000 people, about one-fifth of whom actually lived in shacks built on the garbage. In this 'stench of an eyesore' the inhabitants gleaned what recyclables they could, occasionally finding money or jewellery. The most common luxury item, the report stated, was copper wire, which attracted a higher resale or exchange value with its plastic coating removed. However, the necessity of burning it off created a living atmosphere that was 'a haze of toxic smoke'.[41] Due to the fact that the settlement was built on top of the dump, landslides were always a risk, but on this particular day, as a survivor recounted, he first 'heard a noise like a low-flying aeroplane and then realised that the dump was moving'. The massive landslide that followed buried many dozens of homes and killed hundreds.

Whilst these events – and people – are presented in a way that significantly distances them from us, the recognition of the mere fact that they exist on the familiar and well-used objects we all discard upsets our ability to sustain the repression of the fact. As Anthony Vidler writes, such objects, returned from 'their proper burial . . . break the long process of deterioration and degradation that leads from the familiar, the ordinary, to the banal'.[42] This is the world that the refuse collectors become associated with because they may jolt one into the realization (as garbage objects do) of 'the secret but ever-present reciprocities that bind people to objects in post-technological domesticity'.[43] The symbolism of disconnected, unclaimed objects that reappear in the form of a haunting can only be understood within such a sense of the uncanny. Death appears here, as well, in the absence of stewardship over such objects: which is to say, in the corresponding absence of a human once connected to the objects. Should such lifeless objects not have disappeared with their disconnected owners? Thus, displaced personal belongings – like rubbish one might see in the streets – uncannily remarks upon the universality of death, as Pablo Neruda's poem 'Only Death' suggests:

> To resonance comes death
> like a shoe without a foot, like a suit without a man.[44]

To put the relationship between the material and the psychological into the terms of the various lifestyle gurus, what we dispose of is just a material representation of what used to be; garbage is our 'leavings', a sign of life having moved on, it is life past, representing a death sentence upon these objects. And so in Neruda's poem, too, death is the cleanser: 'But death also goes through the world dressed as a broom, she licks the ground looking for corpses.'

Whilst Freud's essay on the uncanny has been seen as an exercise in literary criticism, it has also been noted that in grappling with this idea, he only reluctantly – near the end of the essay – realizes that psychoanalysis cannot separate itself from uncanniness. It is, after all, to repeat Jean Baudrillard, the first great theoritization of the leftover but not yet jettisoned – the residual.[45] The influence of Freud finds its way to the present in many guises, but none more over-simplified and crass than the varieties of lifestyle psychology that are promulgated in cheap books and in the confessionals of trash television. These lead us to understand that the maintenance of the self actually depends on not allowing the *other* – that which Kristeva says comes to oppose the *I* – to overcome its proper bounds. The presentation of the 'harmful' effects of a failure to clean out rubbish is an interesting development in the psychopathology of modern consumer society, signalling perhaps that changes in fashion, and 'schizophrenic' consumption – that is, consumption as a means of re-making the self – also makes available more objects than one can at any time identify with and, as a consequence, tends toward a gradual unbinding of the self as the accumulation verges on the uncontrollable.[46]

People who are collectors might object to such a judgement, because collecting things – objects of fascination, and so on – to fulfil some desire, to indulge our capacities for self-expression and so on, is also to impose an order. How strange is it that collectors, not unlike philosophers and their systems, have a kind of mania for completion? Collectors favour the sort of things that can, we may infer, be brought together to form some totality: cards from decades-old cigarette packets; toy motor cars; musical recordings; model figures – of 'things' like men, tanks, and trains; living things like butterflies or goldfish; indeed consumable items like wine, or Cuban cigars. The items collected are all objects of value; that is to say in some sense they are use-worthy, or exchangeable.

However, the garbage of the lifestyle cleaner is equated with debilitation. Useless junk is defined by a lapse in value that results in a subjective transformation of this value into indeterminate matter. The neglect of imposing an order on one's life, in hoarding junk, is considered to be indicative of a general dissoluteness that can extend into a tendency to neglect other important parts of life. There is certainly a point to be made here, one that brings to mind again Klíma's masterful novel and the deteriorating relationship between the street-sweeper/ writer and his wife, which falls into decline at the same time as he does into this universe of rubbish. Their neglect of each other is seen to be analogous with the casual nature of disposal in contemporary life; with a blind acceptance that things would continue without requiring any work.

In the contemporary self-help or twelve-step therapies, the disintegration of the love relationship is represented (as it often is with the lifestyle cleaners) as a battle of organization against lazy dissolution. The kind of organization induced by therapy that consists mostly in *bouts of disposal* (the organization and prioritization of time, and so on) establishes a space where one can supposedly fill life with meaning, a 'meaning' that establishes itself *against, and in response* to, a void of laziness. By contrast, the street-sweeping narrator of *Love and Garbage* comes to view his writing vocation as just such a means of grounding his life, as a way of *being* (to call it 'therapy' within this context would demean it). In the sense that his writing reconstituted and gave meaning to life by the careful arrangement (and disposal) of its parts, it was strangely akin to his temporary relationship with the world of garbage; writing was a kind of 'remembrance which lifted the incinerated from the ashes and tried to raise them up to new life'.[47]

However, there is no real equivalence in the depths Klíma's central character reaches, the wisdom he draws from this, and the superficial *keep-busy-and-don't-think-therapy* that drives the mission to cleanse the object world. This latter phenomenon is actually a kind of neo-Lockean view – in that anything not subjected to work or subordinated to a organizing schedule must be waste – and one that is advocated by legions of vacuous 'lifestyle cleaners' who view house-cleaning as the universal antidote to contemporary life's ailments. It is worth quoting at length a list of just how this rubbish affects our lives for the worse. The following list constitutes a fairly accurate summation of the prevailing 'wisdom' of the lifestyle psychology of disposal:

> Having clutter can make you feel tired and lethargic
> Having clutter can keep you in the past
> Having clutter can congest your body
> Having clutter can affect your body weight
> Having clutter can confuse you
> Having clutter can affect the way people treat you
> Having clutter can make you procrastinate
> Having clutter can cause disharmony
> Having clutter can make you feel ashamed
> Having clutter can put a hold on your life
> Having clutter can depress you

Having clutter can create excess baggage
Having clutter can dull your sensitivity and enjoyment of life
Having clutter can cause extra cleaning
Having clutter can make you disorganized
Having clutter can be a health or fire hazard
Having clutter can create undesirable symbology
Having clutter can cost you financially
Having clutter can distract you from the important things.[48]

And so on. This is an exhaustive charge sheet against the ills of useless stuff, yet it seems to lack something in the area of discrimination. One can't help wondering if establishing a hierarchy of threats might help the unfortunate victims find a way of resolving their problems more quickly. Who can say what is more dangerous here – 'undesirable symbology', procrastination, or the possibility that you have unwittingly come to inhabit a combustible warehouse of junk? There is no telling, although we can be sure that none of it *will contribute to your happiness.* The utter vacuity of this is found in the fact that whilst presuming to recast our relationship to the world, it forces the individual to a further point of particularity in pursuit of a happiness that can only result from an unburdening that, like incontinence, produces only waste. (How fitting it seems that Aristotle's notion of *akrasia* or weakness of will is often rendered as moral incontinence.)

Any further movement in this direction and the *failure to dispose* might itself be deemed an illness. The spectre of garbage – of being undone, reduced to nothing, cast aside – has (in its attempt to combat this very effect) paradoxically declared the general disposability of everything in contemporary society. In his recent book, *Liquid Love,* Zygmunt Bauman meditates at length on the wastes of contemporary life through a series of theses that map the span of our 'liquid modern' times, and provides a thoughtful counterpoint to the above list. For example:

Promises of commitment, writes Adrienne Burgess [a relationship guru], 'are meaningless in the long term'.[49]

All that coming together and drifting apart makes it possible to follow simultaneously the drive for freedom and the craving for belonging – and to cover up, if not fully make up for, the short-changing of both yearnings.[50]

Consumerism is not about *accumulating* goods (who gathers goods must put up as well with heavy suitcases and cluttered houses), but about *using* them and *disposing* of them after use to make room for other goods and their uses.[51]

When the quality lets you down, you seek salvation in quantity. When duration is not on, it is the rapidity of change that may redeem you.[52]

Contemporary cities are dumping grounds for the misformed and deformed products of fluid modern society (while, to be sure, themselves contributing to the accumulation of waste).[53]

Modernity turned out and kept on turning out, from the start, huge volumes of human waste.[54]

Spattered all around the globe are 'garrisons of extraterritoriality', the dumping grounds for the undisposed of and as yet unrecycled waste of the global frontier-land.[55]

On one end of a scale we might draw of this notion of 'liquid love' rests the disposed-of lover, and at the other the garrisoned alien. In all events, it seems the remedy to our ills is simply to get rid of the 'trash' (see leaflet on previous page). We reach this state of affairs, as Odo Marquard suggests, because of a key modern phenomenon, what he calls 'the meaning deficit', which results in a need for more fetishes. In other words, a lack of meaning in modern life is met with a mentality of *demands* that leads, inevitably, to an over-accumulation of supposedly 'transforming' objects, exactly because the life one lives in modern society 'is empty', Marquard says. Therefore, we need to prevent the creation of a void:

One needs it [life], and everything in it, at least twice over: the second television, the second automobile, the second home, the second PhD, the second wife or the second husband, the second life (in the form, for example, of vacation).[56]

In other words, the disappearance of meaning in modern life is covered up by a preoccupation with essentially superficial 'things' that are fetishized (endowed with a mystical transforming power) and

One Person's Trash is Another's Treasure. A novel way of getting rid of that lifestyle rubbish, 2001, leaflet advertising a club night at The Garage, Glasgow.

become the true carrier of radically subjective meaning, but rather than substantially replacing the apparent loss of meaning they only add bulk or clutter to life. This, once again, represents an aspect of the uncanny, as the imaginary world of the subjective is confronted by the reality of the possible material disorder of life. Just as the Freudian psychoanalyst helps the patient to sift and organize the residues of memory, so the strategy of the lifestyle cleaners in promoting this dejunking fad is to sort this immanent disorder. By rationalizing our 'space' we can take steps toward improved mental health, they tell us. In a banal sense the ultimate result of this external-internal psycho-physical organization and exclusion is the clearing away of rubbish, but at the extreme, as Bauman implies, it creates a withdrawal into particularity that makes the disposability of everything else a human default reaction to the world we don't recognize any more. And is this, perhaps, this is the real meaning of 'not giving a shit'?

Afterword

'Man that is born of woman hath but a short time to live, and is full of misery. He cometh up, and is cut down, like a flower; he fleeth as it were a shadow, and never continueth in one stay.' We began with this, the First Anthem of the Burial of the Dead from the *Book of Common Prayer*. Garbage is everywhere, I said. Garbage results from the withdrawal that, in a sense, creates our existence as a duplicitous one. Garbage is civilization's double – or shadow – from which we flee in order to find the space to live. Yet this never ends, this fleeing. Since the dawn of philosophy – which originally sought to understand nature, the world, and the non-human, as the source of our human mysteriousness – the separation of the human from the natural is continued and accelerated through modernity. What in the seventeenth century was a retreat from nature (in Kant's terms, represented by the *thing-in-itself*) was devised in order that reason, our faculty of understanding, could be 'hard-wired' into the way we think about humanity, about how the world works, and to *clear the ground* for science.

Because Western culture develops a greater and a more far reaching know-how and a technology that constitutes the efficient disposal of the unusable, it can also be seen as a history of garbage – of cutting off, detachment, and thus retreat into liveable space. Ludwig Wittgenstein – although probably re-administering the purgative that was philosophical scepticism – famously wrote 'what we cannot speak about, we must pass over in silence'. Such a sentiment could almost stand as the leitmotif of Western reason in the modern age, reflecting a constitutional blindness to the remainder of the objectification of the world, to what a eighteenth-century philosopher like Kant would have regarded as the metaphysical wasteland. In Don DeLillo's novel *Underworld,* one of the characters offers the rejoinder to Wittgenstein:

> Something that eludes naming is automatically relegated . . .
> to the status of shit. You can't name it. It's too big or too evil

or outside your experience. It's also shit because it's garbage.[1]

This novel – which approaches biblical proportions in both its bulk and the extent of its vision – contains many parables of modern life. In it, nothing that is detached, like garbage, ever disappears. Rather, things just reappear differently, in new contexts – recycled after their disposal at some earlier time. We see this from the opening scenes, where the winning ball at the 1951 World Series is shot into the crowd, and thereafter reappears throughout the book as, on the one hand, the ordinary (yet, extraordinary) object that speaks history and connects people and events that know nothing of each other. On the other hand this object is a metaphor for the relentless traffic of lives that 'never continueth in one stay', but are constantly broken down, raked over, reassembled and finally buried.

Underworld is principally the story of Nick Shay, and central to his life is the multi-faceted nature of garbage. He is a waste management consultant. His life, we can see, is determined by a present that brings him face to face with his uncomfortable past; the jumble of remembrances that at times threaten to shatter his precarious sense of self and reduce him to bits are the result of his digging around in the past. In Underworld, garbage stands for the final frontier of human autonomy; it should be a sign that no matter how much we separate from ourselves the undifferentiated *stuff* of the world, and despite our skill in disposing of it, the garbage it nonetheless represents secretly represents the underworld we ultimately become part of. In Underworld, garbage 'presents' itself as an obstacle to the forlorn hope that we can be the author of our own biographies when life seems to be more or less trapped by the twin forces of causal necessity (the present) and memory (the past), which, we infer, generate garbage endlessly – the random aberrations of nature beyond our control, the buried waste of the unconscious and so on. Garbage is the objective and material representation of a fear that history, in the form of subjective memory, assumes dominance over the present and future, and is then as inevitable as the bodies we stand in – the past may be repressed, but ultimately cannot be evaded. Striking out against this necessity, a mania for order becomes Shay's guiding principle in life. Like the past that he is continually revisiting, and trying to reconstitute in ways that makes the present real (and not uncanny), his life could be taken to represent the uncomfortable knowledge that self-consciousness may stand alone, but it also proclaims a doubt that burdens the modern mind.

We see Nick Shay flitting between present and past. Having been rescued from a dissolute life by the Jesuits, he appropriately enough becomes a bizarre modern equivalent of these scholastic sorters; an organizer of the unnecessary, a waste consultant. As he travels between continents to observe the workings of landfill sites, so too, in his imagination, he approaches the sites that reopen back into a past he can't get away from, buried, like the reality of the garbage in his landfills, just below the surface. Thus the highly visible character of garbage in his life leads him unavoidably to see the world through the teeming objects of a consumer culture driven by commercial gluttony, and in consequence of which the various products as merely disguised garbage, their future status assured. He remarks at one point on how this extends into his domestic life: 'Marian and I saw products as garbage even when they sat gleaming on store shelves, yet unbought,' he says. The truth he seems to know like only people who deal with waste know, is that he was his garbage; it was indissolubly bound up with the mundane facts of his existence:

> We didn't say, what kind of casserole will that make? We said, What kind of garbage will that make? Safe, clean, neat, easily disposed of? Can the package be recycled and come back as a tawny envelope that is difficult to lick closed?[2]

Shay's preoccupation with the shadowy world of waste marks him out from those of us who don't see the garbage beneath the packaging. In the memory of the consumer who remains ignorant of how life pushes garbage into the shadows and renders it almost invisible, the ultimate connection of the human to garbage remains mysterious. In *Underworld*, we see Nick Shay get himself into a mess because he has, in a sense, unveiled the mystery and made it known to himself, and this leads him now to turn to his mysterious past. His consciousness of the fragility of the bonds that attach past to present reduces him to a state of almost permanent uncertainty. Thus, his acquaintance with the reality of consumption and garbage symbolizes the looming decay of a world that begins to run out of control, that consumes his life. 'Every bad smell is about us,' he says, standing in the shadows of mountains of trash heaped like pyramids as he tries to rationalize the necessity of this sight:

> We make our way through the world and come upon a scene that is medieval-modern, a city of high rise garbage, the hell reek

of every perishable object ever thrown together, and it seems like something we've been carrying all our lives.[3]

But, having been taught by Jesuits, Shay meets the wastes of life with determination and fortitude. Sure, it keeps on coming, but all we need to do is stand up to it, put it in its place. Despite his personal insecurity, what he illustrates is the overestimation of reason's power to secure itself against its wastes, displaying the belief that the proper application of reason can force life to some kind of standstill in order that it can all be controlled. Thus whilst he is highly discriminating in his personal life, in his use of products in a way that consciously reduces waste, Shay meets his fears for society not in advocating less consumption, but rather with fresh holes in which to bury these dead and exhausted products of accelerated hope. Standing over such a hole in the ground, lined with plastic membrane and outfitted with a gas-control system, he listens as his colleague mentions the benefits that would be extracted from the buried debris of modern life. And he feels elated:

> I listened to Sims recite the numbers, how much methane
> we would recover to light how many homes, and I felt a
> weird elation, a loyalty to the company and the cause.[4]

The paradox of the environmental movement, which similarly remains preoccupied with waste, is, by contrast, found in how it shadows the enlightenment rationalism that gives us the landfills, yet at the same time seeks to emerge from its exclusion to be reintegrated within the body of reason itself in order to fine tune it. Where reason created great amounts of waste in making nature efficient, environmentalism would make reason more efficient and reduce waste. Where one aimed to stem the deterioration of human life, the other aims to save the ecosystem (of which humanity, of course, is a fully integrated part). Yet this seems to hold out the hope of a perfectibility, which, as we have seen, becomes problematic because *perfection* is the idea that runs through Western culture; that emerges as the guiding principle of enlightenment reason, and that, in its creation of scientific technology, is ultimately the cause of more garbage.

A clean break with the past still detaches a remainder, and every act of differentiation produces garbage. The relation of garbage, as discussed here, to the ecological crisis, is that the categories of Western thinking prevent us from moving outside the language that designates our world. The very idea of making things better – and the way we express this – unavoidably locks us back into the structure of Western thinking, which postulates this idea of eternity that allows us to distinguish ourselves from nature inasmuch as we assert our permanent dwelling. As Slavoj Žižek wrote, as soon as we locate the ecological crisis with

> disturbances provoked by our excessive technological exploitation of nature, we silently already surmise that the solution is to rely again on technological innovations . . . every concrete ecological concern and project to change technology in order to improve the state of our natural surroundings is thus devalued as relying on the very source of the trouble.[5]

In other words, this is still part of the impulse that historically drove philosophy and science, the desire to fend off death by continually refining and reapplying our knowledge of the world, but which destroys the environment that supports us. There is no criticism of such a relapse offered here, no solution to the deadlock that reason leaves us in – only the sobering reminder that might counter reason's hubris, and that is, *man is nothing but a bit of mud.*

References

1 GARBAGE METAPHORICS

1 F.W.J. Schelling, quoted in David Farrell Krell, *Contagion: Sexuality, Disease, and Death in German Idealism and Romanticism* (Bloomington and Indianapolis, 1998).
2 Ellen Lupton and J. Abbot Miller, 'Hygiene, Cuisine and the Product World of Early Twentieth-Century America', in Jonathan Crary and Sanford Kwinter, eds, *Zone 6: Incorporations* (New York, 1992), p. 499.
3 Christoph Asendorf, *Batteries of Life: On the History of Things and their Perception in Modernity* (Berkeley, Los Angeles and London, 1993), p. 18.
4 For an analysis of the similarity between money and faeces see, for example, Sigmund Freud, 'Character and Anal Eroticism' (originally published in 1908) in *The Standard Edition of the Complete Psychological Works* (London, 1953), pp. 167–76.
5 *The Guardian*, 19 October 2001. The artist later remarked that the mistake was 'fantastic. Very funny.'
6 Compare this to Slavoj Žižek's elaboration of the Lacanian *Real*, which is taken to be that which escapes or eludes the symbolic order, in *The Indivisible Remainder* (London and New York, 1996).
7 Ivan Klíma, *Love and Garbage*, trans. Ewald Osers (Harmondsworth, 1990), p. 33.
8 Klíma, *Love and Garbage*, p. 31.
9 Thomas H. Seiler, 'Filth and Stench as Aspects of the Iconography of Hell', in Clifford Davidson and Thomas H. Seiler, eds, *The Iconography of Hell* (Kalamazoo, MI, 1992), p. 132.
10 Piero Camporesi, *The Fear of Hell: Images of Damnation and Salvation in Early Modern Europe*, trans. L. Byatt (University Park, PA, 1991), p. 36.
11 Cosman, quoted in Seiler, 'Filth and Stench as Aspects of the Iconography of Hell', pp. 135–6.
12 Rem Koolhaas, 'Junkspace', *October*, 100 (Spring 2002), p. 179.
13 David Pascoe, *Airspaces* (London, 2001), p. 221.
14 Pascoe, *Airspaces*, p. 222.
15 Marc Augé, *Non-places: Towards an Anthropology of Supermodernity* (London and New York, 1995), p. 77.
16 Augé, *Non-places*, p. 78.
17 The authoritative source on this is an unpublished PhD thesis by Ruth L. Harris, 'The Meanings of "Waste" in Old and Middle English', University of Washington, 1989.
18 John Calvin, *Commentaries*. This was Calvin's reflection on Genesis 2:15, originally published in 1554, here quoted from Calvin's *Commentary on Genesis*, trans. John King (London, 1965), p. 125.
19 Clarence J. Glacken, *Traces on the Rhodian Shore: Nature and Culture in Western*

Thought from Ancient Times to the End of the Eighteenth Century (Berkeley, Los Angeles and London, 1967), p. 152.

20 Section 32 of the Second Treatise of Government, in John Locke, *Political Writings*, ed. with an introduction by David Wootton (Harmondsworth, 1993), pp. 276–7.

21 Locke, *Political Writings*, s. 42 of the Second Treatise, p. 282.

22 E. G. Wright and R. H. Fuller, quoted in Glacken, *Traces on the Rhodian Shore*, p. 153.

23 Locke, *Political Writings*, s. 32 of the Second Treatise, pp. 276–7.

24 See also Simon Schama's *Landscape and History* (London, 1995). In a discussion of the 'primeval' Lithuanian forest ('a thing of glory and terror'), Schama notes that the chief forest administrator Julius Van Brincken 'had never seen anything like it. Where were the beech trees? For there was *everything* else: ash, aspen, maple, oak, linden, willow, birch, elm, hornbeams and spindle trees, pine and fir, all growing in a crazed jumble, amidst a vast botanical charnel house of rotting trunks, roots, and limbs. The irregularity was dreadful, sublime, perfectly imperfect. What was needed . . . was a methodical forestry that would, over time – and given the size of the wilderness of the place, a very *long* time, perhaps a century and a half – bring it into some kind of proper hierarchy', pp. 49–50.

25 Richard Boyd, 'The Calvinist Origins of Lockean Political Economy', *History of Political Thought*, XXIII/1 (2002), p. 44.

26 Locke, *Political* Writings, s. 38 of the Second Treatise, p. 280.

27 William Blackstone, *Commentaries on the Laws of England* (London, 1830), III, p. 212.

28 Glacken, *Traces on the Rhodian Shore*, p. 388. The idea that no matter ever disappears is one that will reappear at various points below, but also (it is worth mentioning) relates to ideas that can be found in some unusual places. For example, an easily overlooked footnote in Karl Marx's *Capital* rehearses the same idea as support for a view of commodities that underscores Marx's belief that the inherent value in objects, or commodities, does not derive from pre-existing qualities, but rather from something rather more artificial (but nonetheless the result of the general utility of what might be called 'base' matter). The following is a quote from an Italian political economist, Pietro Verri: 'All the phenomena of the universe, whether produced by the hand of man or indeed by the universal laws of physics, are not to be conceived of as acts of creation but solely as a reordering of matter. Composition and separation are the only elements found by the human mind whenever it analyses the notion of reproduction; and so it is with the reproduction of value and wealth, whether earth, air and water are turned into corn in the fields, or the secretions of an insect are turned into silk by the hand of man, or some small pieces of metal are arranged together to form a repeating watch.' Marx, *Capital* (Harmondsworth, 1992), p. 133.

29 In Glacken, *Traces on the Rhodian Shore*, p. 385.

30 Glacken, *Traces on the Rhodian Shore*, p. 411.

31 David Matless, *Landscape and Englishness* (London, 1998), p. 26.

32 Matless, *Landscape and Englishness*, p. 28.

33 In Niccolò Machiavelli, *The Portable Machiavelli*, ed. and trans. P. Bonadella and M. Musa (Harmondsworth, 1979). In chapter 24 of *The Prince*, Machiavelli writes, 'These princes of ours who have lost [their principalities] must not blame Fortune but instead their own idleness', p. 158.

34 Klíma, *Love and Garbage*, p. 98.

35 Don DeLillo, *Underworld* (New York, 1997), p. 539.

36 The term 'Physico-Theology' is Clarence J. Glacken's. See Glacken, *Traces on the Rhodian Shore*, pp. 375–428.

37 As Maurice Cranston notes: 'Oxford men of Locke's generation [Locke went to Oxford in 1652] had to hear at least two sermons a day, and remember them. All undergraduates, and Bachelors of Arts as well, had to go every Sunday evening between six and nine o'clock to "give an account to some person of known ability and piety (to be appointed by the Heads of the Houses) of the sermons they had heard."' In *John Locke: A Biography* (London, New York and Toronto, 1957), p. 31.

38 Klíma, *Love and Garbage*, p. 83.

39 Klíma, *Love and Garbage*, p. 83.

40 Klíma, *Love and Garbage*, p. 101.

41 John Keats, 'Ode on Indolence', in Elizabeth Cook, ed. and intro., *John Keats: Major Works* (Oxford, 1990), p. 283.

42 Michel de Montaigne, *Essays*, trans. J. M. Cohen (Harmondsworth, 1958), p. 26.

43 Montaigne, *Essays*, p. 27.

44 On the destructive potential of gambling, for example, see John Scanlan, 'Combustion: An Essay on the Value of Gambling', in Gerda Reith, ed., *Gambling: Who Wins, Who Loses* (New York, 2003), pp. 348–53.

45 Tim Cresswell, *The Tramp in America* (London, 2001), p. 52.

46 William Shakespeare, 'Capricious Time', in Kenneth Muir, ed., *The Oxford Shakespeare: Troilus and Cressida* (Oxford, 1982), pp. 128–9.

47 See William Rathje and Cullen Murphy, *Rubbish! The Archaeology of Garbage* (New York, 1992) for a discussion of historical methods of dealing with garbage.

48 Don DeLillo, *Underworld* (London and New York, 1997), p. 121.

49 Susan Strasser, *Waste and Want: A Social History of Trash* (New York, 2000), p. 275.

50 M. Calinescu, *Five Faces of Modernity: Modernism, Avant-Garde, Decadence, Kitsch, Postmodernism* (Durham, NC, 1987) pp. 61–2.

51 Calinescu, *Five Faces of Modernity*, p. 63.

52 See Hans Blumenberg, *The Legitimacy of the Modern Age* (Cambridge, MA, 1983).

53 F. Nietzsche, *The Complete Works of Friedrich Nietzsche, II: Unpublished Writings from the Period of Unfashionable Observations* (Stanford, CA, 1999), p. 89.

54 Jean Baudrillard, *Simulacra and Simulation*, trans. Sheila Faria Glaser (Ann Arbor, 1994), p. 145.

55 S. Freud, 'The Uncanny', in *The Standard Edition of the Complete Psychological Works of Sigmund Freud*, trans. James Strachey, XVII (London, 1953), p. 241.

56 M. Heidegger, *The Question Concerning Technology and Other Essays* (New York, 1977). For example: *Techne* means, 'to be entirely at home in something, to understand and be expert in it. Such knowing provides an opening up. As an opening up it is a revealing' (p. 13). And the demand of *techne* as a way of knowing the world 'banishes man into that kind of revealing which is an ordering. When this ordering holds sway, it drives out every other possibility of revealing.' (p. 27).

57 Gilles Lipovetsky, *The Empire of Fashion: Dressing Modern Democracy* (Princeton, NJ, 1994), p. 24.

58 See Vance Packard, *The Wastemakers* (Harmondsworth, 1960).

59 Ellen Lupton and J. Abbott Miller, 'Hygiene, Cuisine and the Product World of Early Twentieth-Century America', pp. 496–515.

60 Quoted in Rosalie L. Colie, 'Some Paradoxes in the Language of Things', in

J. A. Mazzeo, ed., *Reason and Imagination: Studies in the History of Ideas, 1600–1800* (New York and London, 1962), pp. 93–128.

61 Lorraine Daston and Katherine Park, *Wonders and the Order of Nature, 1150–1750* (New York, 1998), p. 290.

62 Francis Bacon, quoted in Daston and Park, *Wonders and the Order of Nature, 1150–1750*, p. 317.

63 Odo Marquard, *In Defence of the Accidental: Philosophical Studies* (New York and Oxford, 1991), pp. 38–9.

64 Peter Burke, *A Social History of Knowledge* (Cambridge, 2000), p. 103.

65 Burke, *A Social History of Knowledge*, p. 109.

66 Friedrich Nietzsche, *Beyond Good and Evil*, trans. R.J. Hollingdale, and with a new intro. by Michael Tanner (Harmondsworth, 1990), p. 152.

67 Jean Baudrillard, *Simulacra and Simulation*, p. 143.

68 Baudrillard, *Simulacra and Simulation*, p. 144.

69 Baudrillard, *Simulacra and Simulation*, p. 143.

70 Geoffrey Bennington, *Legislations: The Politics of Deconstruction* (London and New York, 1994), p. 65. This is not to equate the work of Marx with the ideology of Marxism.

71 Soap found on a street market in Mexico City. See, 'Lather, rinse, repeat', *The Independent*, 2001 (precise date unknown).

72 Mary Douglas, *Purity and Danger: An Analysis of Concepts of Pollution and Taboo* (London and New York, 1966), p. 36.

73 Douglas, *Purity and Danger*, p. 2.

74 Michael Thompson, *Rubbish Theory: The Creation and Destruction of Value* (Oxford, 1979), pp. 11–12.

75 Compare with Clarence J. Glacken's comments on views of nature in the ancient *Hermetica* to the effect that evil is taken to like dirt that gathers on a body: 'It is not God that creates evil, but the "lasting on" of things causes "evil to break out on them"', that is to say, continuation without change, or the assertion of an order, eventually contaminates. See Glacken, *Traces on the Rhodian Shore*, pp. 75–6.

76 Dominique Laporte, *History of Shit* (Cambridge, MA, and London, 1999), p. 84. A point made apparent recently, in 2003, as *The Washington Post* of 7 September reported that Marseilles had 'found itself in the middle of a trash collectors' strike, with tons of garbage rotting in the streets [and that in response] the French government leapt into action. It sprayed the garbage with perfume' (p. W14).

77 Adrian Forty, *Objects of Desire: Design and Society since 1870* (London, 1986), p. 156.

78 See, for example, Michelle Passoff, *Lighten Up! Free Yourself from Clutter* (New York, 2000).

79 See Greil Marcus, *Dead Elvis: A Chronicle of a Cultural Obsession* (Cambridge, MA, and London). And a demonstration of the 'white trash' cultural horizon is demonstrated by the reported reaction of Elvis's one time producer, Felton Jarvis, to his death – a death that was mourned in every corner of the world: 'It's like someone just told me there aren't going to be anymore cheeseburgers in the world', p. 163.

80 John Hartigan, 'Unpopular Culture: The Case of White Trash', *Cultural Studies* XI/2 (1997), p. 318.

81 Thompson, *Rubbish Theory*, p. 47.

82 Matless, *Landscape and Englishness*, p. 40.

83 Matless, *Landscape and Englishness*, p. 40.

84 Tim Cresswell, *The Tramp in America* (London, 2000), pp. 80–86.

85 Simon Sadler, *The Situationist City* (Cambridge, MA, 1998), pp. 93–4.
86 See Tom McDonough, ed., *Guy Debord and the Situationist International: Texts and Documents* (Cambridge, MA, 2002), p. 248.
87 See John Scanlan, 'Duchamp's Wager: Disguise, the Play of Surface and Disorder', in *History of the Human Sciences*, XVI/3 (2003), pp. 1–20.
88 In Matthew Collings, *This is Modern Art* (London, 1999), p. 145–7.
89 Julian Stallabrass, *Gargantua: Manufactured Mass Culture* (London, 1996), p. 175.
90 Stallabrass, *Gargantua*, p. 175.
91 Mark C. Taylor, *Hiding* (Chicago, 1997), pp. 213–14.
92 Svetlana Boym, *The Future of Nostalgia* (New York, 2001), p. 206.
93 Klíma, *Love and Garbage*, p. 43.
94 László Krasznahorkai, *The Melancholy of Resistance*, trans. George Szirtes (London, 1989), p. 117.
95 Krasznahorkai, *The Melancholy of Resistance*, p. 287–8.
96 Paul Binski, *Medieval Death: Ritual and Representation* (London, 1996), p. 144.
97 Binski, *Medieval Death*, p. 145.

2 GARBAGE AND KNOWLEDGE

1 Luciano Floridi, *Philosophy and Computing: An Introduction* (London and New York, 1999), p. 161.
2 Floridi, *Philosophy and Computing*, p. 161.
3 Floridi, *Philosophy and Computing*, p. 161.
4 Jonathan Barnes, ed., *Early Greek Philosophy* (Harmondsworth, 1987), p. 19.
5 From Theophrastus' *Metaphysics* (7a10–15), quoted in Barnes, *Early Greek Philosophy*, p. 123.
6 Barnes, *Early Greek Philosophy*, p. 39.
7 Barnes, *Early Greek Philosophy*, p. 16.
8 Richard Padovan, *Proportion: Science, Philosophy, Architecture* (London and New York, 1999), p. 105.
9 Immanuel Kant, *Critique of Pure Reason*, trans. and ed. Paul Guyer and Allen W. Wood (Cambridge, 1998), p. 508 (A486/B514).
10 John Locke, *An Essay Concerning Human Understanding* (London, 1976), pp. xlii–xliii.
11 Maurice Cranston, *John Locke: A Biography* (London, New York and Toronto, 1957), p. 265.
12 In J. W. Yolton, *Locke and the Compass of Human Understanding* (Cambridge, 1970), p. 62.
13 Quoted in Karsten Friis Johansen, *A History of Ancient Philosophy: From the Beginning to Augustine* (London and New York, 1998).
14 Rosalie Colie, 'The Essayist and his Essay', in J. W. Yolton, *John Locke: Problems and Perspectives* (London, 1969), p. 242.
15 Marcus Tullius Cicero, *The Nature of the Gods* (I.84), trans. and intro. by H. C. McGregor (Harmondsworth, 1985), p. 59.
16 Ludwig Wittgenstein, *Tractatus Logico-Philosophicus* (London, 2001), p. 89.
17 Members of the Royal Society such as Sprat and Hooke used almost identical words to express the under-labouring task. See Yolton, *Locke and the Compass of Human Understanding*, p. 56.
18 David Hume, *An Enquiry Concerning Human Understanding*, section XII part 3.
19 Rosalie L. Colie, 'The Essayist and His Essay', p. 244.
20 Roy Porter, *The Enlightenment* (Harmondsworth, 2000), p. 53.

21 Charles Taylor, *Sources of the Self* (Cambridge, MA, 1989), p. 166.
22 Simon Critchley, *Continental Philosophy: An Introduction* (Oxford, 2001), p. 5.
23 Locke, *Essay*, 1.iv., s. 24.
24 Wittgenstein, *Tractatus Logico-Philosophicus*, p. 8
25 Odo Marquard, *In Defence of the Accidental: Philosophical Studies* (New York and Oxford, 1991), pp. 38–9.
26 Dominique Laporte, *History of Shit* (Cambridge, MA, 1999), p. 7.
27 Laporte, *History of Shit*, p. 3.
28 And beyond. It seems that no change is ever effected without a clear out, as Richard Rorty demonstrates in a swipe at the empiricist legacy in twentieth-century philosophy: 'British empiricism may well seem an unfortunate distraction, a parochial and unimportant movement whose only impact on contemporary philosophy has been to provide piles of rubbish for us to sweep away', in *Truth and Progress: Philosophical Papers, III* (Cambridge, 1998), p. 123.
29 R. I. Aaron and Jocelyn Gibb, *An Early Draft of Locke's Essay Together with Excerpts from his Journals* (Oxford, 1936), p. 84.
30 For the emergence of commercial culture in eighteenth-century Britain and its relation to thinkers like Locke, see Roy Porter, *The Enlightenment*, pp. 40–44.
31 Sir Walter Scott, *Rob Roy* (Harmondsworth, 1995), p. 10.
32 Scott, *Rob Roy*, p. 9.
33 Scott, *Rob Roy*, pp. 20–21.
34 Interestingly, Dominique Laporte makes this same point, except the values are reversed and the language of commerce represents filth. See *History of Shit*, p. 18.
35 Locke, quoted in Lorraine Daston and Katherine Park, *Wonders and the Order of Nature* (New York, 1998), p. 341.
36 Peter Burke, *A Social History of Knowledge: From Gutenberg to Diderot* (Cambridge, 2000), p. 110.
37 In Jacques Derrida, 'Freud and the Scene of Writing', in *Writing and Difference*, trans. Alan Bass (London and New York, 1978), p. 248.
38 Jacques Derrida, *Of Grammatology*, trans. Gayatari Chakravorty Spivak (Baltimore and London, 1997), p. 11.
39 Derrida, *Of Grammatology*, p. 5.
40 See John Locke, *Some Thoughts Concerning Education and Of the Conduct of the Understanding*, ed. Ruth W. Grant and Nathan Tarcov (Indianapolis and Cambridge, 1996).
41 This is expressed in Kant quite clearly, when he suggested that the young need to be taught the dangers of dogmatic – that is, metaphysical – writing: 'until their power of judgement has matured or rather the doctrine that one would ground in them has become firmly rooted'. See Kant, *Critique of Pure Reason*, p. 651 (A754/B782).
42 The words of Moses Mendelssohn in a letter to Kant of 25 December 1770, in Zweig, *Kant: Philosophical Correspondence, 1759–99* (Chicago, 1997) p. 67.
43 Zweig, *Kant: Philosophical Correspondence*, p. 76.
44 Kant, *Critique of Pure Reason*, p. 667 (A787/B815).
45 Robert Pippin, *Modernism as a Philosophical Problem* (Oxford, 1991), p. 117.
46 Letter to J. H. Tieftrunk, 11 December 1797, in Zweig, *Kant: Philosophical Correspondence*, p. 245.
47 Kant, *Critique of Pure Reason*, p. 654 (A761/B789).
48 Kant, *Critique of Pure Reason*, p. 100 (AX, Preface).
49 Kant, *Critique of Pure Reason*, p. 703 (A855/B883).
50 The emphasis in this passage is mine. J. H. Lambert to Kant, 3 February 1766. In Zweig, *Kant: Philosophical Correspondence*, p. 52.

51 See Pippin, *Modernism as a Philosophical Problem*, p. 46.
52 Letter to Marcus Herz, dated 24 November 1776, in Zweig, *Kant: Philosophical Correspondence*, p. 86.
53 To quote Kant: 'By an *architectonic* I understand the art of systems. Since systematic unity is that which first makes ordinary cognition into science, i.e., makes a system out of a mere aggregate of it, architectonic is the doctrine of that which is scientific in our cognition in general, and therefore necessarily belongs to the doctrine of method.' In *Critique of Pure Reason*, p. 691 (A832/B860).
54 The emphasis here is mine. Karl Jaspers, *Kant* (San Diego, New York and London, 1962), p. 145.
55 Ernst Cassirer, *Kant's Life and Thought*, trans. James Haden (New Haven and London, 1981), p. 126.
56 Jaspers, *Kant*, p. 39. As Jaspers adds, 'there is greatness in Kant's vicious circles [because] they open up the path to every aspect of philosophical consciousness' (p. 40). The vicious circles of philosophy cannot be avoided because in the act of confining itself to its own 'self-legitimated' domain 'philosophy obviously runs into vicious circles, tautologies, and contradictions, because it strives to perceive the whole through the whole, not through something else, and to understand its own thinking through itself, not through something that went before' (p. 40).
57 Cassirer, *Kant's Life and Thought*, p. 131.
58 Mark C. Taylor, *Hiding* (Chicago, 1997), p. 286.
59 Letter to Christian Garve, 21 September 1798, in Zweig, *Kant: Philosophical Correspondence*, p. 252.
60 Kant, *Critique of Pure Reason*, p. 497 (A464/B492).
61 Letter to Moses Mendelssohn, 8 April 1766, in Zweig, *Kant: Philosophical Correspondence*, p. 55.
62 Letter to Marcus Herz, about 11 May 1781, in Zweig, *Kant: Philosophical Correspondence*, pp. 95–6.
63 Kant, *Critique of Pure Reason*, pp. 692–3 (A835/B863).
64 Cassirer, *Kant's Life and Thought*, p. 138.
65 Letter to Moses Mendelssohn, 16 August 1783, in Zweig, *Kant: Philosophical Correspondence*, p. 105.
66 Letter to J. H. Lambert, 2 September 1770, in Zweig, *Kant: Philosophical Correspondence*, p. 60.
67 Letter to Moses Mendelssohn, 16 August 1783, in Zweig, *Kant: Philosophical Correspondence*, p. 107.
68 The emphasis on 'polish' and 'wasteland' here is mine. Letter to Christian Garve, 7 August 1783, in Zweig, *Kant: Philosophical Correspondence*, p. 103. It is also worth noting in the quoted passage how Kant refers to Garve as if he is not the person that the letter is addressed to ('*Garve, Mendelssohn,* and *Tetens* are the only men I know . . .'). He does this elsewhere in his letters, as if appealing to the recipients' vanity in order that they may accede to his requests.
69 Letter to Christian Garve, 21 September 1798, in Zweig, *Kant: Philosophical Correspondence*, p. 251.
70 Kant says: 'The whole [i.e., the scientific rational concept] is therefore articulated and not heaped together; it can, to be sure, grow internally but not externally, like an animal body, whose growth does not add a limb but rather makes each limb stronger and fitter for its end without any alteration of proportion.' *Critique of Pure Reason*, p. 691 (A833/B861).
71 Ludwig Feuerbach, quoted in Hans Blumenberg, *The Legitimacy of the Modern Age* (Cambridge, MA, and London, 1983), p. 120.

72 David Roochnik, *Of Art and Wisdom: Plato's Understanding of Techne* (University Park, PA, 1996), p. 15.

73 On this matter, see also Nicholas Royle's chapter 'Nigh Writing' in *The Uncanny: An Introduction* (Manchester, 2003), pp. 112–23.

74 Friedrich Nietzsche, *Beyond Good and Evil*, trans. R. J. Hollingdale, intro. Michael Tanner (Harmondsworth, 1990), p. 51.

75 Theodor Adorno and Max Horkheimer, *Dialectic of Enlightenment* (London, 1979), p. 12.

76 Pippin, *Modernism as a Philosophical Problem*, p. 55.

77 Terry Pinkard, *German Philosophy, 1760–1860: The Legacy of Idealism* (Cambridge, 2002), p. 77.

78 In Roochnik, *Of Art and Wisdom*, p. 15 (my emphasis).

79 Kant, quoted in Pippin, *Modernism as a Philosophical Problem*, p. 55.

80 Martin Heidegger, *The Question Concerning Technology*, trans. W. Lovitt (New York, 1977), p. 13.

81 Heidegger, *The Question Concerning Technology*, p. 13.

82 Heidegger, *The Question Concerning Technology*, p. 23.

83 Heidegger, *The Question Concerning Technology*, p. 14.

84 Heidegger, *The Question Concerning Technology*, p. 16.

85 Adorno and Horkheimer, *Dialectic of Enlightenment*, p. 4.

86 Heidegger, *The Question Concerning Technology*, p. 21.

87 Pippin, *Modernism as a Philosophical Problem*, p. 141.

88 Pippin, *Modernism as a Philosophical Problem*, p. 135.

89 Slavoj Žižek, *The Ticklish Subject* (London and New York, 2000), p. 310.

90 Slavoj Žižek, *The Ticklish Subject* (London and New York, 2000), p. 310.

3 GARBAGE AESTHETICS

1 See Dore Ashton, *A Joseph Cornell Album* (New York, 1974), p. 4. 'As early as 1936 he responded unabashedly to the Museum of Modern Art's biographical inquiry: EDUCATION – Went to Andover. No art instruction. Natural talent . . . Twenty-four years later he was saying, "I never called myself an artist. On voter registration I call myself a designer."'

2 On the history of three-dimensional boxes see Alex Mogelan and Norman Laliberté, *Art in Boxes* (New York, 1974).

3 On Cornell's relation to Surrealism, see Rosalind Krauss, 'Joseph Cornell's Transcendental Surrealism', in Kynaston McShine, ed., *Joseph Cornell* (New York, 1980), and Lindsay Blair, *Joseph Cornell's Vision of Spiritual Order* (London, 1998), pp. 38–45.

4 Blair, *Joseph Cornell's Vision of Spiritual Order*, pp. 26–7.

5 See John Scanlan, 'Duchamp's Wager: Disguise, the Play of Surface and Disorder', in *History of the Human Sciences*, XVI/3, pp. 1–20.

6 Octavio Paz, *Marcel Duchamp: Appearance Stripped Bare* (New York, 1990).

7 See Pierre Cabanne, *Dialogues With Marcel Duchamp* (London, 1971). Speaking to Cabanne in the 1960s, Duchamp said: 'To talk about truth and real, absolute judgement – I don't believe in it at all,' p. 70.

8 Duchamp's final work was titled *Given 1. The Waterfall, 2. The Illuminating Gas (Etant donnés 1° la chute, 2° le gaz d'éclairage)*, 1946–66, although it is not at all clear *what is given* – because what is 'there' is determined in the end only by the viewer. This work, from the title to the conditions under which one views, is a puzzle that the viewer has to work out (it is viewed behind a large wooden door, and accessed only through a 'peep' hole on the same door).

See Eric Cameron, 'Given', in Thierry De Duve, ed., *The Definitively Unfinished Marcel Duchamp* (Cambridge, MA, 1991), pp. 1–29.

9 G. W. Leibniz, *Philosophical Essays* (Indianapolis, 1989).

10 See Mark C. Taylor, *Disfiguring: Art, Architecture, Religion* (Chicago, 1992). In chapter 6 Taylor reveals a difference between *logocentrism* and the *logo-centric*.

11 G. W. F. Hegel, *Phenomenology of Spirit* (Oxford, 1977), p. 14.

12 Jonathan Dollimore, *Death, Desire and Loss in Western Culture* (London, 1998), pp. xx–xxi.

13 See Hans Blumenberg, *The Legitimacy of the Modern Age* (Cambridge, MA, 1983).

14 Rosalind Krauss, 'Grids', *October*, 9 (1979), pp. 50–64.

15 Cornelia Parker, *Cornelia Parker/Institute of Contemporary Art Boston* (London, 2000). Parker also used the residue from the record mastering process to create a work called 'The Negatives of Sound'. The swarf was placed between two pieces of glass.

16 Calvin Tomkins, *The Bride and the Bachelors* (London, 1965), p. 232.

17 Given his reputation now it is easy to forget how long it took for Duchamp to be accepted. For instance he never had a single solo exhibition until 1964 in Pasadena, California, and many of his works remained in private ownership.

18 See Daniel Belgrad, *The Culture of Spontaneity* (Chicago, 1998). For an eloquent defence of Abstract Expressionism, see T. J. Clark, *Farewell to An Idea: Episodes From a History of Modernism* (New Haven and London, 1999).

19 Cf. Taylor, *Disfiguring: Art, Architecture and Religion.*

20 Belgrad, *The Culture of Spontaneity*, p. 23.

21 This modification of collage techniques was the continuation of a trend that is associated with modern painting of the early twentieth century, but which seems to have origins prior to modernism. As Eddie Wolfram notes: 'In the curio cabinets of wealthy collectors of the seventeenth century strange objects made from the most bizarre materials might be found: Mosaic pictures constructed from beetles, corn kernels, coffee beans and fruit stones.' See E. Wolfram, *A History of Collage* (London, 1975), p. 8.

22 Paz, *Marcel Duchamp: Appearance Stripped Bare*: '[Duchamp's] fascination with language is of an intellectual order; it is the most perfect instrument for producing meanings and at the same time for destroying them', p. 5.

23 Mary Lynn Kotz, *Rauschenberg: Art and Life* (New York, 1962), pp. 78–9.

24 Tomkins, *The Bride and the Bachelors*, p. 209.

25 Kotz, *Rauschenberg*, pp. 78–9.

26 See Walter Hopps, 'Rauschenberg's Art of Fusion', in Walter Hopps and Susan Davidson, eds, *Robert Rauschenberg: A Retrospective* (New York, 1998), p. 22.

27 Quoted in Hopps and Davidson, *Rauschenberg: A Retrospective*, p. 29.

28 See Tomkins, *The Bride and the Bachelors*, p. 233. Rauschenberg said: 'When I get the silk screens back from the manufacturer the images on them look different from the way they did in the original photographs, because of the change in scale, so that's one surprise right there. Then, they look different again when I transfer them to canvas, so there's another surprise. And they keep on suggesting different things when they're juxtaposed with other images on the canvas, so there's the same kind of interaction that goes on in the combines and the same possibilities of collaboration and discovery.'

29 Quoted in Tomkins, *The Bride and the Bachelors*, p. 200.

30 See Scanlan, 'Duchamp's Wager'.

31 See Hillel Schwartz, *The Culture of the Copy: Striking Likenesses, Unreasonable Facsimiles* (New York, 1996), p. 92. He quotes Erasmus on this matter: 'What an enormous amount of a real person is missing from the portrait! . . . Where are

the brain, the flesh, the veins, the sinews and the bone, the bowels, blood, breath, humours? Where are life, movement, feeling, voice and speech? Where finally are man's special characteristics, mind, intelligence, memory and understanding?'

32 Schwartz, *The Culture of the Copy*, p. 92
33 See Paz, *Marcel Duchamp: Appearance Stripped Bare*, p. 16. See also Harriet Ann Watts, *Chance: A Perspective on Dada* (Ann Arbor, 1980), p. 33.
34 George Basalla, 'Transformed Utilitarian Objects', *Winterthur Portfolio*, XVII/4 (1982), p. 189.
35 See Celeste Olalquiaga, *The Artificial Kingdom* (London, 1999), pp. 38–9, fn.8, who explains that the etymology of 'kitsch' includes '*verkitschen*, to make cheap, and *kitschen*, to collect junk from the street'.
36 One interesting outcome of this lack of housework was Man Ray's well known photo known as *Dust Breeding*, taken in Duchamp's apartment, and featuring a section from Duchamp's *Large Glass*, which the photograph shows to have been colonized by dirt. The image is reproduced in many places, but see Dawn Ades *et al.*, eds, *Duchamp* (London, 1999), p. 91.
37 See Helen Molesworth, 'Work Avoidance: The Everyday Life of Marcel Duchamp's Readymades', in *Art Journal*, L/1 (1996), p. 51.
38 Bruce Altshuler, *The Avant-Garde in Exhibition: New Art in the 20th Century* (Berkeley, CA, 1994), Chapter 11.
39 Altshuler, *The Avant-Garde in Exhibition*, Chapter 11.
40 See *Tony Cragg*, exh. cat., Société des Expositions du Palais des Beaux-Arts (Brussels, 1985), p. 16.
41 *Cragg*, exh. cat., Société des Expositions du Palais des Beaux-Arts, p. 31.
42 *Tony Cragg*, exh. cat., Fifth Triennale India, (New Delhi, 1982).
43 In *Cragg*, exh. cat. Fifth Triennale India, p. 4.
44 *Cornelia Parker*, exh. cat., ICA Boston 2 February–9 April, The Arts Club, Chicago, 8 June–21 July and ICA Philadelphia, 15 September–12 November, 2000 (2000), p. 4. In homage to her childhood passion, the coins were run over by a train before being suspended into the form.
45 In *Cragg*, exh. cat., Fifth Triennale India, p. 2.

4 GARBAGE MATTERS

1 See Karl Marx, *Early Writings* (Harmondsworth, 1974), p. 358.
2 Marx, *Early Writings*, p. 354.
3 See Aristotle, *Metaphysics*, trans. H. Tredennick (Cambridge, MA, 1983), V.IV. 1–6. Here *phusis* is taken to refer to 'nature' or 'the primary stuff, shapeless and unchangeable from its own potency, of which any natural object consists or from which it is produced', and *techne* refers to human knowledge of the operations of nature. See also Martin Heidegger, *The Question Concerning Technology and Other Essays* (New York, 1977). For Heidegger *techne* means, 'to be entirely at home in something, to understand and be expert in it', p. 13.
4 See Carlo Cipolla, *Miasmas and Disease: Public Health and the Environment in the Pre-industrial Age* (New Haven and London, 1992), p. 81.
5 See Jean Baudrillard, 'Consumer Society', in *Selected Writings*, ed. Mark Poster (Cambridge, 2001) pp. 32–59. On theories of consumption, see Mike Featherstone, *Consumer Culture and Postmodernism* (London, 1991). On technology and the perception of the world in industrial society, see Christof Asendorf, *Batteries of Life* (Berkeley, CA, 1993).
6 See also Slavoj Žižek, *The Indivisible Remainder* (London, 1996).

7   Cipolla, *Miasmas and Disease*, p. 81; Dominique Laporte, *History of Shit* (Cambridge, MA, 2000), Chapter 1.
8   Laporte, *History of Shit*, pp. 119–20.
9   William Miller, *Anatomy of Disgust* (Cambridge, MA, 1997), pp. 60–88.
10 Miller, *Anatomy of Disgust*, p. 69.
11 See Lawrence Wright, *Clean and Decent* (Harmondsworth, 1960); Laporte, *History of Shit*, pp. 27–49; Norbert Elias, *The Civilizing Process*, I (Oxford, 2000), pp. 45ff. See also Miller, *Anatomy of Disgust*, pp. 143–78.
12 Harvie Ferguson, 'Me and My Shadows: On the Accumulation of Body Images in Western Society. Parts 1 and 2', *Body & Society*, III/3, pp. 1–31 and III/4, pp. 1–31.
13 Manuel DeLanda, *A Thousand Years of Nonlinear History* (New York, 2000), pp. 42–3.
14 See the discussion in Harvie Ferguson, *Modernity and Subjectivity: Body, Soul, Spirit* (Charlottesville, VA, and London) pp. 44–9.
15 A claim made forcefully in William Rathje and Cullen Murphy, *Rubbish! The Archaeology of Garbage* (New York, 1992).
16 Wright, *Clean and Decent*, p. 50.
17 Wright, *Clean and Decent*, p. 50.
18 Wright, *Clean and Decent*, p. 47.
19 Wright, *Clean and Decent*, p. 49.
20 Wright, *Clean and Decent*, p. 51.
21 For example, see Baudrillard, *Selected Writings*, pp. 32–60.
22 Rathje and Murphy, *Rubbish!*, pp. 75–8.
23 Zygmunt Bauman, *Liquid Modernity* (Cambridge, 2000), pp. 2–14; Marshall Berman, *All That Is Solid Melts Into Air* (London, 1982), pp. 15–36.
24 Ralph Lewin, *Merde: Excursions into Scientific, Cultural and Socio-Historical Coprology* (London, 1999), p. 61.
25 Cf. José Saramago, *Blindness* (London, 1995).
26 Cf. F. Nietzsche, 'On the Utility and Liability of History for Life', in *The Complete Works of Friedrich Nietzsche, II: Unfashionable Observations*, trans. Richard T. Gray (Stanford, CA, 1995), pp. 83–168.
27 Gilles Lipovetsky, *The Empire of Fashion: Dressing Modern Democracy*, trans. C. Porter (Princeton, 1994), p. 24.
28 Jean Baudrillard quoted in Mike Gane, *Baudrillard's Bestiary* (London, 1991), p. 56.
29 Adrian Forty, *Objects of Desire: Design and Society since 1750* (London, 1986).
30 Thomas Hine, *The Total Package* (Boston, 1995), pp. 150–51.
31 Mark C. Taylor, *Hiding* (Chicago, 1997), p. 167.
32 Matei Calinescu, *Five Faces of Modernity* (Durham, NC, 1987).
33 W. Benjamin, *The Arcades Project* (Cambridge, MA, 1999), p. 63; Taylor, *Hiding*, pp. 211–14.
34 Lipovetsky, *The Empire of Fashion*. Subjective desire will remain the elusive product of 'intimate and existential motives, psychological gratification, personal pleasure, and product quality and usefulness', p. 147.
35 Martin Heidegger, *The Question Concerning Technology and Other Essays*, trans. W. Lovitt (New York, 1977), pp. 3–35.
36 Lipovetsky, *The Empire of Fashion*, p. 135.
37 As Wittgenstein may have supposed when he wrote that 'There must be objects, if the world is to have an unalterable form.' See Ludwig Wittgenstein, *Tractatus Logico-Philosophicus* (London, 2001), s. 2.023, p. 8.
38 Taylor, *Hiding*. Modernity, he argues, can be summed up by the obsolescence of fashion, which affirms every present as always passé, pp. 167–217.
39 Lipovetsky, *The Empire of Fashion*, p. 148.
40 Taylor, *Hiding*, p. 211.

41 Stewart Ewen, *All Consuming Images* (New York, 1988), p. 245.
42 Rathje and Murphy, *Rubbish!*, p. 45.
43 John Bunyan, *The Pilgrim's Progress* (London, 1900), p. 11.
44 Rathje and Murphy, *Rubbish!*, p. 14.
45 Rathje and Murphy, *Rubbish!*, p. 22.
46 Rathje and Murphy, *Rubbish!*, p. 57.
47 'Well designed and managed landfills seem to be far more apt to preserve their contents for posterity than to transform them into humus or mulch. They are not vast composters; rather they are deep filled mummifiers', Rathje and Murphy, *Rubbish!*, p. 112.
48 See Asendorf, *Batteries of Life*. In discussing Marx's explanation of commodity circulation he observes that 'while the goods [in exchange] are indeed active within social relations as if they were living, living social relations transform themselves into petrified, objective relations', p. 36.
49 See Marx, *Early Writings*. In the 'Economic and Philosophical Manuscripts' (p. 324) Marx explains it thus: 'The externalization of the worker in his product means not only that his labour becomes an object, an external existence, but that it exists outside him, independently of him and alien to him, and begins to confront him as an autonomous power; that the life that which he has bestowed on the object confronts him as hostile and alien.'
50 Kevin D. Mitnick and William L. Simon, *The Art of Deception: Controlling the Human Element of Security* (Indianapolis, IN, 2002), p. 156.
51 Don DeLillo, *Underworld* (New York, 1997), p. 290.
52 Taylor, *Hiding*, p. 18.
53 Weberman claims to have invented the term 'garbology', although this is strictly applied to the methodology devised by William Rathje and Cullen Murphy. The *Oxford English Dictionary* (2nd edn, 1989) suggests that dustmen in the 1960s were the first to use this term, describing themselves, in some cases, as garbologists.
54 A. J. Weberman, *My Life in Garbology* (New York, 1980), pp. 6–7.
55 In Howard Sounes, *Down the Highway: The Life of Bob Dylan* (New York, 2001), p. 262.
56 In *Don't Look Back*, D. A. Pennebaker's famous film of a 1965 tour of England, we can see earnest journalists ask Dylan what his 'message' was. With a mixture of exasperation and contempt he responds at one point: 'always keep a clean head and carry a light bulb'.
57 Sounes, *Down the Highway*, p. 264.
58 Sounes, *Down the Highway*, p. 265.
59 Weberman, *My Life in Garbology*, p. vii. Weberman may be the source for Don DeLillo's 1960s 'garbage guerrilla', Jesse Detwiler. See DeLillo, *Underworld*, p. 286ff.
60 Ivan Klíma, *Love and Garbage*, trans. Ewald Osers (Harmondsworth, 1990), p. 9.
61 In Anthony Scaduto, *Bob Dylan* (London, 2001), p. 278.
62 See Weberman, *My Life in Garbology*, p. 14–17. Dylan also compared him to 'government phone-tappers'.
63 In Pat Hackett, ed., *The Andy Warhol Diaries* (New York, 1991), p. 359.
64 That publicity was Weberman's main objective is notable throughout his book, and was reflected in his choice of associates, who turned out to be equally adept at grabbing their own headlines: 'In order to stay ahead of the competition I was forced to train an associate garbologist – Aron Morton Kay (who would later achieve notoriety as the man who throws pies at celebrities)', *My Life in Garbology*, p. xii.
65 Weberman, *My Life in Garbology*, p. 117.
66 Ellen Schrecker, *Many are the Crimes: McCarthyism in America* (New York, 1998), p. 225.

67   Ever since Niccolò Machiavelli composed *The Prince* in the early sixteenth
     century as a guide to maintaining power against external threats, there has
     been an acceptance that statecraft can be a dirty business. Like the physical
     organism, it was recognized that the political commonwealth, often described
     as an 'organism', or 'body', was subject to attack from debilitating elements.

5 GARBAGE AND THE UNCANNY

1   Kevin Lynch, *The Image of the City* (Cambridge, MA, 1960), p. 46.
2   M. Christine Boyer, *The City of Collective Memory* (Cambridge, MA, 1995),
    pp. 490–91.
3   Marc Augé, *Non-Places: Introduction to an Anthropology of Supermodernity*
    (London and New York, 1995), p. 78.
4   Sigmund Freud, 'The Uncanny', in *The Standard Edition of the Complete
    Psychological Works of Sigmund Freud*, XVII, ed. J. Strachey (London, 1953).
5   Edward Ruscha, *Thirty-Four Parking Lots in Los Angeles* (New York, 1967).
6   Anthony Vidler, *The Architectural Uncanny* (Cambridge, MA, 1994), p. 180.
7   Vidler, *The Architectural Uncanny*, p. 217. As David Frisby has written, the
    emergence and existence of a literary and cultural figure such as the detective
    presupposes both the illusory nature of such a blank order, and also the fact
    that the city is intelligible; that it presents itself as a text that can be read, or
    deciphered. See David Frisby, *Cityscapes of Modernity* (Cambridge, 2001), p. 53.
8   See Vidler, *The Architectural Uncanny*, p. 200: 'places receive the imprint of
    people'.
9   Nicholas Royle, *The Uncanny: An Introduction* (Manchester, 2003), p. 2.
10 Iain Sinclair, *London Orbital* (London, 2002), p. 52.
11 Joyce M. Ellis, *The Georgian Town, 1680–1840* (Basingstoke and New York,
    2001), p. 104.
12 J. C. Wylie, *The Wastes of Civilization* (London, 1959), pp. 33–4.
13 Ellis, *The Georgian Town*, p. 105.
14 Michael Faraday, letter to *The Times*, 7 July 1855. The story of the origins of
    London's sewage system following the collapse of parliamentary business due
    to the stench of the river Thames is recounted in detail in Stephen Halliday,
    *The Great Stink of London: Sir Joseph Bazalgette and the Cleansing of the
    Victorian Metropolis* (Stroud, 1999).
15 Wylie, *The Wastes of Civilization*, p. 23.
16 Wylie, *The Wastes of Civilization*, p. 23.
17 There is no room here to give an account of how people have dealt with
    wastes in other times and places, but see William Rathje and Cullen Murphy,
    Rubbish! The Archaeology of Garbage (London and New York), pp. 30–52.
18 Friedrich Nietzsche, 'On the Utility and Liability of History', in *The Complete
    Works of Friedrich Nietzsche, II: Unfashionable Observations* (Stanford, CA,
    1988), p. 84.
19 Freud, 'The Uncanny'.
20 Vidler, *The Architectural Uncanny*, p. 186.
21 Marcel Mauss, 'Techniques of the Body', in Jonathan Crary and Sanford
    Kwinter, eds, *Zone 6: Incorporations* (New York, 1992), pp. 455–77.
22 Julia Kristeva, *Powers of Horror: An Essay on Abjection*, trans. Leon S. Roudiez
    (New York, 1982), pp. 1–2.
23 Kristeva, *Powers of Horror*, p. 2.
24 For a full account of the dread and disgust of matter, see William I. Miller, *The
    Anatomy of Disgust* (Cambridge, MA, and London, 1997).
25 Ivan Klíma, *Love and Garbage*, trans. Ewald Osers (Harmondsworth, 1990),
    p. 128.

26 Michael Walzer, *Spheres of Justice* (New York, 1984), p. 176.
27 Freud says: 'the *unheimlich* is what was once familiar; the prefix 'un' [un-] is the token of repression', 'The Uncanny', p. 245.
28 For a full account of the origin and uses of these terms, see Nicholas Royle, *The Uncanny*. On this point he notes that 'the similarities between English (or Scottish English) and German, regarding the ways in which uncanny (*unheimlich*) haunts and is haunted by what is 'canny' (*heimlich*) are themselves perhaps uncanny', p. 11.
29 Julia Kristeva locates 'our own foreignness' – the recognition of 'strangers' – with Kant's political cosmopolitanism, or in her apposite phrase this cosmopolitanism was supported by 'the notion of *separation* combined with *union*'. See *Strangers to Ourselves*, trans. Leon S. Roudiez (New York, 1991), p. 171.
30 It may also be the case that garbage, and I discuss this below as well, is simply obliterated from consciousness as far as possible because it is disgusting and must be avoided. See, e.g., Miller, *The Anatomy of Disgust*.
31 Klíma, *Love and Garbage*, p. 77.
32 Andrew Davies, *Leisure, Gender and Poverty: Working Class Culture in Salford and Manchester, 1900–1939* (Buckingham, 1992), p. 147.
33 Klíma, *Love and Garbage*, p. 5.
34 Klíma, *Love and Garbage*, p. 2.
35 Klíma, *Love and Garbage*, p. 5. These days only small time criminals (traffic violators, and the like) are required to pick up garbage as a punishment.
36 Karl Marx and Friedrich Engels, *The Communist Manifesto* (Harmondsworth, 1967), p. 92.
37 Karl Marx, 'The Class Struggles in France 1848–50', in *Surveys from Exile. Political Writings, II* (London, 1973), p. 52.
38 Karl Marx, *The Eighteenth Brumaire of Louis Bonaparte* (Moscow and London, 1984), for remarks on the lumpen proletariat, see part 5.
39 Henry Mayhew, *London Labour and the London Poor, I: The London Street Folk* (London, 1851), p. 1.
40 Mayhew, *London Labour and the London Poor*, p. 2.
41 'Life and Death on a Rubbish Dump', *The Guardian*, 14 July 2000.
42 Vidler, *The Architectural Uncanny*, p. 163.
43 Vidler, *The Architectural Uncanny*, p. 163.
44 Pablo Neruda, 'Only Death', in *Residence on Earth* (New York, 1973).
45 Jean Baudrillard, *Simulacra and Simulation*, trans. Sheila Faria Glaser (Ann Arbor, 1994), p. 145.
46 This kind of fleeting identification is also found in the transient nature of the self as 'drifting' or of oneself being 'drugged', under the influence of mind-altering substances, which, like fashion, institute a temporary sorting of existence on the condition that this is only temporary, and does not take over – *unsort* – the self.
47 Klíma, *Love and Garbage*, p. 101.
48 Karen Kingston, *Clear Your Clutter with Feng Shui: Space Clearing Can Change Your Life* (London, 1998), pp. 19–50.
49 Zygmunt Bauman, *Liquid Love: On the Frailty of Human Bonds* (Oxford, 2003), p. 13.
50 Bauman, *Liquid Love*, p. 34.
51 Bauman, *Liquid Love*, p. 49.
52 Bauman, *Liquid Love*, p. 58.
53 Bauman, *Liquid Love*, p. 116.
54 Bauman, *Liquid Love*, p. 123.
55 Bauman, *Liquid Love*, p. 136.

56 See Odo Marquard, *In Defence of the Accidental* (Oxford, 1991), pp. 35–6.

AFTERWORD

1 Don DeLillo, *Underworld* (London, 1997), p. 77.
2 DeLillo, *Underworld*, p. 121.
3 DeLillo, *Underworld*, p. 104.
4 DeLillo, *Underworld*, p. 285.
5 Slavoj Žižek, *The Ticklish Subject* (London and New York, 2000), p. 12.

Bibliography

Adorno, Theodor, and Max Horkheimer, *Dialectic of Enlightenment* (London, 1979)

Ammons, A.R., *Garbage* (New York and London, 1993)

Asendorf, Christoph, *Batteries of Life: On the History of Things and Their Perception in Modernity*, trans. Don Reneau (Berkeley, CA, 1993)

Ashton, Dore, *A Joseph Cornell Album* (New York, 1974)

Augé, Marc, *Non-Places: Introduction to an Anthropology of Supermodernity*, trans. John Howe (London, 1995)

Barnes, Jonathan, ed. and trans., *Early Greek Philosophy* (Harmondsworth, 1987)

Baudrillard, Jean, *Simulacra and Simulation*, trans. Sheila Faria Glaser (Ann Arbor, 1994)

Bauman, Zygmunt, *Liquid Modernity* (Cambridge, 2000)

Bauman, Zygmunt, *Liquid Love* (Cambridge, 2003)

Benjamin, Walter, *Illuminations*, trans. Harry Zohn (London, 1992)

Berman, Marshall, *All That Is Solid Melts Into Air: The Experience of Modernity* (London, 1982)

Blair, Lindsay, *Joseph Cornell's Vision of Spiritual Order* (London, 1998)

Blumenberg, Hans, *The Legitimacy of the Modern Age* (Cambridge, MA, and London, 1983)

Boym, Svetlana, *The Future of Nostalgia* (New York, 2001)

Burke, Peter, *A Social History of Knowledge* (Cambridge, 2000)

Calinescu, Matei, *Five Faces of Modernity: Modernism, Avant-Garde, Decadence, Kitsch, Postmodernism* (Durham, NC, 1987)

Camporesi, Piero, *The Fear of Hell: Images of Damnation and Salvation in Early Modern Europe*, trans. L. Byatt (University Park, PA, 1991)

Cassirer, Ernst, *Kant's Life and Thought*, trans. James Haden (New Haven and London, 1981)

Compagnon, Antione, *The Five Paradoxes of Modernity*, trans. Franklin Philip (New York, 1994)

Tony Cragg, exh. cat., Société des Expositions du Palais des Beaux-Arts (Brussels, 1985)

Tony Cragg, exh. cat., Fifth Triennale India, (New Delhi, 1982)

Cranston, Maurice, *John Locke: A Biography* (London, New York and Toronto, 1957)

Crary, Jonathan, and Sanford Kwinter, eds, *Zone 6 Incorporations* (New York, 1992)

Daston, Lorraine, and Katherine Park, *Wonders and the Order of Nature, 1150–1750* (New York, 1998)

DeLillo, Don, *Underworld* (London and New York, 1997)

Dollimore, Jonathan, *Death, Desire and Loss in Western Culture* (London and New York, 1998)

Douglas, Mary, *Purity and Danger: An Analysis of Concepts of Pollution and Taboo* (London and New York, 1966)

Ferguson, Harvie, *Modernity and Subjectivity: Body, Soul, Spirit* (Charlottesville, VA, and London, 2000)

Glacken, Clarence J., *Traces on the Rhodian Shore: Nature and Culture in Western Thought from Ancient Times to the End of the Eighteenth Century* (Berkeley, Los Angeles and London, 1967)

Heidegger, Martin, *The Question Concerning Technology and Other Essays*, trans. W. Lovitt (New York, 1977)

Jaspers, Karl, *Kant* (San Diego, New York and London, 1962)

Kant, Immanuel, *Critique of Pure Reason*, trans. and ed. Paul Guyer and Allen W. Wood (Cambridge, 1998)

Klíma, Ivan, *Love and Garbage*, trans. Ewald Osers (Harmondsworth, 1990)

Koolhaas, Rem, 'Junkspace', *October*, 100 (2002)

Krasznahorkai, László, *The Melancholy of Resistance*, trans. George Szirtes (London, 1989)

Kristeva, Julia, *Powers of Horror: An Essay on Abjection*, trans. Leon S. Roudiez (New York, 1982)

Kristeva, Julia, *Strangers to Ourselves*, trans. Leon S. Roudiez (New York, 1991)

Laporte, Dominique, *History of Shit* (Cambridge, MA, 1999)

Lewin, Ralph A., *Merde: Excursions into Scientific, Cultural and Socio-Historical Coprology* (London, 1999)

Lipovetsky, Gilles, *The Empire of Fashion: Dressing Modern Democracy*, trans. C. Porter (Princeton, 1994)

Locke, John, *An Essay Concerning Human Understanding*, abridged, ed. and intro. John W. Yolton (London, 1976)

Locke, John, *Political Writings*, ed. and intro. David Wooton (Harmondsworth, 1976)

Lupton, Ellen, *The Bathroom, the Kitchen, and the Aesthetics of Waste: a Process of Elimination* (New York, 1992)

McShine, Kynaston, ed., *Joseph Cornell* (New York, 1980)

Matless, David, *Landscape and Englishness* (London, 1998)

Marquard, Odo, *In Defence of the Accidental: Philosophical Studies* (New York and Oxford, 1991)

Marx, Karl, *Capital: A Critique of Political Economy*, ed. Frederick Engels, trans. Samuel Moore and Edward Aveling (London, 1954)

Miller, William I., *The Anatomy of Disgust* (Cambridge, MA, and London, 1997)

Montaigne, Michel de, *Essays*, trans. J.M. Cohen (Harmondsworth, 1958)

Nietzsche, Friedrich, *Beyond Good and Evil*, trans. R.J. Hollingdale, intro. Michael Tanner (Harmondsworth, 1990)

Nietzsche, Friedrich, *The Complete Works of Friedrich Nietzsche, II: Unfashionable Observations* (Stanford, 1998)

Neruda, Pablo, *Residence on Earth*, trans. Donald D. Walsh (New York, 1973)

Cornelia Parker, exh. cat., ICA Boston 2 February–9 April, The Arts Club, Chicago, 8 June–21 July and ICA Philadelphia, 15 September–12 November, 2000.

Pinkard, Terry, *German Philosophy 1760–1860: The Legacy of Idealism* (Cambridge, 2002)

Pippin, Robert B., *Modernity as a Philosophical Problem* (Oxford, 1991)

Porter, Roy, *The Enlightenment: Britain and the Creation of the Modern World* (Harmondsworth, 2000)

Rathje, William and Cullen Murphy, *Rubbish! The Archaeology of Garbage* (New York, 1992)

Royle, Nicholas, *The Uncanny: An Introduction* (Manchester, 2003)

Sadler, Simon, *The Situationist City* (Cambridge, MA, 1998)

Saramago, José, *Blindness*, trans. Giovanni Pontiero (London, 1995)

Schama, Simon, *Landscape and Memory* (London, 1995)

Schwartz, Hillel, *The Culture of the Copy: Striking Likenesses, Unreasonable Facsimiles* (New York, 1996)

Sinclair, Iain, *London Orbital* (London and New York, 2002)

Taylor, Mark C., *Hiding* (Chicago, 1997)

Thompson, Michael, *Rubbish Theory: The Creation and Destruction of Value* (Oxford, 1979)

Vidler, Anthony, *The Architectural Uncanny: Essays on the Modern Unhomely* (Cambridge, MA, 1994)

Weberman, A.J., *My Life in Garbology* (New York, 1980)

Wittgenstein, Ludwig, *Tractatus Logico-Philosophicus* (London, 2001)

Wright, Lawrence, *Clean and Decent: The Fascinating History of the Bathroom and the Water-Closet* (London, 1960)

Wylie, J.C., *The Wastes of Civilization* (London, 1959)

Yolton, J.W., *Locke and the Compass of the Human Understanding* (Cambridge, 1970)

Žižek, Slavoj, *The Indivisible Remainder* (London and New York, 1996)

Zweig, Arnulf, *Kant: Philosophical Correspondence, 1759–99* (Chicago, 1967)

Acknowledgements

Thanks go to Harvie Ferguson, Gerda Reith and Bridget Fowler at the Sociology department of Glasgow University. I'd also like to express my gratitude to Charles Woolfson for all his encouragement over the last few years. Finally, thanks to John Clark and Claire Jack at the AHRB Centre for Environmental History at the University of St Andrews for allowing me the time to finish work on the manuscript, and to Steve Rosenberg for the Dow Chemical advert reproduced in Chapter Two.

Photographic Acknowledgements

The author and publishers wish to express their thanks to the following sources of illustrative material and/or permission to reproduce it:

Photo © ADAGP, Paris and DACS London 2004: p. 113; photo by the author: p. 6; photo by permission of the British Library, London/ © British Library Reproductions: p. 54; photo courtesy of Cathouse Promotions, Glasgow: p. 177; photograph collection of the Centre for Creative Photography, The University of Arizona: p. 91; photo Private First Class Walter Chichersky, courtesy of the US National Archives, Washington, DC: p. 11; photo courtesy of Glasgow City Council: p. 10; photo courtesy of the artist (John Hilliard): p. 115; photo © The Joseph and Robert Cornell Memorial Foundation/VAGA, New York/DACS, London 2004: p. 93; photo William Kuykendall/US National Archives, Washington, DC: p. 153; photo collection of Alex S. Maclean: p. 137; photo National Gallery Picture Library/© National Gallery, London Picture Library: p. 159; photo courtesy the artist (Cornelia Parker) and Frith Street Gallery, London: p. 101; Phoenix Art Museum, Texas: p. 101; Fondation Rau, Paris (painting by 'Der Meister der Verherrlichung Mariae'): p. 21; photo © Robert Rauschenberg/VAGA, New York/DACS, London 2004: p. 105; collection of Steve Rosenberg: p. 85; reproduced courtesy of the artist (Ed Ruscha): p. 156; photo Norbert Schoener, courtesy of the the Saatchi Collection, London: p. 20; photo © Tate, London 2004; photo courtesy of the United States Postal Service: p. 144; University of Arizona Press: p. 139; photo courtesy of the US National Archives, Washington, DC: p. 29.

Index